Acting to Manage Conflict and Bullying
Through Evidence-Based Strategies

Bruce Burton • Margret Lepp
Morag Morrison • John O'Toole

Acting to Manage Conflict and Bullying Through Evidence-Based Strategies

 Springer

Bruce Burton
Chair in Applied Theatre
Griffith University Mt. Gravatt Campus
Mt. Gravatt, QLD, Australia

Margret Lepp
Institute of Health and Care Sciences
University of Gothenburg
Göteborg, Sweden

Morag Morrison
Faculty of Education
University of Cambridge
Cambridge, UK

John O'Toole
Formerly Chair of Arts Education
The University of Melbourne
South Brisbane, QLD, Australia

ISBN 978-3-319-17881-3   ISBN 978-3-319-17882-0   (eBook)
DOI 10.1007/978-3-319-17882-0

Library of Congress Control Number: 2015941733

Springer Cham Heidelberg New York Dordrecht London

Printed on acid-free paper

Springer International Publishing AG Switzerland is part of Springer Science+Business Media (www.springer.com)

Contents

Contents

Author Biography

Bruce Burton, Ph.D. is Professor Emeritus at Griffith University, Australia, and has been an academic, teacher, playwright and theatre director. He was the first Chair in Applied Theatre in Australia. He has been the recipient of six Australian Research Council grants investigating the impact of theatre and drama education on conflict and bullying management, healing the consequences of childhood abuse in institutions and assisting refugee re-settlement. He is the author of ten books in the fields of drama education and applied theatre and has trained a generation of drama teachers in Australia. He has received four national university teaching awards including the national Award in 2007 for excellence in teaching in the Humanities and the Arts. Internationally, Bruce has been a Visiting Scholar at Cambridge University in the UK and a Visiting Professor at both University of Borås and the Institute of Health and Care Sciences, The Sahlgrenska Academy, University of Gothenburg, Sweden.

Morag Morrison, Ph.D. is a lecturer in Arts Education in the Faculty of Education, University of Cambridge U.K. where she teaches and supervises on undergraduate, graduate and postgraduate courses in Drama, Creativity and Arts Education. Morag co-ordinates the MPhil in Arts, Creativity, Education within the faculty and is Director of Studies in Education at St John's College in Cambridge. Morag has been involved in on-going research in Pupil Voice, Conflict Management and Democratic Teaching and Learning through creative practice; and most recently in developing an understanding of the role Applied Theatre pedagogy can play across diverse educational contexts and international settings. Morag is involved in an on-going ERASMUS exchange with the University of Gothenberg, Sweden where she teaches in the Institute of Health and Care Sciences, The Sahlgrenska Academy, University of Gothenburg, Sweden, and she is currently also utilizing Drama pedagogy in International Teacher Development work through her involvement in a programme of national education reform in Kazakhstan.

John O'Toole was Foundation Chair of Arts Education at the University of Melbourne from 2005 to 2010, and before that Professor of Drama and Applied Theatre at Griffith University. A schoolteacher for 12 years, then actor-director in theatre in education, he has spent nearly 40 years as a teacher-educator and academic, teaching on every continent and at every age level. He has written and co-written many standard research texts and student textbooks in drama and arts education, and was Lead Writer for the Arts and Drama in the Australian Curriculum. He was a founder-member of IDEA, and earlier of Drama Australia and Drama Queensland. He is also a playwright and director in applied theatre. In 2001 he was awarded the American Alliance for Theatre and Education Lifetime Research Award. In 2014 he was awarded the Order of Australia for services to drama education.

Margret Lepp, RN RNT Ph.D. is Professor in Caring Sciences at the Institute of Health and Care Sciences, The Sahlgrenska Academy, at the University of Gothenburg, Sweden. For over 20 years she has used drama for professional development in her work as a researcher and consultant involving students, patients, academics, nurses and other health care professionals. She was a key researcher in the international DRACON (Drama and Conflict Management) project between 1994 and 2005. She was a Special Interest Group leader at four IDEA conferences and has published original articles, books, chapters of books and other reviewed publications. During the years 2008–2012 she was Associate Editor of the Scandinavian Journal of Caring Sciences. She was a founder of the European Network Nursing Academies (ENNA) for European Academies cooperating in the context of Nursing Science. She is the current vice president of Sigma Theta Tau International (STTI), the Tau Omega Chapter, and the Chair of the STTI Education Advisory Council since 2014.

Chapter 1
Introduction

The research related to conflict and bullying reported in this book has been on-going in a number of countries on three continents and in a range of contexts for two decades, and continues to expand and evolve as new and continuing projects develop.

The extensive application of the research over the past 20 years has produced a number of fundamental concepts and strategies that have proved effective wherever they have been applied. The *first* strategy is the use of formal theoretical and practical teaching to generate understanding about conflict and bullying. The *second* is the use of a range of Drama techniques and activities, including improvisation, role and process drama to explore conflict and bullying in a safe, fictional environment. *Thirdly,* an adaptation of Augusto Boal's Forum Theatre, developed by the authors and described as Enhanced Forum Theatre (EFT), has proven effective in enabling a range of participants to experiment with alternative and constructive ways of handling conflict and bullying situations. Finally, the *fourth* strategy that is crucial to the success of the research and learning process, is the use of peer teaching, where participants in the projects first learn how to manage conflict and bullying through the language of Drama, and then teach what they have learned to others.

The length of time and the variety of investigations characterised by the research are due to the significance and complexity of its nature. The focus of the research throughout had been the development of research-based strategies and methods that can be utilised in different cultures and different educational and professional settings to enable participants to learn about and reduce bullying and conflict.

International research collaboration is a crucial, fragile and complex process taking time, valuing diversity, developing co-operative goals and promoting collaborative dialogue. There is a need to focus on teamwork, collaboration, and managing the inevitable conflicts that arise. In our international work across several continents and representing different disciplines, the success of the research has been driven by a number of factors. The first vital factor has been the involvement of a significant number of leading researchers from international universities. Their contributions have led to new discoveries and innovative applications of the research. Secondly, there has been extensive interest in the research from governments, non-government

© Springer International Publishing Switzerland 2015
B. Burton et al., *Acting to Manage Conflict and Bullying
Through Evidence-Based Strategies*, DOI 10.1007/978-3-319-17882-0_1

organisations and a range of educational and commercial organisations which have provided funding and research sites for the investigations. Finally, the willing engagement of many thousands of participants in schools, universities and workplaces in different countries has resulted in consistently positive outcomes in each phase of the research.

The authors of this book have been involved in the complex evolution of the research throughout, and have been the chief investigators responsible both for cooperative experiments across countries and for individual projects on a number of sites. A significant number of these projects are on-going, whilst new implementations of the strategies are also occurring in new sites and settings.

1.1   The Core Strategies

1.1.1   Teaching About Conflict and Bullying

Formal, structured teaching about the nature of conflict and bullying, and the core concepts related to managing and resolving them, has been fundamental in all the research projects associated with the development of the effective strategies explored in this book. The concepts that are taught are drawn from the fields of conflict resolution and bullying management. The first core strategy that was developed was therefore to provide all participants, through structured teaching, with an effective cognitive understanding of the nature and consequences of bullying and conflict and a range of strategies for dealing with them.

Participants of all ages – school children, students and professionals – have been able to effectively apply the knowledge and the language of conflict resolution and bullying management in addressing these issues. In particular, the understanding that the use and misuse of power is central to both has enabled them to identify and deal with their own conflict and bullying agendas, and to address them in a range of fictional scenarios and real life experiences during their participation in the projects.

The realisation that both conflict and bullying escalate in clearly recognisable stages – latent, emerging and manifest, also provided participants with the ability to identify the most effective and appropriate time to intervene or take action in dealing with these issues. Participants in the research projects were able to use the language of conflict management and apply the concepts to a range of situations, both real and fictional, during the ongoing projects.

An understanding of some of the important contrasting elements of conflict and bullying have also been significant in empowering participants to deal with them effectively. The realisation that conflict is an inherent part of human experience, and not necessarily negative, has meant that many of the participants in the adult iterations of the projects have been able to manage their own conflicts, both personal and professional, in more positive and constructive ways. At a school level, an awareness of the escalating, harmful nature of bullying has led to significant numbers of bullies to consciously modify both their attitudes and their behaviour.

1.1.2   The Use of Drama Techniques

The content of Drama is human relationships, interactions containing both conflict and power. Drama operates through invoking both cognitive understanding and emotional empathy, where participants imitate and refract life through improvised, fictional contexts and situations, integrating thoughts, actions and feelings. By using improvisation to create and explore power, conflict and bullying, both individual participants and groups were able to develop and enact realistic events and characters that could be manipulated and reflected upon, and investigate issues of relationships in a safe, fictional context. It became increasingly apparent in the research that a crucial factor in developing both engagement in the learning and competence in managing conflict and bullying was the use of Drama as the central learning method. Some key Drama strategies and techniques were identified as most successful in providing participants with a safe learning environment and a creative structure for effectively investigating and managing conflict and bullying. These included improvisation and mainly naturalistic, experiential role work. Because the purpose of the Drama was to empower the participants themselves with strategies to manage conflict and bullying in their lives, such as in school, at home or at work, process drama was also used extensively as a strategy.

A significant part of educational drama is process drama, which has no formal audience or performance outcome, and is created and enacted by the participants themselves. This proved particularly effective in allowing those involved in the different projects to be both actors and audience, able to experience fictional roles and situations related to conflict and bullying whilst observing and reflecting on the meaning of these experiences at the same time.

Drama is also able to effect behavioural change by providing learners with opportunities to experience reality from different perspectives. By taking on fictional roles in invented scenarios, based on real conflict experiences, but fictionalised to make them safe, participants were able to see themselves as others, and step into those others' shoes. At the same time emotional distance was preserved, distance needed for reflection and learning, to understand the other person's perspective. Participants in all the projects were also able to distance themselves from their own personal and cultural belief systems, and explore a range of experiences and issues related to conflict, and/or bullying from other perspectives than their own. By later reflecting on these perspectives and critically analysing their personal responses to them, significant numbers of students and adults were able to modify or even transform their attitudes and behaviour in regard to conflict and bullying.

1.1.3   Enhanced Forum Theatre

Enhanced Forum Theatre (EFT) was developed and refined by the authors from Augusto Boal's (1979) original participatory form of Theatre of the Oppressed, widely used in Theatre for Development around the world. Enhanced Forum Theatre involves the creation of a realistic play in three scenes, showing the latent, emerging and manifest stages of a conflict or bullying situation, rather than the single scene structure of Boal's version. Enhanced Forum Theatre also encourages members of the audience who intervene to take on the role of any of the characters involved in the play, not just the protagonist as in Boal's original form. Enhanced Forum Theatre was used in most of the research projects to provide participants with the opportunity to demonstrate in practice their understanding of the nature and consequences of conflict, and/or bullying, and to explore their ability to effectively and constructively manage a range of these issues. Enhanced Forum Theatre was also an integral part of the peer teaching strategy which proved effective in schools as reported in the student-based projects.

The structure of Enhanced Forum Theatre allowed participants in the projects to represent the three parties to bullying, the bully, the bullied and the bystander, and to identify the three identifiable stages of escalation in conflict and bullying- latent, emerging and manifest, by representing each stage as a separate scene in the play. A number of participatory techniques from process drama were incorporated, to provide a deeper understanding of context, a wider range of appropriate interventions and create richer reflective discussion. The modifications to Boal's original form proved remarkably effective in the many performances of the Enhanced Forum Theatre plays about conflict and bullying that were created and performed in different contexts and countries.

1.1.4   Peer Teaching

The discovery of the efficacy of peer teaching as a strategy for addressing conflict and bullying in schools occurred by accident in an early stage of the research. However, from its first application through to the current international research projects, the use of peer teaching, used in conjunction with the other three core strategies of formal teaching, Drama and Enhanced Forum Theatre, has empowered school students, and adults, to deal with conflict and bullying. This should be unsurprising, given that extensive research over the past 30 years has found clear and convincing evidence that having students teach each other can be an extremely effective tool for improving learning in the classroom.

Extensive international research has identified that peer teaching has a powerful positive effect on student self-esteem, particularly for the students acting as teachers, enabling intellectual, social and personal growth, and this proved to be a major finding in its use as an effective strategy for dealing with conflict and bullying in schools. The range of specific benefits for students doing peer teaching are described in the literature as: an increase in social and intellectual awareness; significant gains in empathy; the clear recognition that students can change habitual patterns of behaviour, and an increasing sense of mastery and self-esteem in participants in peer teaching. All these benefits were consistently demonstrated in the research projects conducted in the schools which are investigated in this book.

Other research has focused on the effects of peer teaching on the students being taught, and studies show that peer learners had higher test scores than students who studied alone and that there was an increase in positive attitudes to their learning and completion rates higher in comparison to traditionally taught students. Furthermore, being helped by older children acting as peer teachers motivates younger children to adopt a helping relationship towards other people, and this outcome was particularly significant in the bullying research projects.

The potency of peer teaching in empowering school students of all ages to understand and manage conflict and bullying situations in their lives is explored in detail in the reports on a number of the projects. The consistent success of peer teaching in enabling participants, and particularly school students, to manage conflict and bullying in their lives is an especially significant finding.

1.2   The Research Projects in Sequence

Chapter 2: *In the Beginning: The DRACON Project*, gives an account of the establishment of DRACON, the international collaboration that initiated the research. The DRACON (DRAma and CONflict resolution) project aimed to find effective means of dealing with conflict in schools in Sweden, Malaysia and Australia. The chapter explores how the researchers developed a co-operative process for sharing ideas and strategies and began to experiment with approaches to conflict management in schools in their own countries.

Chapter 3: *The DRACON Project in Brisbane* examines a particular application of the DRACON project in a school in Brisbane, Australia which led to the evolution of a number of the strategies which became central to the later research into conflict and bullying. The chapter also analyses the outcomes of an experiment in Theatre In Education which explored conflict in schools.

Chapter 4: *From DRACON to Cooling Conflicts* analyses in detail the Cooling Conflicts research in Australian schools. This project initially employed the effective strategies discovered in the DRACON research to implement a successful conflict management program in a country school in Australia where a serious racial conflict between indigenous and other students had spread to the town. Cooling Conflicts then became a major research project that was eventually implemented in over 100 schools in Sydney.

Chapter 5: *Conflict and Negative Leaders in Schools,* details a research project in the United Kingdom that drew specifically on the use of peer teaching and drama to focus on addressing conflict related to negative leaders in schools. The case study conducted as part of a major research project at Cambridge University demonstrated how these strategies can transform the behaviour of aggressive and disengaged school students.

Chapter 6: *Acting Against Bullying in Schools*, evaluates the success of the use of drama and peer teaching to empower adolescent students to deal with bullying in schools in Australia. The chapter reports on the overall outcomes of the 3 year research project in a total of 18 schools, and also examines the detailed data from three specific case studies of the impact of the research on individual schools.

Chapter 7: *Moving On* shifted the focus of the research from schools to the use drama and theatre performance in addressing post-traumatic stress and psychological dysfunction in the lives of adults who had been abused as children in orphanages and foster homes. This 3 year action research project conducted in partnership with professional counsellors encountered serious challenges in avoiding re-traumatisation of the participants, but eventually assisted them to address their trauma and develop new and effective behaviours.

Chapter 8: *Drama for Learning in Professional Development Contexts: A Global Perspective* explores the techniques in three quite different cultural and professional contexts. The chapter investigates research carried out in the UK with university students training to be teachers, nursing education in the health sector in Sweden, and the professional development of teachers in Kazakhstan.

Chapter 9: *The Use of Core Conflict Competency in Nursing Education* examines the impact of drama as one of several pedagogical methods in conflict management for practitioners in the field of Health Care in Jordan, as part of a preceptor training program in Clinical Nursing Education conducted in collaboration with Gothenburg University, Sweden.

In Chap. 10: *Acting Against Social and Cyber Bullying,* the focus of the research returns to schools, this time in a case study of female students which demonstrates how covert forms of bullying can be endemic amongst older adolescent girls in Australia. The chapter analyses the success of the research in producing transformational changes in behaviour in this specific group of female students.

Chapter 11: *Conflict and Bullying Management for Adolescent Refugees* analyses another application of the Acting against Bullying program, but this time in the context of its impact on newly-arrived adolescent refugees being re-settled in Australia. The chapter reveals how the combination of teaching about bullying, drama and peer teaching was just as effective in empowering these participants as the students in all the earlier projects.

Chapter 12: *The Conclusion*. This chapter summarises the nature and extent of the research and examines the emergence of newly started projects based on the research model and strategies explored in previous chapters. These projects provide further evidence of the effectiveness of the strategies that have been developed, and also indicate the validity of these strategies in diverse contexts.

The extensive explorations of the numerous research projects detailed in this book indicate how the implementation of evidence-based, successful conflict and bullying strategies can be complex, demanding and time-consuming. The analysis of the projects also demonstrates that the implementation of these strategies must be sensitive to each new context where they are applied. An on-going process of action research is presented as crucial to the process of implementation and evaluation of the strategies. Despite these complexities and constraints, the evidence clearly reveals that effective conflict and bullying management can be implemented and sustained in schools and workplaces around the globe.

Chapter 2
In the Beginning: The DRACON Project

The DRACON (DRAma and CONflict) project was an international research project that was established in 1994 and formally ended in 2005 with the publication of the book: *DRACON International: Empowering students to handle conflicts through school-based programs* (Löfgren and Malm 2007) that detailed the research conducted over more than a decade in three countries into Drama and Conflict Management in schools. The DRACON project was the genesis of the conceptual framework and many of the techniques that led to the development of the effective, evidence -based programs explored in this book.

2.1   1994: DRACON Begins

The DRACON project was officially initiated in May 1994 by a Swedish industrial consultant, *Jöns Andersson*. He had retired from his profession with the vision of linking the two academic and practical fields of drama and conflict resolution. This idea had come to him much earlier when he attended a drama workshop in Penang, Malaysia, where he lived for most of the year. The workshop leader, Janet Pillai, was the theatre director at the Five Arts Centre and the Young Theatre, Penang; also a lecturer at the local University of Sains Malaysia.

At the first International Drama/Theatre and Education Association (IDEA) Congress in Porto, Portugal in 1992 Andersson represented Malaysia, as Pillai could not participate, and here he met Margret Lepp from Malmö University, Sweden, and they decided to meet again in Sweden to further discuss plans for a drama and conflict management project. A meeting was set up later in 1992 with Anderson's friend and colleague Mats Friberg, from the Department of Peace and Development Research at the University of Gothenburg; for some years they had been working together on major Peace Research projects between Malaysia and Sweden. Friberg became the initial leader of DRACON. Two more experts were added to the team: Anita Grünbaum, a drama education specialist and Head of

© Springer International Publishing Switzerland 2015
B. Burton et al., *Acting to Manage Conflict and Bullying Through Evidence-Based Strategies*, DOI 10.1007/978-3-319-17882-0_2

drama teacher education at Storvik College, and Horst Löfgren, Professor of
Education at Malmö University, who took over leadership of the DRACON project
from 2001 to 2005. In 2001, Birgitte Malm from Malmö University became the last
member of the Swedish DRACON team. Although the initiative for the DRACON
project initially came from Sweden, it was not until 2001 that the Swedish team was
given a grant from The Swedish Council of Scientific Research for 3 years research.
Leadership for the project and economic responsibility was given to the School of
Teacher Education at Malmö University.

As Jöns Andersson believed that drama would be the perfect medium in which to
work with conflicts he organized contacts between Swedish conflict researchers and
Malaysian drama specialists with a meeting in Kuala Lumpur in May 1994. Sadly
Andersson had no further influence on the development of the project because of his
death in 1995.

2.2   1996: DRACON International is Born

The scope of the program has been cross-cultural, based as it is on the collaboration
between researchers in Australia, Malaysia and Sweden (Bagshaw et al. 2007). One
focus of the study from its inception was to map cultural manifestations of conflict
and their implications for conflict resolution (Burton and Lepp 2003), as this had
been a major theme of the original Sweden/Malaysia Peace Projects. At the Kuala
Lumpur meeting it was decided to further broaden the research by including
Australia. Mats Friberg invited Dale Bagshaw, a conflict resolution specialist from
the University of South Australia in Adelaide to join, and Margret Lepp invited John
O'Toole, a drama specialist from Griffith University in Brisbane, Queensland. These
invitations developed into two separate teams, each with specialists in both fields of
drama and conflict resolution, and both practitioners and researchers. The South
Australian DRACON team primarily consisted of: Bagshaw herself, drama consultant Rosemary Nursey-Bray, and Ken Rigby, a well-known expert on bullying in
schools, also from the University of South Australia. Janet Pillai teamed up with her
University of Sains colleague Latif Kamaluddin, a conflict management specialist,
along with a group of researchers from the university, and a team of four artists: a
dramatist, a visual artist, a dancer and a musician, to become the Malaysian
DRACON team. The Brisbane team based at Griffith University comprised O'Toole,
his drama colleague Bruce Burton, with strong initial input from police social worker
and academic Merrelyn Bates, and major overlapping contributions from local
schoolteachers Morag Morrison and Anna Plunkett (O'Toole et al. 2005).

At a meeting held in January 1996, in Aldinga, South Australia, DRACON
International was established by a core group of researchers from the three countries, with the formal brief:

> DRACON is an interdisciplinary and comparative action research project aimed at improv-
> ing conflict handling among adolescent school children by using the medium of educational
> drama. (Löfgren and Malm 2007, p. 13)

The essential hypothesis in this project is that drama can be an effective way to learn conflict handling. Because teenagers often find it difficult to handle their own conflicts, the project focused on students aged 13–16 years in selected schools, but also aimed to involve teachers and school counsellors. The school became a strategic arena for learning, practising and spreading conflict competence. The main purpose of DRACON has been to:

> develop an integrated program using conflict management as the theory and practice, and drama as the pedagogy in order to empower students through an integrated, school-based program to manage their own conflict experiences in all aspects of their lives. (Löfgren and Malm 2007, p. 422)

To further the aims and operation of DRACON, these international meetings were held annually throughout the project, eight in all, in all three countries, but mainly in Penang, as notionally the mid-point between the four far-flung project centres.

2.3 Aims, Principles and Research Questions

The two overall aims of DRACON International are:

- to develop and research integrated programs using conflict management as the content and drama as the pedagogy
- to empower students through integrated, school-based programs to manage their own conflict experiences in all aspects of their lives.

Marking the Millennium, twenty-first century research studies carried out in the field of drama and conflict, confirm that conflict handling is one of the most important skills of life needed today. Swedish schools do not have adequate strategies to trouble shoot in areas concerned with conflict situations. Many students are exposed to harassment of various kinds. Violence in schools seems to increase and become more severe every year (Fjellström 1998; Skolverket 1999).

> There are certain results in the survey, which indicate that the climate in schools has worsened. The teachers are mainly responsible for conveying this picture: almost one teacher in three states that he or she has witnessed increasing problems with violence, victimisation and racism, and almost half of them perceive an increasing problem with shortcomings in ethics and morals. (Fjellström 1998, p. 148)

There is an urgent need for social innovations such as creative ways of managing and handling conflicts. The schools surveyed in the DRACON research in Australia, Malaysia and Sweden indicated a need for new and creative programs, including strategies such as drama and other arts, for conflict resolution among adolescents. The theoretical thinking and practical work within DRACON were informed by a social philosophy that can be summarised in five basic principles:

- it is possible to improve conflict literacy handling through drama;
- the school is a strategic arena for learning conflict handling and literacy skills;

- early adolescence is a critical period for learning conflict resolution strategies, as there is a high frequency of conflicts;
- ways of handling conflicts are culturally conditioned;
- empowerment of students is needed in order to build up self-help as well as intervention capacities.

The first task of the DRACON project has been to develop research methods that could map students' conflicts and strategies for handling conflicts and study the effects of various drama exercises at individual, class and whole-school levels. Another major task has been to contribute to the development of a theory of conflict processes in different cultures in order to explain the effects of different types of interventions in adolescent conflicts. The third task has been to develop and test integrated drama programs, giving adolescents in the three different countries the opportunity of handling conflicts in a more constructive way.

The DRACON International project formulated the following eight general research questions relevant to all four DRACON teams:

1. What are the most common types of conflicts among adolescents? How do they perceive their conflicts and how do they behave in typical conflict situations?
2. How can adolescents explore their own conflicts through the medium of drama?
3. Can the development of relevant drama methods and programs in schools improve adolescents' capacities for handling conflicts?
4. How resilient are these drama methods and programs? Will they function under troublesome conditions, such as in 'problem' classes and in ethnically divided schools?
5. Can the same or similar drama programs be used for schoolteachers and counsellors to stimulate their participation as facilitators in the drama programs?
6. Under what conditions and to what effect can the drama programs be implemented in a whole school? Can they be taken over and run by the school itself, and under what conditions?
7. What kind of observations/measurements can be developed for studying the long and short-term effects of drama programs?
8. What are the effects of different background or contextual factors (national and ethnic cultures, school systems etc.) on the design and outcomes of the field studies? (Löfgren and Malm 2007, p. 29)

Questions 1 and 2 are preliminary questions that provide a baseline for dealing with the other questions. Question 3, about how to improve conflict handling among adolescents through the medium of drama, is the central DRACON question and most efforts in all research teams have been devoted to this question. Question 4, about how resilient the proposed drama processes are, is also a central question that has been faced by almost all teams. The other questions are also important as follow-up questions, but it has not been possible for all the teams to do systematic research on them. The last question (no. 8) is of a different nature. As a comparative question it cannot be answered by each field study taken separately. It is a matter for joint analysis.

2.4 Specific Focus for Each DRACON Team

In addition to the three aims, principles and eight research questions for the DRACON International project, each of the four teams: Sweden, Malaysia, Adelaide and Brisbane had a different and specific focus, partly by choice, partly because of the particular expertise available and partly through practical constraints. The Malaysian DRACON team investigated creative arts in conflict exploration, using theatre in education (TIE) performance and a broader offering including music, dance and visual arts. The South Australian team concentrated first on gathering baseline data about the types and frequency of conflict among adolescents and in schools, then creating classroom drama specifically addressing the results of the data generated. The Swedish DRACON team focused its investigation on teenagers as third-party mediators in conflicts among adolescents themselves within the school environment and with friends, setting up classroom explorations of this through drama activities. Brisbane from the beginning took an action research approach to teaching about all kinds of conflict involving young people, at home or in school, using drama and peer teaching within the school curriculum to create 'conflict literacy'. They then extended and refined their research during and beyond DRACON's life to include bullying and a focus on a whole-school approach to conflict.

Financial, logistical and human exigencies played differing parts in the long-term sustainment of all of the teams, with changes in personnel also playing a major role in several of the projects. Inevitably in such a large, widespread and multi-contextual study as DRACON International, there were tensions. One such was a major and irreconcilable difference, mainly philosophical, and ironically among the conflict resolution specialists, which resulted in leadership issues that were never fully resolved, but did not in the end derail DRACON or any of the projects. All four projects produced valuable results and insights, and interesting convergences: for instance, the Swedish and Brisbane projects independently developed basically very similar drama strategies, and the Swedish and Adelaide classroom survey research also reveal considerable correlation of student opinions and concerns. In this book we have chosen mainly to focus on the research related to members of the Swedish team and the Brisbane team, as these two projects were the most sustained and continuous throughout DRACON, and the personnel from both are still active in the combined field of drama and conflict management today, including the authors of this book. However, it is appropriate at least to introduce here the main aims, focus and considerable achievements of the other two projects. A comprehensive account of the research and its outcomes, for each of the four projects, can be accessed in the final published DRACON International Report, already mentioned.

2.5 DRACON in Adelaide

The DRACON project in Adelaide effectively ran from 1997 to 1999, and Dale Bagshaw remained one of the key members and conflict advisers throughout the DRACON International project. In South Australia as in the rest of Australia, the arts are within the curriculum, and Drama is taught as a discrete subject within schools, especially at the secondary level. Previous research by Rigby and others (e.g. Rigby and Slee 1991) had identified that conflict within school settings, particularly aggressive behaviour and bullying, were matters of deep concern to teenagers, and the DRACON team's preliminary consultation with senior educators identified Year 9 (13–14 years old) as generally the most conflict-ridden year in schools. The team therefore decided to concentrate on 'the nature, incidence and perceived sources of conflict for at school for students in Year 9' (Löfgren and Malm 2007, p. 230). The Adelaide project consisted of two components: a large-scale classroom research project inquiring into Year 9 students' perceptions of conflict and how to handle it (1997–1998), and a practical pilot project consisting of school-based action research in a metropolitan Year 9 Drama classroom (1999). Lack of funding and the limited availability of the drama specialist involved meant that the pilot project could not be extended beyond this time.

However, the 2-year South Australian data-gathering project (1997–1998), of all the four DRACON projects, produced the most detailed profile of student perspectives, concerns and opinions, and was particularly influential in the later developments of the Brisbane project, *Cooling Conflicts* and *Acting Against Bullying* (See Chaps. 4 and 6). Almost 800 students were involved from single-sex and co-educational schools across South Australia, either in extensive surveys comprising 30 items of information, or focus group discussions. The study examined aggressive behaviour, consisting of physical (including the use of weapons), relational, verbal and psychological, as well as types of bullying. When cross-referenced with gender, useful and sometimes surprising information appeared – for instance that boys' reactions to conflict was more strongly influenced by peer pressure and the hegemonic expectations of others than girls (unsurprising), and that physical aggression among girls was more prevalent than expected and was deemed by both boys and girls to be more serious than among boys (both surprising). A model of five styles of conflict handling was used to analyse students' reactions to conflict: *problem-solving, compromising, forcing, withdrawing* or *smoothing*, and analysis indicated that adolescents used all five quite extensively, with girls predictably a little more likely to problem-solve, compromise or smooth, and boys more likely to force.

These five styles became the basis of the practical exploration of concepts that formed the 1999 action research project. The research team had noted that in schools drama teachers were often appealed to in order to help students solve conflicts, perhaps because of the very nature of drama, dealing in issues of conflict and involving collaborative discussion and action. A mixed Year 9 class was selected, deliberately in a school with escalating conflict issues and many disadvantaged and non-English-speaking backgrounds; a class identified by the teachers as 'difficult': often uncooperative, boisterous and even hostile to each other and to drama. In 13 sessions over 10 weeks the students explored types of conflict and styles of conflict handling through dramatic exercises and improvisations, structured role-plays, play-building and finally small-group performances, and a resulting video, displaying their understanding of particular conflicts and how to handle them. By the end students demonstrated an improved understanding of conflict management strategies and concepts.

Perhaps more importantly, from a beginning where the students' own behaviour was challenging, pushing boundaries and teachers' tolerance levels, there were observable shifts in levels of attentiveness and self-confidence in the individual students, including appreciation of the confidence that had been placed in them to accomplish the learning tasks. There was 'profound' cooperation within the working sub-groups. Most significantly, it was clear to the team that interpersonal understanding and friendship had begun the grow among members of what had been discrete sub-groups in the class – with the indication that this might lead to more pleasant social relations in the future between members of the class. Though the project was too limited in scale to make definitive inferences, there were indications that drama is an effective medium for introducing possibilities for change by allowing adolescents to explore conflict, and its resolution, from a variety of perspectives.

2.6 DRACON in Malaysia

The DRACON project in Malaysia ran from 1995 to 1998, and took a somewhat different path from the other three regional projects, although, like all of them, gathering data on young people's attitudes to conflict and action research were major components. There were logistical, cultural and environmental reasons for this disparity. Malaysia and most of its schools are multi-cultural and multi-ethnic, but each of the various ethnic groups has distinct cultural and religious practices, with strong pressures on young people to adhere to these cultural norms. These are usually hierarchical, authority-centred and seniority-based, unlike the other two countries involved in the project, and Malaysia is correspondingly more a communal than individualistic society, with an emphasis on 'we' rather than 'I'. In matters of conflict: restoring harmony, saving face and relationship-building are seen as more important than resolution of the content of the dispute. This has led to the establishment of strong Counselling services in Malaysian schools, and the DRACON team decided to work primarily towards and through these, rather than through curriculum teachers. There was another reason for this: The arts are not in the mainstream curriculum in schools, apart from a little music and visual arts. Drama is not taught, though like the other arts it flourishes in the co-curriculum. Drama and theatrical performance are not seen as a discrete subject, unlike in Australia and Sweden, but as components of a much more integrated approach to all the arts. They therefore decided that the action research would take place outside the curriculum, through extracurricular creative arts workshops and theatre-in-education visits.

The Malaysian team organised their research in three cycles. In the first, the team worked with a group of 20 young people in the participatory 'Teater Muda' form, on social and conflict issues The aim was to survey the various creative arts exercises and activities involved, and identify which of them, across a range of art forms – creative movement, visual arts and drama – might relate to the exploration of conflict and conflict interventions; and also how young people use the arts in dealing with their own conflicts. The second cycle initially involved 60 volunteer students from three schools, and it started – as in Sweden and Adelaide – with a survey, but part of this took the shape of a 2-day practical workshop using the art forms of dance, drama, music and visual arts – each led by a specialist in that art form – to identify and reveal some of the conflicts these adolescents were involved in, and their understanding of conflict. By then for various reasons the group had shrunk to 34, which was further reduced to 26 by the second 2-day workshop, which was strongly focused on expression: exploration through the arts of the students' real conflict problems, the values, needs and interests that they attached to them, and their feelings about them. This work formed the basis of presentations which allowed the students to reflect on the experiences; it was noted that the visual arts was the preferred form of expression, followed by drama, with music least popular – at least in this small and brief sample. One of the more valuable research aspects of this cycle was identifying the reasons for the drop-off in numbers: partly logistical and the result of time problems and other priorities for the participants; partly structural, relating to insufficient time and attention given to scaffolding the experiences for the students to build their confidence in the work; and partly, the research team realised, through inadequate briefing by themselves of the participant teaching artists, because they were more concerned with their research priorities than concerned for the artists or the students. These factors were reinforced in discussion with the teacher counsellors who observed both workshops, and the team recognised that a different, more intensive approach would need to be taken to assist such teacher-counsellors to adopt these arts-based methods in their practice.

The third cycle therefore took a different tack, devising a participatory theatre-in-education (TIE) performance. This was preceded by a focus group enquiry involving three groups of 15 volunteer teenagers using creative arts exercises, and a survey questionnaire, to gather specific information and stories of conflict from the participants. That information was then used in devising the interactive TIE and accompanying educational resources kit. The resulting performance had some of the participatory components that also emerged in the Swedish and Brisbane DRACON projects – the use of techniques drawn from forum theatre and process drama, which will be described in more detail in succeeding chapters. In fact, an interesting synergy and congruence emerged here within DRACON: in the same year, 1998, another interactive performance formed the major practical output of the Brisbane project, independently using several of the same techniques, and, identically centred on four fictional narratives of conflict situations of young people in situations outside schools (See Chap. 3). The Malaysian TIE, entitled *Stop! Look! Go!,* was presented over ten performances in school time to 1,300 students in working-class, multicultural schools, 300 of whom took part in a pre- and post-performance survey. The team was pleased that the audiences were found to be more engaged by the stories of conflict and the characters' emotions than by the theatrical trappings of sets, costumes etc. and nearly 80 % of these students were able to identify the theories of conflict demonstrated in the performance. However, only half of these showed awareness of the model of emotions presented in the piece, and fewer still that they could apply them to their own conflicts. As for the educational resource kit, this worked well to reinforce the concepts underlying the performance when the teachers had been properly briefed in advance, but not working at all when this did not happen.

The Malaysian project overall revealed that process-oriented creative arts can be combined with conventional conflict management processes to broaden those processes and make them more participatory, more empowering, and, when carefully implemented, more comfortable and safer. Furthermore, it revealed that current problem-solving conflict resolution models in use in Malaysian schools need serious rethinking, if not reinvention. Unfortunately, the follow-up work envisioned by the research team was not realised, owing to lack of further funding, and the unavailability of key research team personnel.

2.7 DRACON in Sweden

Sweden has a long history of peaceful solutions to internal and external conflicts, although it was once the homeland of the Vikings and built an empire in the North in the seventeenth century. The last international war Sweden took part in ended in 1814. Sweden is a technologically advanced country with a population of almost nine million inhabitants (2005) on the northern periphery of Europe. Sweden is one of the oldest states in Europe and emerged as a Lutheran nation state already in the sixteenth century. There have been almost no religious, ethnic, linguistic or regional divisions until the recent immigration. About 15 % of the population has been born outside the country. Sweden belongs to the Nordic community – together with Norway, Denmark, Iceland and Finland. Since 1995 Sweden has also been a member of the European Union.

The Swedish school system comprises compulsory as well as various types of voluntary schooling. The compulsory school program is directed to all children between the ages of 7 and 16 years, although parents may request that their child start school a year earlier, i.e. at the age of 6. In Sweden approximately 10 % of students in compulsory schools reported that they are bullied, half of them by schoolmates and half of them by teachers (Eriksson et al. 2002; Skolverket 2002). The frequency of bullying in school has increased over the last years. Swedish schools do not have adequate strategies to manage in areas concerned with conflict situations. Many students are exposed to harassment of various kinds. Violence in schools appears to increase and become more severe every year (Fjellström 1998; Skolverket 1999).

The Swedish DRACON project shares the same general research questions with the other countries' projects. The aim has been to study how teenagers usually handle conflicts and to test whether a combination of conflict theory and educational drama can enhance Year 8's (13–14 years old) understanding of conflicts among students, and their ability to manage them. However, the specific focus has been on third-party roles, in particular the role of the mediator.

2.7.1 A Survey Study in Sweden

In order to learn more about typical conflict situations among Swedish school children, prior to designing specific drama exercises, a survey was conducted among Swedish students at the higher level of the comprehensive school to identify general, basic ways of handling conflict. Students were asked how they usually handled a conflict with classmates in school or with friends in their leisure time. In the first study data was collected from 13 schools and from 48 different classes. Over 1,200 students, approximately 900 from Grade 8, answered the questionnaire. The statements were presented as a Likert scale with the alternatives 'almost never', 'seldom', 'sometimes', 'often', and 'almost always'. A second study was carried out where the most appropriate items from every factor in the previous study were kept and some new ones were added – 61 statements in all. Data was collected from 5 schools and from 30 different classes with a total of 674 students. Although only five schools were chosen, we consider this to be a fairly representative sample of Grade 8 students in Sweden.

Analysis of the statements about conflict handling in the two studies showed very similar results. Three distinct types of aggressive behaviour were identified. These were: *physical aggression, psychological aggression*, and *displaced aggression*. These three types were labelled **confronting** alternatives. Three types of **avoidance** could also be identified. These were named *wait/ignore/ withdrawal, hide/mask*, and *postpone/avoid person*. Four types of **fronting** behaviour were found: *give up, win-win/co-operate/ compromise, assistance seeking/third party* and *self-blame*.

A second-order factor analysis showed these three components very clearly: **confronting, avoidance** and **fronting**. Under **confronting** behaviour we found, besides the general factor of aggression, the same three specific types: *physical aggression, psychological aggression*, and *displaced aggression*. Under the general **avoidance** factor three specific types of behaviour could also be identified. The first was defined by the words *wait, ignore* and *withdrawal* and consisted of six identifying items. The second specific can be understood by the words *hide or mask*. The third specific factor was termed *postpone or avoid person* and included three identifying items. The third main factor in students' conflict handling was **fronting.** This was a way of acting, however not aggressively. Also here we found three specific behaviour types. These three factors were termed *give up, assistance seeking/third party,* and *self-blame*.

Another aim of the study was to study differences between boys and girls concerning both the structure of their conflict handling strategies and the frequencies of using these strategies. No differences could be found regarding the structure of strategies. Some differences could be found, however, when frequencies were studied. There were three differences between boys and girls that were significantly large. A big difference became evident, as might have been expected, concerning physical aggression and threats. Girls used this kind of strategy more seldom. As many as one third of all girls said that they never used any of these kinds of aggression mentioned in the test items. Instead, girls more often used some kind of fronting behaviour. The difference was also significant in items measuring win-win/ co-operative/compromising behaviour. The third difference worth observing was that of psychological aggression. Girls did not appear to use this strategy as much as boys do.

In a follow-up study we were interested in studying the relationships between teacher competence, school attitudes and self-esteem as determining factors in conflict handling strategies. A number of indicators of teacher competence were summarised into seven sub-scales: discipline and structured learning, subject knowledge, teaching skills, social competence, positive attitudes to students, feedback and individualised teaching and fairness. Attitudes to schooling were measured using four indicators, as was self-esteem. We found clear causal relationships between teacher competence, school attitudes, self-esteem, gender and ways of handling conflicts.

2.7.2   The DRACON Program in Sweden

The Swedish DRACON project focused on third-party roles, in particular the role of the mediator. The first phase in our study was to design a program for dealing with conflicts through drama work and to test if it worked in a few school classes. This resulted in six studies. The final program was developed as the six studies were carried out between 1996 and 2000, and applied a second time with adult participants over a period of 5 (whole) days. The program thus showed itself to be applicable to both teenagers and adults. The second phase was about efforts to implement the program in schools.

The DRACON classroom program consisted of the following eight stages; (1) Building a positive working environment, (2) Learning the languages of drama and conflict, (3) Constructing and performing conflict role-plays, (4) Interventions in role-plays (video-recorded), (5) Self-confrontation and analysis of video-recordings, (6) Role-playing peer-mediation, (7) Peer teaching (inspired by the Brisbane team), and (8) Evaluation.

In total the program consisted 12 sessions over 5 whole days. The content was related to the eight stages starting with stage 1 on the first day and ending at stage 8 on the fifth day. Sessions 1–12 comprised the following activities:

1. getting to know one another, making verbal contracts and activities involving painting a conflict and exploring different parties in an ongoing conflict;
2. learning the ABC conflict model used as a starting point by all the DRACON teams, and involving concepts such as *escalation* and *de-escalation* and *symmetric* and *asymmetric* conflicts: *The ABC-model* provides basic conflict theory: escalation, de-escalation and conflict resolution. A stands for attitudes, the feelings and imaged the parties have to each other. B stands for behaviour, what the parties do to each other, their action. C stands for contradiction or the content of the conflict that the parties are arguing about. A model of conflict

escalation with three steps from C, A to B is presented. De-escalation is the reverse process, from B, A to C;

3. continuing the ABC-model and other theory (detailed further in Löfgren and Malm 2007, Chap. 2), and role-plays in pairs related to basic strategies for handling conflicts applying the ABC-model. These examples of typical conflicts were extracted from situations given by the students;

4. exploration of the research model of conflict styles and personal involvement using the analogies of: lion, turtle, camel, fox and owl;

5. 'third party body sculptures' of people in conflict situations: in this exercise, every person gets a number 1, 2 or 3 in the changeable sculpture. Number one, in angry conflict with somebody, takes a position that expresses the feelings of the protagonist and stays in a frozen position; Number two reacts to the protagonist and takes a position as an antagonist; finally, Number three is the third party who can make one or two changes of the statue to improve the relationship between the protagonist and the antagonist. All three participants try all the different roles. They choose one sculpture situation to be shown to the other groups. This fifth session also included role plays on escalated conflicts – these were videotaped.

6. further role-plays depicting interventions in the conflicts – also videotaped;

7. analysis of the video-recorded interventions in conflicts;

8. analysis of four different types of third party interveners or mediators, followed by preparation for mediation;

9. training in mediation within a fictitious conflict;

10. preparation for peer teaching with Grade 7 students;

11. peer teaching with Grade 7; and finally

12. evaluation and closure.

2.8   Results and Conclusions

The DRACON team in Sweden achieved a number of significant outcomes. These included mapping the conflicts and conflict handling styles of teenagers in Sweden; integrating conflict theories that were quite advanced for teenagers with drama pedagogy in an educational program; creating a step-by-step program with a specific focus on third party roles and mediation; and demonstrating that teenagers can gain new knowledge about conflict handling by participating in a program such as DRACON. In addition, the Swedish DRACON program showed that adult participants could also be supplied with new knowledge about conflict handling through drama in education. The Swedish DRACON program is described in full in book form in Swedish: *DRACON I SKOLAN. Drama, konflikthantering och medling* (Grünbaum and Lepp 2005, also translated into Danish), and also in more detail in Löfgren and Malm (2007).

2.9   DRACON in Brisbane

Of the four projects that made up DRACON International 1996–2005, the Brisbane research had the greatest longevity and widest reach, not least because it was the most effectively supported institutionally and financially. Chapters 3, 5 and 6 relate in detail the three main stages of the formal association with DRACON: 1996–1998 (locally still named DRACON); 1999–2002 (when it became Cooling Conflicts); and 2003–2005 (Acting Against Bullying, which continued beyond the life of the formal DRACON International collaboration).

2.10   Conclusion: DRACON International

In terms of DRACON International, many people from two disciplines and three countries have managed to work together on a complex research design for 10 years (1995–2005). DRACON has included around 4,000 students in survey studies and hundreds more in interviews and focus groups. A further 2,500 students, 150 teachers and 20 school counsellors have participated in intensive drama programs and 1,300 students have experienced a DRACON program about conflict handling. This work has generated about 100 working papers, besides the already mentioned comprehensive report of the project: *DRACON International Bridging the Fields of Drama and Conflict Management: Empowering students to handle conflicts through school-based programs* (Löfgren and Malm 2007). A fuller account of the outcomes, developments and publications to emerge from the DRACON decade can be found in the conclusion (Chap. 11).

References

Bagshaw, D., Lepp, M., & Zorn, C. R. (2007). International collaboration: Building teams and managing conflicts. *Conflict Resolution Quarterly, 24*(4), 433–446.

Burton, B., & Lepp, M. (2003). Playing against violence – Cooling conflicts. In H. Heikkinen (Ed.), *Special interest fields of drama, theatre and education. The IDEA dialogues* (pp. 114–124). Jyväskylä/Bergen: University of Jyväskylä, Department of Teacher Education/IDEA Publications.

Eriksson, B., Lindberg, O., Flygare, E., & Daneback, K. (2002). *Skolan– en arena för mobbning* [The school – An arena for bullying]. Stockholm: Skolverket.

Fjellström, C. (1998). Trots hårdnande klimat trivs elever och lärare I skolan [In spite of a worsening climate students and teachers get on well in school]. In: *Vem tror på skolan?* [Who to trust in school?]. Stockholm: Liber Distribution.

Grünbaum, A., & Lepp, M. (2005). *DRACON I skolan: Drama, konflikthantering och medling* [DRACON in the school: Drama, conflict management and mediation]. Lund: Studentlitteratur.

Löfgren, H., & Malm, B. (Eds.). 2005, rev. (2007). *DRACON International: Empowering students to handle conflicts through school-based programs* (Studia psychologica et paedagogica, series altera, Vol. CLXX). Malmö: Malmö University Electronic Publishing. http://dspace.mah.se/ bitstream/2043/5975/1/drac06nov.pdf

O'Toole, J., Burton, B., & Plunkett, A. (2005). *Cooling conflict. A new approach to managing bullying and conflict in schools*. Frenchs Forest: Pearson Education Australia.

Rigby, K., & Slee, P. (1991). Bullying among Australian schoolchildren: Reported behaviour and attitudes towards victims. *Journal of Social Psychology, 131*, 615–627.

Skolverket. (1999). *Läget i grundskolan 1999* [The situation in the compulsory comprehensive school 1999]. Stockholm: Liber Distribution.

Skolverket. (2002). *Relationer i skolan – en utvecklande eller destruktiv kraft* [Relations in school – A developing or destructive power]. Stockholm: Skolverket.

Chapter 3
The DRACON Project in Brisbane

The involvement of Brisbane's Griffith University researchers John O'Toole and Bruce Burton in the DRACON project described in the previous chapter commenced when John O'Toole was approached by Dale Bagshaw of the University of South Australia on behalf of the Project, to provide some drama advice and possibly input in an Australian component of DRACON, exploring the possibilities of drama for conflict resolution in schools. As it happened, Griffith university was very well placed to respond. The relationship between drama and conflict was one which it was already investigating on a long-term basis in two contexts, one not dissimilar to DRACON.

Two years earlier, we had been approached by Shirley Coyle, a drama-trained education officer working for the Northern Territory Department of Education, proposing a program using drama to mitigate inter-racial conflict in schools there – many of them with an uneasy mix of Aboriginal and Non-Aboriginal students. Owing to financial exigencies the plan had been shelved pro tem. However, Shirley Coyle was to make another vital appearance in this narrative, detailed in the next chapter.

Meanwhile, for over a decade Griffith University researchers had been running drama-based training exercises for the local Police Academy, which were aimed at helping trainee and probationary officers with communication skills, and to manage conflict of various kinds. The training consisted of a whole day off the Police Academy campus in the apartments and salons in the halls of residence of the University, where the trainees had to deal in quick succession with four 'calls', of the kind that officers might receive over a police radio: one each dealing with domestic conflict, with a victim of crime, with a suspect of crime, and with a sudden death enquiry or notification. The drama students had backgrounded these fictionalised situations in great detail, each based on real stories collected from serving officers, and each with plentiful sub-texts and human relations complications. By 1996, the Police training and the Human Relations work had been incorporated into the University, and the Griffith researchers had learned a great deal about HR and the theory and practice of conflict management in real-life contexts.

© Springer International Publishing Switzerland 2015
B. Burton et al., *Acting to Manage Conflict and Bullying Through Evidence-Based Strategies*, DOI 10.1007/978-3-319-17882-0_3

However, we were deeply concerned from the start by the phrase 'conflict resolution', which was part of DRACON's original aim for using drama. We were aware that in the connected world of psychodrama and drama therapy, dramatising real-life situations of stress, conflict and trauma is frequently seen as a way of helping clients to resolve, exorcise or at least manage them (for example Blatner 2000, p. 124; Nolte 2001, pp. 211–218). However, some practitioners in these fields are also aware of the possible hazards (eg Landy 1994, p. 134). For us as drama educators, we believe that drama cannot help in the resolution of real-life conflicts, at least in 'normal' situations, and might actively exacerbate them, because of the very nature of emotion in the art form, and how it works. This may seem odd, when it is a truism to state that conflict is usually at or near the centre of any drama.

However, drama demands emotional identification or *empathy* – that participants step into another person's shoes; conversely, drama also demands emotional *distance*, the capacity to reflect coolly and as it is an imagined world, without the fear of real consequences following the drama. In serious real-life contexts, the antagonists are rarely if ever capable of either empathy or emotional distance, or freedom from the threat of real consequences following turns in the drama. This does not mean, however, that drama has no place in helping to *understand* and *manage* real-life conflicts in schools, just as in the police service. The key is in that first characteristic: we can certainly suspend the real world to explore fictional or fictionalised conflicts, in order to get to understand the nature of conflict, feel with the protagonists, experiment with changing viewpoints and try out possible solutions. So long as it is fictional, the emotions and changing viewpoint are all vicarious, and there need be no repercussions in the real world when the participants step back – obviously vital in school classrooms where students and teacher are engaged in long-term relationships, some of which might well contain real conflict.

Accordingly, before we agreed to join the DRACON Project, we insisted that for our part of it at least, we would be investigating conflict *management* or *handling*, and definitely not *resolution*. The Swedish and Malaysian drama specialists on the DRACON project backed us up, the psychologists accepted our reasoning, and without dispute or fuss the whole project became about conflict *management*. We then had to work out what we might mean by this. The notion of *managing* entails the ability to understand and control – and effective management means understanding and controlling consciously: in other words acts of cognition. Could drama – more readily recognised in school contexts for providing emotional expression – provide cognitive knowledge and explicit skills practice instead? If so, might that knowledge and those skills be transferable, so that students could call on them when they were involved in a real conflict? Our aim crystallised: to investigate the use of drama to give students the tools for them to manage the real life conflicts which they encountered or in which they were involved.

Through our work with the Police trainees, we had ourselves learned quite a lot about conflict. Conflicts do not arise by accident, and they have causes, elements and structures that can be recognisable. Gaining the cognitive understanding and skills to manage conflicts among the public with whom they deal was the prime purpose of our long-running Police drama work. Together with Merrelyn Bates, our

Human Services adviser from the Police, we sat down and identified a set of key concepts which we thought needed to be taught, in as simple a form and sequence as we could. These concepts have remained unchanged throughout the formal project and beyond to the present day, and have proved a sufficient cognitive basis through all its iterations, and with all the age groups and cultural groups involved.

- Conflict develops through clashes of rights, interests and/or power; as a result of misunderstanding, misplaced expectations and/or stereotyping.
- Conflicts develop in three discernible stages:

  - *latent* (when the conditions – the clash or misunderstanding – are present, but those involved are not conscious of it or explicitly responding to it);
  - *emerging* (when some of the participants are aware of it and beginning to respond to it – in the early stages of the project we used the term *brewing*);
  - *manifest* (when most or all of the participants are aware of and responding to it).

- Responses to conflict fall into four categories:

  - *avoidance* (withdrawing or pretending the conflict is not happening);
  - *accommodation* (giving in and yielding);
  - *fronting* (facing the problem, highlighting the differences);
  - *aggression/confrontation* (returning antipathy in equal measure).

- Any of these responses can lead to *escalation* (worsening) or *de-escalation* (lessening) of the conflict, depending entirely on the context.
- Some conflicts can be resolved by the parties themselves through negotiation and trade-offs; some need a mediator to resolve them.
- Some conflicts – particularly those involving multiple clashes and deep misunderstandings – cannot be resolved, but all can be de-escalated.

To these basic definitions, at the end of the first phase of our investigation, we added one more:

- Conflict is natural and not always a bad thing.

Before we tried out any of these theories that we were developing, we needed to take stock of how conflict was managed in schools at the time, and whether in fact it needed improving. From our own observations and the literature we identified that some schools and education systems already used a range of strategies and behaviours to deal with conflict. However, we also identified a number of shared and more or less unspoken assumptions, which we felt might be worth questioning or even countering. In the years since the program started, many of those assumptions have been widely questioned and more schools are explicitly addressing both conflict and bullying, but they were current at the time in many schools and systems:

- That schools are or should be basically conflict-free sites, and conflict is an unnatural state;
- That adults understand more about conflict and how to deal with it than young people, who need to copy and learn from them.

- That conflict management strategies are top-down, and involve invoking various forms or levels of authority, usually teachers and 'the school' – though this frequently clashes directly with the strong cultural imperatives among children and adults alike not to 'dob' or tell tales.
- That conflict is best left unacknowledged and suppressed, until it becomes manifest, so conflict management strategies are reactive and ad hoc rather than integral to school structures;
- That learning about conflict, if dealt with at all, is extra-curricular, not part of the school's core business to teach.

Methods are being tried in schools to make the management of conflict more democratic, particularly *peer mediation*. Though widely used in primary schools, its results are equivocal, and it is proving less successful in secondary schools. The reasons can be summed up as many conflicts in schools not responding easily to appeals to authority, for reasons of student culture and of the imbalance of power that is often integral to conflicts. Peer mediation seems to some students just to impose another level of authority figure, one whom they perceive as not having the experience or skills to address serious conflict (Powell et al. 1995).

We decided that a worthy aim for our project would be to challenge all of these assumptions, and seek to offer the alternative of providing some tools for young people themselves to manage (i.e. gain understanding and take control of) their conflicts. To begin with, we had little idea of how to go about this, but decided to take on the last one first, and find a place in the curriculum to teach it.

3.1   1996: The Pilot Project

We also decided to start with a pilot project, with the odds on our side, in a school supportive of drama and without exceptional conflict issues, and approached Morag Morrison, head of drama in a local secondary school with a performing arts speciality, that we will call 'Thistle State High'. She offered us her mixed Year 11–12 Drama class (senior students), who were studying Greek Tragedy, which we figured would be an excellent starting place to explore the nature and causes of conflict. We experimented with various drama forms and techniques, exploring the themes of the plays and the genre they were studying, through improvisation, process drama, rehearsal exercises, working with script, and forum theatre.

The students enjoyed it and felt they were still learning their drama curriculum and more, till two factors stopped us: the students' need to concentrate on their final assessment, and our own growing realisation that while Greek tragedy was good for exploring the causes of conflict, it was not so good for exploring effective human management of the conflict! Nonetheless, in externally conducted interviews following the teaching, the students not only approved of our teaching, but a surprising percentage explicitly described, unsolicited, what they had found useful in dealing with their own real conflict issues – a strong preliminary affirmation.

I've started to define conflict better for myself at home and at school. I can see something happening and say 'hey, that's a latent conflict – look out' or 'We're into a manifest conflict – better butt out of this'. (Year 11)

I've talked to my sister about it. I was using some techniques on her and asking her if it would help. She was very helpful in that way and she even understands a little bit of it too, just by me understanding what I do to create conflicts, that has stopped a lot of fighting at home. Yeah, if I know there's going to be an argument with my mom I'll just walk off and I'll just think of a few things to say and then I'll come back with a few different points I can say instead of my bad temper. (Year 11)

They also expressed regret that they could not continue. More than one suggested that the work would be useful for younger students and because of the drama both engaging and easily grasped. One even suggested that she felt confident enough with some of the drama techniques and her understanding of conflict to run some sessions, given time. This brave offer triggered the brainwave that we immediately had together with Morag the teacher in our follow-up discussion, which became the vital second component of the project: *peer teaching.*

The use of peer teaching to enhance learning is not uncommon in primary and secondary schools in the field of sports coaching, and more occasionally in a range of other formal and informal learning environments. Although peer teaching can involve students of the same age teaching each other, or even younger peers instructing older students, the most common and successful application in schools has involved older peers teaching younger students. There has been considerable research into its effectiveness in schools as educators search for more effective ways of engaging students in their learning (eg. Bilson and Tiberius 1991; Goodlad and Hirst 1989, 1998). These studies have found clear and convincing proof that peer teaching can be an extremely effective tool for improving learning in the classroom, in a wide a variety of subject areas and teaching environments.

Major educational benefits have been identified in all these settings (Svinicki 1991; Rubin and Herbert 1998). For those doing the teaching there are: an increase in both social and intellectual awareness; significant gains in empathy; the clear recognition that they can change habitual patterns of behaviour; and finally, evidence that peer teaching empowers the students, increasing their sense of mastery and self-esteem. The writers conclude that it would be hard to think of another method that would enable so much intellectual, social and personal growth.

Other research has focused on the effects of peer teaching on the students being taught, producing clear evidence that teenagers often learn more effectively from their peers than from traditional, teacher-centred instruction. Simmons et al. (1995) found that this was particularly evident with students with low academic achievement and learning difficulties. Despite clear evidence that peer teaching is effective in both enhancing learning and empowering students, it has been a neglected resource in the field of conflict management. In particular, when we took up the suggestion of those students, there was little evidence in the literature on conflict in schools that peer teaching had been empirically tested as a mechanism to address cultural conflict or bullying – two kinds of conflict that were already showing themselves to be of major concern to the students in our pilot class.

3.2   1997: Taking Shape

The following year, armed with a small faculty research grant, we returned to Thistle High school, Morag and her senior drama class (including some of the previous year peers than from Year 12), whom we dubbed the 'Key Class'. This year we picked a curriculum unit much more amenable to exploring conflict: Political Theatre. We narrowed the drama techniques down to two extended improvisational forms, *process drama* and *forum theatre*, which we taught not only to embed the conflict understanding, but also with an eye to making the techniques and skills that were involved in using and managing these two genres transferable to the students themselves.

* *Process drama* is a genre of drama mainly used in primary educational settings, with no outside audience, where the participants use a range of types of role-play interspersed with theatre techniques to explore a dramatic situation or a story by enacting it, with no predetermined conclusion. The central method is usually experiential role-play, where the participants together identify and empathise with the characters and step into their shoes to act out their roles in the story.
* *Forum theatre* is a participatory theatre technique mainly used in adult educational settings, made popular by the Brazilian founder of Theatre of the Oppressed, Augusto Boal. A group of actors creates and performs a scene depicting oppression of some kind, introduced and controlled by a 'Joker' or 'Host' as we re-christened the role. Members of the audience are invited by the Host to stop the scene at any point in order to intervene as 'spect-actors' by stepping into the role of the oppressed protagonist in order to lessen or overcome the oppression by behaving differently. If the intervention is far-fetched or right out of character, the audience is encouraged to shout 'Magic!' and the scene starts again from where it was interrupted.

Using both of these genres entailed identifying what the students regarded as significant conflicts, ensuring that they were thoroughly fictionalised, and then problematising them, leading always to complex dramas and much reflective discussion, which became the place where the learning crystallised for the students. We then divided the class up into four groups of about six students, two groups each to devise a piece of forum theatre and a process drama, through which they would teach conflict management to younger students. At the same time, Morag lined up for us four Year 9 (14 year old) English classes whom we called the 'Focus classes'. We chose another subject rather than drama, to make the statement that study of conflict has a broader curriculum application; conveniently, these students were already studying 'Conflict in literature'! Before sending the four Key class groups into the firing line with their prepared drama work, one into each Focus class, we in-serviced their teachers. Two of these were ignorant of practical drama, and one very doubtful about the wisdom of delivering their classes into the hands of other students. We were ourselves somewhat apprehensive, but tried not to show it, and we spent time worrying about how the three of us could accompany and support the four groups for the whole time in separate classrooms. More than one of the Key class students later admitted in interview that

...we were terrified, when we walked over to that Year 9 classroom...

They remembered only too well the volatility and potential unruliness of themselves as Year 9 students (famously defined in a contemporary piece of Theatre in Education as *Year 9 are Animals*).

None of us need have worried. In the event, all the classes went off without a hitch; there were virtually no instances of misbehaviour at all during the fortnight; we needed to intervene only very occasionally, and the class teachers not at all. The Focus class students were enthusiastic, co-operative and participated in everything willingly. We noticed a spin-off effect: that some of the Year 9 students (especially the girls) started hanging around the Key class common room hoping to engage the older students in conversation (especially the boys). While this was in itself charming, it gave us the seeds of a vision which was to become a major focus of later stages of the project, the idea that this work could begin to change the culture of a school (see Chap. 5).

Where the Key class students became stuck, they invariably found their way out – one or other would come to the rescue. An interesting observation we made in several classes was that some Key class students who had taken a back seat in the planning and initial contact gradually grew in assertiveness and leadership. It was the Year 12 students who had led all the planning, and initiated the first peer teaching – in three of the four classes, it was Year 11 students who ended up the team leaders. The exception was in one class where an exceptionally capable Year 12 student ended up voluntarily coming back the following week for the next two sessions and teaching them solo, while the Focus class teacher looked on admiringly. Those non-drama Focus class teachers, including the two who had initially expressed reservations, all ended up extending the drama work with their classes. Most important, there were a number of significant effects identified in the externally conducted interviews with all the Key class students, selected students from all the Focus classes, and the questionnaire used with one class:

- strong evidence of the Key class students having reinforced their own learning by having to teach it to other students;
- further evidence of the Key class students applying their learning to their own real-life conflicts;
- evidence that the Focus class students had learned quite accurately the basic concepts about conflict from the Key class students;
- explicitly stated evidence that the Focus class students had felt that being taught by their peers was in this context preferable to having teachers, because the Key class 'teachers' were much closer to themselves, and better understood their problems, attitudes and conflicts;
- strong evidence that the Focus class students had both enjoyed the experience and felt they had learned from it. (In the questionnaire, every student expressed strong approval for the peer teaching, and all except one expressed at least approval for the drama – who said s/he hated it but felt s/he had learned a lot from the peer teaching!)

In our evaluation of this cycle, we began to give consideration to the possible further downward extension of the project, with the Focus classes peer-teaching primary students. We also felt it was time to expand the project beyond the protected walls of this school, with its Performing Arts focus, its helpful and flexible administration, its relative freedom from major contexts of social conflict and its exceptional drama staff. However, neither opportunity nor funding presented themselves immediately, and we found another line of practical action research with Morag's class the following year: to peer teach not downwards, but outwards and upwards. The conflicts that the students were intent on exploring were by no means restricted to school settings – many of them focussed on family tensions. We wondered: what if the students could impart their new understanding to their families – teach their parents? This demanded a new strategy, and we were fortunate to have available a distinguished British theatre-in-education director, Steve Ball, to provide a different kind of drama expertise. We withdrew, and Morag took over, as she will now take over this narrative.

3.3   1998: A Step Sideways

In this project we were working with my Year 12 Theatre class, a group of students who included both those involved in Theatre Arts, the specialist Performing Arts students in the school, and a general cohort of students who had selected Theatre as a subject from a wider range of other options. This group were more mixed than the previous 2 years' DRACON classes in terms of their ability and motivation as drama students, and in terms of gender and ethnic diversity. In retrospect it became evident that this serendipitous situation impacted on the evolution of numerous wider insights into how exploring conflict through drama opens up a range of wider personal learning for adolescents. In fact, three of the young women involved in this project became the focus for my own doctoral research, their experiences providing significant insights into gender, self-esteem and empowerment.

The central aim of the 1998 project was not only to continue to explore, through drama, conflict management issues relevant to the young people participating in the project but also to develop a form of dramatic performance in which their insights could be shared with others (and not just other students in the school through peer teaching). As a result, this third project was very different in structure to its predecessors and successors, and in many ways stands alone in terms of its form. Unlike the approaches of the previous 2 years, which focussed on the learning of the participant students, this project sought a wider audience for learning and it was decided activities should culminate in an interactive performance for an audience of parents, school peers and the community in a setting outside the school. This 'performance' outcome has not been replicated in subsequent approaches, and indeed from the next year onwards the research returned to the shape of the earlier peer-teaching project when exploring conflict management in schools and subsequently in other contexts. There were, nevertheless, some critical lessons learned for DRACON in the evolution of the performance, *As One Door Closes*.

This decision to shape a performance was in large part driven by the demands of the curriculum for the Year 12 Theatre students involved i.e. there was an expectation that their year should end with a performance for an audience, and while the group did explore conflict through process drama and other strategies, the end game was to transform their insights into something to be shared. A modest amount of funding was available for research, and this allowed the employment of English theatre-in-education specialist Steve Ball as director/artist in residence, and he played a significant role in shaping the final production. Also valuable here and in the following 2 years was the involvement of Griffith PhD student Anna Plunkett, who co-planned and taught some of the earlier sessions in the project, and gathered data throughout, including conducting pre- and post-project student interviews. Anna's work has informed many of the insights in this discussion.

As One Door Closes focused on the specific conflicts that adolescents experience as they reach the end of school and begin to make the transition away from the influence of parents and seek to find their identity in the wider world. At the beginning of the project the Year 12 Theatre class had been given a questionnaire which asked them to identify any issues or conflicts at home or in school that concerned them. Interestingly, it was not social problems or school conflict that were most worrying them but inner, emotional issues, particularly the pressure to do well in their final year. One student in pre-project interview, following up the questionnaire, asked how she was coping with Year 12, responded

> *Stressing out. I've had breakdowns every so often – I just can't handle it very well. There's a lot of emotional stresses when you get to Grade 12, a lot more stress than people realise and I think that most people go through that.* (Kelly)

The feedback also indicated that one of the biggest battlegrounds for adolescents was at home where conflicts often erupted with parents:

> *I just can't handle it at home. I come home and just start fighting with everyone.. My Dad told me to revise my studies that (I) have just done…they just come down on me at one time, you know?* (Mark)

DRACON research found fertile ground at Thistle High for exploring adolescent experience, and family conflicts clearly emerged as a key focus for exploration. It is significant that the Thistle students chose to focus on personal adolescent conflict, rather than bullying or peer related conflict. The research of authors such as Bagshaw (1998) and Bagshaw and Halliday (1999) has identified that although students and teachers are aware of and concerned by conflict, they often feel powerless and ill-equipped to deal with it. Rigby (1996, p. 276) reinforces this concern: 'many students are, in fact, deeply concerned about seeking solutions to the problem'. He suggests (p. 6) that the best way to empower young people is to teach them how to understand conflict and tackle the problem for themselves. This research indicates that conflict management education was at that time and, we believe, still remains a vital component of the curriculum, but one neglected in most secondary schools in Australia. In fact DRACON and subsequent project work, in school contexts in all its incarnations in other parts of the world too, has tapped into an essential need.

As in previous years, we began with a series of workshops that introduced students to the conflict management concepts described earlier in this chapter: e.g. the *latent, emerging* and *manifest* stages of conflict. As in previous years the students seemed to enjoy learning the terminology and they were able to call on key words as they identified the stage of conflict operating in shared performances. We were off to a good start, further supported early in the project by the success of a process drama we devised to explore the kinds of issues they had raised in their surveys. It was entitled the *Leaving Home Drama* and used the Lennon and McCartney song *She's Leaving Home* as a pre-text. The process drama engaged the students very deeply, with positive outcomes. It provided them with an opportunity to reflect on their own conflicts and it had a deep and lasting impact on several students, one of whom in an essay written much later recalled it vividly:

> *The process drama ended in listening to the song (pretext) for one last time, was the icing on the cake. The uproar of sensation I had never felt or experienced during the process drama. Feelings and emotions had come together to create a dramatic tension that words can't even describe. As the song went on so did my emotions for this girl Charlotte that (it) felt as though I had knew her and in some cases felt like her. Only realise when the song had ended that this girl was just make believe and only existed in the fictional world.* (Tina)

For the students the situation held an element of truth and was therefore not entirely fictional in terms of their own experiences, so it was unsurprising that they identified with roles explored in the process drama.

It was about half-way through the project that we were joined by Steve Ball, our artist in residence, and planning began on the shape of the performance that the students would develop. At this point students were developing a series of short scenes, based on their own experiences of conflict, to explore through forum theatre. Steve as director considered how the range of ideas explored could be narrowed down into possibly four key situations. It was decided that each of these would form the basis for an interactive theatre performance and that if all were performed in the same space, a kind of promenade theatre approach could be taken i.e. where the audience could move from one scene to another to watch the action and interact with the cast. Four scenarios of conflict were developed and in each the adolescent was the central figure.

> *A young man of migrant parents frustrated and limited by his parents' reluctance to let go of traditional values, and their continued reliance on him as English translator.*
> *A young woman in constant dispute with her parents because of their lack of trust and unwillingness to offer the freedom she felt she needed to be regarded by her peers as a young woman and not a closeted child.*
> *A young man who, despite his own desires, was being pressured by parents into a applying for a university course he did not wish to do.*
> *A young woman of migrant parents required to take on considerable responsibility for her younger siblings on top of the weight of expectation from her parents to achieve outstanding academic results.*

Although the students had enjoyed exploring their ideas through Forum Theatre in class, they were not confident that it would be an appropriate form to utilise in a public performance. It was hard for them to let go of more traditional approach to taking something out of the classroom, as Anna noted:

When forum theatre was first introduced at Thistle in 1998 the ease, confidence and swe the students from Thistle displayed towards process drama was noticeably lacking when attention was focused on forum theatre. In fact they were very wary and on occasion even hostile towards the concept of non-realistic forms of drama, which aim to release audience members from what is traditionally a passive role of receiver of information. (Plunkett 2002, p. 197)

The students, very conscious they would be performing for an audience, had a tendency to concentrate on form at the expense of the content and considerable work had to be done to ensure they did not push roles and situations into exaggerated, one-dimensional or stereotyped forms. The interactive performance, under the guidance of the experienced T-I-E director, had taken a very flexible approach to forum theatre, which had added further challenge. In traditional or more classic forum theatre, audience members are limited to stepping in and taking over the role of the central protagonist (in this case it would have been those four adolescent main subjects of the scenarios), to try and impel the other characters to offer alternative responses to drive the scenario toward resolution. In the form developed for our performance it was decided that not only could the audience (the spect-actors) replace any character, they could also stop the action to 'hot-seat' any of the characters to ask them questions about their perspectives, background and motivations (a technique borrowed from process drama). Thus students were left without the security of preset dialogue or predetermined pace and structure, and were expected to prepare and think through multiple possibilities in terms of audience response. Students found it difficult to let go of more traditional performative aspects, and so the form was challenging:

The performing was hard and it's unusual for me to be nervous about performances – but the actual performance was difficult. It was so personal with the audience – how we had to get them in groups. It was (a) little intimidating to have to get so close to them and to have to deal directly with the audience. (Mary)

Despite their misgivings, the final production was deemed a success and they did appreciate the journey in hindsight:

Like, that actually turned out really well. I didn't know that it would turn out that good... I wasn't very keen on doing that. I was more keen on doing, like, just like a realistic play. (Tina)

Students only really learnt the potential power of the form from the experience of actually performing the scenes and interacting with their audience. The realisation that the form could have a strong impact on their audience was only identified later because during preparation the challenge of rehearsing interactive elements, and their inability to control or anticipate the outcome of those, overshadowed for them the more positive and concrete aspects of the dramatic form:

When we actually did the performance, when I saw the responses of people, I saw that they actually meant what they were saying; they actually tried to help. (Goran)

Goran, whose story one of the scenarios was based on, subsequently made the link between the fictional world and his own experience in recognising the audience had offered insights into his own behaviour, not just that of his character.

*I never expected what other people were going to ask me as a character because, like I just
never knew what they were thinking about me. And when they made those suggestions I was
thinking 'wow, you know, this is really...' I was thinking, 'Is that what they really think?' It
made me realise what people really think about what I'm doing.* (Goran)

In the performance the less tightly structured forum theatre and the elements of
process drama, hot-seating in particular, encouraged audience members to be more
responsible for shaping the performance. This seemed to foster more critical reflection from students as they considered how audience interventions revealed some of
the complexities of conflict.

*Like the protagonist could be the one that's causing the problem, or the protagonist could
be the one that's the victim.* (Emily)

Another student reinforced this view, offering further justification for why Boal's
limited intervention opportunities may not be ideal.

*One person can't fix a conflict. All parties have to be willing (to modify their behaviour and
conduct).* (Mary)

Bolton (1995) has questioned Boal's preference for allowing audience members
to identify with only the victim(s) of oppression in Forum Theatre, and suggests a
more meaningful approach would enable participants to identify and respect *both*
sides involved in a conflict, offering the observation that, 'Curiously, taking the
conflict *out* of an event can be very exciting' (p. 33). Although a less flexible
approach to forum theatre may have worked extremely well in South America with
dispossessed and oppressed peasants i.e. where there was clear injustice and immediate action necessary, it was less successful in classrooms in the economically
developed world for the conflict management purposes of the DRACON Study.
This theme and its implications for the ongoing project will be explored further in
Chap. 3. The way forum theatre was structured in the 1998 project provided insights
into how drama could be used to open up rather than close down explorations of
conflict.

All the drama approaches used had the potential to foster dialogue. Anna recognised the significance of this evolution and offered the following observation in her
thesis:

Fortunately, the existing dramatic structures are extremely flexible which readily allows for
fine-tuning and other experimental approaches to be added to the mediation repertoire. Had
the research placed a direct emphasis on resolving conflict, this could have proved restric-
tive by concentrating on the very limited applications of drama that can operate in forum
theatre. (Plunkett 2002, p. 214)

In the 1998 DRACON study, the pressure of developing a final polished public
presentation did ultimately prove a challenging but revealing decision. This third
project in Thistle High School provided some very significant insights, and indeed
influenced the shape of what was to be one of the central components in much of the
later work, the key drama strategy that evolved into what we labelled 'Enhanced
Forum Theatre'. On the other hand, some of the issues and questions that arose from
the pressures which the students faced leading up to the performance did, at the

time, pull focus away from other key insights. We felt the public production approach had not been ideal in providing the deepest levels of conflict learning, and so some of the most valuable things that were embedded in the structure of the project were overlooked or undervalued. The full significance of this project to the development of key ideas in later research was only fully recognised in hindsight, as Anna points out:

> At this time the research had not yet evolved to the extent that the drama had, and as a result, I did not recognise the importance and significance of this innovative approach until after almost another year of further research. Although it was these factors which led to the development of *Enhanced Forum Theatre* (sic) by the researchers following the 2000 phase of the research, it is extremely important to note that in actual fact it had already been implemented – albeit sub-consciously – at Thistle State High School during As One Door Closes in 1998. (Plunkett 2002, p. 208)

Acknowledgment We are indebted to Dr Anna Plunkett for much of the retrieved data, and for her insights, throughout the 1998 phase of the program, and also the phases 1999–2000, described in Chap. 4. The pseudonyms for the schools and all students in both chapters are also taken from her PhD thesis (Plunkett 2002).

References

Bagshaw, D. (1998). What adolescents say about conflict in schools. *Children Australia, 23*(3), 17–22.

Bagshaw, D., & Halliday, D. (1999). Teaching adolescents to handle conflict through drama. *NJ – Journal of Drama Australia, 24*(2), 87–104.

Bilson, J., & Tiberius, R. (1991). Effective social arrangements for teaching and learning. *New Directions for Teaching and Learning, 45*, 87–109.

Blatner, A. (2000). *Foundations of psychodrama: History, theory, and practice*. Amsterdam: Springer.

Bolton, G. (1995). *Drama for learning: Dorothy Heathcote's mantle of the expert approach to education*. Portsmouth: Heinemann.

Goodlad, S., & Hirst, B. (1989). *Peer tutoring: A guide to learning by teaching*. London: Kogan Page.

Goodlad, S., & Hirst, B. (Eds.). (1998). *Mentoring and tutoring by students*. London: Kogan Page.

Landy, R. (1994). *Drama therapy: Concepts, theories and practices*. New York: Thomas.

Nolte, N. (2001). Re-experiencing life. In J. O'Toole & M. Lepp (Eds.), *Drama for life*. Brisbane: Playlab Press.

Plunkett, A. (2002). *The art of cooling conflict: Using educational drama and peer teaching to empower students to understand conflict*. Ph.D. thesis, Griffith University, Brisbane

Powell, K., Muir-McClain, L., & Halasyamani, L. (1995). A review of selected school-based conflict resolution and peer mediation projects. *Journal of School Health, 65*(10), 426–432.

Rigby, K. (1996). *Bullying in schools and what to do about it*. Melbourne: Australian Council for Educational Research.

Rubin, J., & Herbert, M. (1998). Peer teaching – Model for active learning. *College Teaching, 48*(1), 26–30.

Simmons, D., Fuchs, L. S., Fuchs, D., Mathes, P., & Hodge, J. (1995). Effects of explicit teaching and peer tutoring on the reading achievement of learning-disabled and low-performing students in regular classrooms. *The Elementary School Journal, 95*(5), 387–408.

Svinicki, M. D. (1991). Practical implications of cognitive theories. *New Directions for Teaching and Learning, 45*, 30.

Chapter 4
From DRACON to Cooling Conflict

The next 3 years of Australian research (1999–2002) continued to develop from the basic foundations laid in the 1996–1998 Brisbane DRACON Project, focusing on researching conflict management in the classroom. In particular, this phase of the research, which we named Cooling Conflict, implemented and evaluated the effects of the combination of drama and peer teaching first developed in the research at Thistle High School. Increasingly positive results emerged as the teaching and drama structures were refined. The core concepts taught to the participants about conflict and how to manage it (Chap. 3) did not change at all, but the drama and the peer teaching were adapted and refined to give students and schools appropriate tools for conflict management.

There were two separate Cooling Conflict projects, the first in 1999 and the second from 2000 to 2002, and a major outcome of both was the discovery that involvement in the research project could be life-changing for certain students and for the ethos of conflict in selected schools. Not all students or all schools; but by the end of 2001 there was overwhelming evidence that the students were learning something that they believed was useful about conflict. For instance, after the second project, 95 % of the participants could accurately identify and define the three stages of conflict, and the principal ways of de-escalating them. This was not just a rote-learned familiarity with the key words themselves, though the project certainly made a feature of teaching and reinforcing the specialist terminology, which appeared from the responses to be appreciated and welcomed by the students. The students' language in defining and explaining the terminology, often under pressure of peer teaching, showed that they had internalised the concepts, as this example by a Year 11 student peer-teaching Year 9s clearly indicates, through its articulate syntax and controlled use of vivid metaphor, as well as the accurate use of the specialised terminology:

> There are three stages of conflict: which are latent, emerging, and manifest. So, say you've got a pot. The water's cold: that's latent; emerging is when it's bubbling; and manifest, which is the next stage, is when it's overflowing. These can escalate or de-escalate and what we want to do is de-escalate them so there's no conflict left at all. (Kylie)

© Springer International Publishing Switzerland 2015
B. Burton et al., *Acting to Manage Conflict and Bullying
Through Evidence-Based Strategies*, DOI 10.1007/978-3-319-17882-0_4

Even more striking is the depth of understanding shown by this year 5 student, who had participated in the drama work itself, but not had the opportunity to reinforce it for himself by peer teaching it to others (the liberal scattering of the phatic 'like' indicates that he was still processing it for himself as he went along):

Latent is when you are, like, talking and arguing, and then, like, emerging is when it gets a bit more serious, and then, like... Oh yes, and manifest is when you can, like ... you start punching people to hurt them emotionally or physically really badly. [This definition received spontaneous applause from the whole class, as well as the Year 8 peer teachers]

Other qualitative data from students, teachers, parents and school administrators was strongly supportive and positive too, again affirming that the students were applying to real life conflict what they had learned in the projects. However, the sample was very small, and the odds were stacked in the researchers' favour with the choice of school and participant teacher. Cooling Conflict began in 1999, purposely situated in a school without Thistle High's exceptional drama program, profile of conflict management and geographical convenience for frequent visits. These advantages we perceived had provided an untypical environment for the research so far. The opportunity came with a renewed offer to fund the project from our original Education Officer contact Shirley Coyle, who had moved from the Northern Territory to the New South Wales (NSW) Multicultural Programs Unit, with a particular brief for resolving cultural conflict in schools.

A new research question:

1. To what extent can drama assist students in the management of cultural conflict through deconstruction of cultural stereotypes and construction of multicultural perspectives?

was therefore added to the three original ones that had driven the DRACON research:

2. Can drama assist in empowering students through developing conflict literacy?
3. Can peer teaching assist this process?
4. Can drama and peer teaching strategies assist in developing whole-school improvement in conflict management?

The first two questions had received quite emphatic positive responses from our earlier work, and as our research plan for 1999 unfolded, we were hopeful of gaining some useful information about the third, as well as the new one. The literature on the use of drama for cultural conflict management and resolution in schools identifies a number of successful experiments, including Elyse Dodgson's work in London schools (1982) and Anita Manley's in Ohio (Manley and O'Neill 1997), both addressing black schooling in predominantly white communities; however, the literature also contains a number of cautionary tales, such as the less successful experiments described by Shifra Schonmann in Israel (1996) and Hamish Fyfe in Northern Ireland (1996). While drama advocates such as Sharon Grady (2000) argue for the use of drama to celebrate cultural diversity, this is offset by warnings (such as Bharucha 1996) against drama's natural tendency towards cultural appropriation and colonisation – encapsulated in the commonly expressed maxim defining drama as 'putting oneself in another's shoes'.

The drama techniques that we were refining involved gathering instances of conflict from the students themselves, to be fictionalised and used as the case studies for learning about how to handle conflict. As well as the literature, our own experience in drama and theatre in education had taught us that drama works obliquely and metaphorically better than directly and didactically, especially with sensitive subject matter. To approach or elicit discussion on cultural conflict directly and explicitly could be dangerously counter-productive and might exacerbate racist attitudes. Accordingly, we negotiated with the initially reluctant NSW Multi-Cultural Programs Unit that we would not single out or highlight cultural conflicts, but just deal with them as they arose naturally from the students, along with school, family and community issues. And they did emerge, but only as one key theme along with other sensitive issues, such as family violence and peer pressure.

4.1 1999: Cooling Conflict at Clifton High School

The school chosen for the first implementation of Cooling Conflict provided significant challenges. First, 'Clifton High School' in Northern New South Wales had a serious endemic cultural conflict problem in the school which was also evident within the town community. A recent incident of racism in the school had involved national publicity, with staff and students forced to leave, which had left the school destabilised and trying to recover. It was therefore an appropriate research site for collecting data addressing our sub-theme of racism and cultural conflict, and there was strong support for the project among the staff and administration. The continuing conflict problem was between the two dominant cultural groups: the majority traditional white rural farming community, mainly Anglo-Celtic with few recent migrants, and an Indigenous population, mostly at the lower socio-economic end of the town. There were internal tensions among the disparate groups in this Aboriginal population, following historical resettlements that had disturbed traditional ownership patterns over the previous century. These conflicts were exacerbated by local social and economic disadvantages: the dominant dairy industry was shrinking, and the major employer in the town, a meat works, (controversially) only employed men. There was significant domestic violence in the town: 52 Apprehended Violence Orders had been taken out in the previous year, in a town of 10,000 inhabitants, some of them by the school students against each other (NSW 1998).

The research team from Griffith University of Bruce Burton and John O'Toole was augmented by the DRACON PhD student, Anna Plunkett, which made it possible in this phase of the research to collect some longitudinal data by identifying students of interest, and re-interviewing them 6 months after the program had been completed – and in one case a further 1 year and 2 years on. This longitudinal data was particularly valuable in the evaluation of the effectiveness of the action research, which continued to be our primary research methodology, and in beginning to show patterns of sustained, long-term and residual learning, as well as some pointers that suggested both personal and institutional behaviour change as a result of the project.

A crucial pre-condition for the success of the research in this school, and in fact in all the schools that were the subjects of the DRACON, Cooling Conflict, and subsequently Acting Against Bullying research, was that the school administration should be keen and supportive. School administrators needed to support the staff and students involved in the project, to make timetabling rearrangement for peer teaching possible, and to drive the emergence of a whole-school ethos of interest and encouragement. As at Thistle High, Clifton's principal, the administration and the Key drama teacher were genuinely committed to the project, but with the added hope that it might be able to help the healing process following the racial unrest in the school. How much the principal and the teaching staff were in sympathy on this issue became apparent immediately, when we held a 2-day in-service course for the coordinator and the key teachers involved, and any other interested teachers – perhaps the relevant year coordinators, we thought. More than 50 teachers, over half the school staff, enthusiastically volunteered to attend. Part of the incentive might have been 2 days out of school at a beachside resort, but they all came ready and willing to involve themselves in what for many of them was an unknown approach and pedagogy in order to deal with the school's problems.

> *A lot of the kids that are having problems come from family situations where there would be a lot of ...yelling and screaming... a lot of physical stuff... So I was fairly pleased to be able to be part of something that might offer an ongoing structure for ... providing guidelines – a model to work with. (Principal, Clifton)*

This in-service course provided us with valuable contextual information and understanding about the school, and an extensive fund of examples of conflict within the school to draw on. That overall support became very important during the project, when the human and logistical problems that typically arise in schools threatened its success.

Whilst the year's research in Clifton school produced strongly positive results, it also revealed some of the serious problems and issues associated with the implementation of the core strategies for managing conflict and bullying that had already emerged from the Brisbane DRACON Project. Major logistical problems were encountered, that in spite of the initial and continuing goodwill amongst staff and students threatened on a number of occasions to derail the whole project. The researchers did not have the choice of students and classes involved in the project, and in addition, there were serious problems of ongoing absence – of staff and students.

Once the project was established, we had intended to withdraw from the day-to-day running of the program, and leave it in the hands of the staff and students in the school, concentrating on the gathering and analysis of the data, and only providing supportive intervention if it was required as a safety net. Instead, sustained engagement by all three research team members in the implementation of the project itself was required throughout, with weekly visits to the school to assist in each phase of the learning and peer teaching. At one point the doctoral student team member, Anna, spent 2 weeks in residence, teaching intensively, to stop the program imploding completely. Although these logistical issues challenged the existence of the project, being forced to find solutions and adapt the techniques to the reality of the research site worked in the long run to make the Cooling Conflict program much more robust and self-sufficient.

4.2   Implementing the Project at Clifton

The administration assigned a Key class of Year 11 drama students, and two Focus classes, one Year 9 Aboriginal Studies and one Year 8 English, to be the research participants. As at Thistle, we had insisted that the younger participants should not be drama students, so as to increase the 'whole school' impact of the project. It was arranged that these Focus classes would continue the downward peer teaching in special sessions with the Year 6 students from the local primary schools, on their annual orientation visit to the high school – an innovation welcomed by all. However, in keeping with the on-going problem of staff absences which challenged this phase of the project, none of the Year 6 teachers from the primary schools was present to watch their students being peer-taught, so there was no opportunity for them to be encouraged to reflect on their experience of the peer teaching, or continue the project in their own schools.

The key teacher at Clifton was a competent and experienced male drama teacher, but his senior drama class – the Key class – comprised twelve Year 11 students, all girls (though the school was coeducational), all timid and insecure in terms of self-presentation and far less mature than the 'Thistle' students. Apart from two, they had no previous drama experience and only rudimentary drama skills, and there was a remarkably high non-attendance rate – on occasions only four students came to the class. We inferred from this that drama was not a high-status subject in terms of students' choices and career ambitions. Unlike the Thistle students, the Year 11 girls at Clifton were only moderately interested in the project and at times appeared overwhelmed by it – which was not helped by their own absenteeism and the unfortunate prolonged absence of the Key drama teacher. When they attempted a trial run of the peer teaching they had planned for the Focus classes with a Year 10 drama class, they discovered for themselves how inept their planning had been and how inadequate their class management was, and the session fell apart humiliatingly:

> We didn't bother – we thought we could improvise as we went along. Well our first lesson was terrible, we were really embarrassed… we had no idea how to explain … so they knew what we meant. What made the lesson worse was that three people didn't show up to help. (Sharly, Year 10)

4.3   The Peer Teaching

However, most of the Year 11 Clifton drama students were motivated by this failure, and redesigned their work for the Focus classes with intelligence and determination. The absenteeism continued, though startlingly almost all the Key class did turn up for the first lesson, for the first time in the whole project. However, ironically the two most capable and committed student leaders were unavoidably absent (on a school mission) for the first three Focus class sessions. As a result, for one lesson with the very problematic Year 8 class only one Year 11 student, Katrina, was left entirely alone to cope. With the help of Anna, Katrina rose to the occasion. As Anna observed:

> When teaching, Katrina seemed to be able to draw on a seemingly internalised lesson plan and ultimately fall on her feet – an ability that was repeated by many of the Focus class students when they taught the Relay students (Plunkett 2002, p. 158).

This positive outcome for Katrina, who had not been previously identified as either a leader or significantly resourceful, indicated that the drama strategies at the heart of the program were manageable by the majority of students and that, when challenged and motivated, students were capable of effective peer teaching. Moreover, on-going observations of the peer teaching revealed that the most successful teachers were not necessarily either the most effective group leaders nor the highest academic achievers. The peer teaching experiences of the Clifton students confirmed what Mann (in Briggs 1998) emphasises, that if peer teaching is to be successful, students must develop a rapport with those they are to teach. The Clifton data confirmed that an age difference of 2 or 3 years appeared to be an appropriate gap between the peer teachers and the peer learners. A key finding in the data from all the research sites was the consistent appearance of a natural two way tendency for respect and attention in the peer teaching episodes, from Key to Focus, and Focus to Relay. The older students took their responsibilities seriously because their targets were significantly younger, and the younger students looked up to their elders, even more than teachers, because as one anonymous Focus class student put it vividly about his peer teachers:

> *It's ages since teachers were young, but they [the Key class] have been through what we are just a couple of years ago and have survived, so they must know something!*

However, from the logistical and teaching difficulties which some of the students experienced at Clifton, we realised that we needed to build into the key teaching some basic skills about how to teach, and behaviour management techniques – some students seemed to have them instinctively, but others struggled and needed procedures to fall back on. In later developments, our final preferred drama convention, Enhanced Forum Theatre, which finally crystallised 2 years later, incorporates these techniques and skill training organically within its structure. At the time of the Clifton experiment, we were still teaching standard process drama and forum theatre to the key class, and then dividing them into groups to use process drama with one focus class and forum theatre with the other, as we had at Thistle – gathering valuable data about the advantages and disadvantages of each form.

4.4   The Impact of the Project at Clifton

The two Focus classes provided an interesting and revealing contrast. One was a Year 9 Aboriginal Studies class of 16 students about half of whom were Aboriginal, and an even gender mix, with a very keen and cooperative teacher. Most of the students were as enthusiastic as the teacher, but he too had a period of extended absence from the school during his students' preparation to teach their Relay classes, and his relief teachers seemed to have received no briefing on the project, which entailed our further intervention to rescue the project in this classroom.

There was a cultural behavioural characteristic of the Aboriginal students which impacted significantly on the teaching and therefore on the research. The Aboriginal girls found it difficult to take a lead in activities, and especially discussion, and for some of them it was too much even for them to participate actively. In this Aboriginal Studies class it was therefore several of the boys who took a lead in the work from the beginning, with most of the girls very passive, and one, 'Alexia', seemingly unwilling or unable to take part at all, sitting out of most activities, silent and apparently detached. Especially during the absence of their teacher, the Aboriginal boys dominated all activities and implemented their peer-teaching with more enthusiasm than thought.

The Year Six students they taught were an enormous group – over 40 lively and excited primary students on their first visit to the high school, and the Year 9 boys had planned to begin with some high energy warm-up games. As the younger children became over-excited, the boys lost control, and started to panic. Confidently and unobtrusively, Alexia, who had as usual been sitting on the sideline, walked over to them, peremptorily motioned the boys to sit down, and took over the class, getting immediate calm and obedience from the unruly primary class, and with quiet organisational skill moving the session into the next phase. Interviewed afterwards, she mentioned that she only realised she had done something exceptional when we had complimented her, and she still couldn't really explain what had motivated her to intervene and take over.

Well, I thought the day was pretty cool, how I handled it – I dunno – I just said it – it just come natural.

Alexia was one of the students interviewed the following year as part of the longitudinal study. She was no more articulate or reflective about her intervention.

Like, it just, yeah, came naturally, like, I wasn't ready for it but, like I just did it.

However, since her involvement in the Cooling Conflict project, her teachers had noted a marked change in her public assertiveness and sociability, and to their astonishment she had even auditioned for a major part in the forthcoming school musical.

The implementation of the project with the Year 8 Focus class was an extraordinary experience, from its inception to at least one remarkable outcome. The school had been unable to find an appropriate class in the timetable for the peer teaching, so with the best of intentions they arranged a 'special' class for the project, consisting of 28 students, all those who had been identified as having serious problems with conflict. This was a major challenge to the intention of the research, which was to investigate in normal class settings the effectiveness of the conflict management strategies developed in the DRACON project. Two male students, who objected to being put into a class of 'bad kids', withdrew from the project with their parents' approval. Surprisingly, the other 26 students chosen for this' conflict' class appeared to find the project interesting enough to be worth trying, and willingly engaged in it. As the project continued, the extra attention they were receiving became a source of pride in being chosen for this 'special' class. Unluckily, this class suffered more even than the other classes from teacher absence – there did not seem to be a specific teacher assigned to them, and once again members of the research team had to take the class, introduce the Key class and supervise the peer teaching in every session.

A remarkable outcome of this phase of the case study involved Tracey, a physically strong and imposing girl reported to us as having an uncontrollable temper and a history of violence inside the school and beyond, who was under threat of final expulsion at the time of her involvement in the project. The Key class students designated to peer teach this class were extremely apprehensive about Tracey, and the research team was ready to step in at any point if Key class students found themselves unable to teach the class or control her behaviour.

Intervention proved completely unnecessary. The active approach of the peer teaching using drama gave Tracey an outlet for her enormous physical energy, and she demonstrated real expertise when it came to learning about and exploring conflict. The class as a whole enjoyed the drama lessons given by the Key class and came to relish their special status, but levels of motivation varied, with some of the boys easily distracted. The Key class students were at times not very expert or organised (this was the class where Katrina was stranded by herself). However, Tracey not only took a leading role in all the drama activities, but kept the class organised and on task – we could see that the other students were scared of crossing her. When the time came for peer teaching the Year 6 students, Tracey and her best friend – another "negative leader" with a police record – led the planning and the activities. At one point in the first of the two classes they led, she made a teaching error, and partially lost control of the class and her teaching plan, so that one of us had to step in and rescue the lesson. She was distraught and in tears, something nobody had ever seen, and it took the whole hour before the next peer class of Year 6 students was due, to persuade her to face her demons and try it again. She carried it off with aplomb and without a mistake.

Even before these peer teaching episodes, during the work with the Key class, a number of teachers had noticed a change in Tracey. '*What have you been doing to Tracey?*' observed 1 Year 8 teacher to us 1 day: '*She was almost civil to me this morning in class!*'

The Year 9 Focus class teacher noticed with admiration:

Tracey came to me a number of times [when there was no Year 8 teacher with them] ... too much for a girl of that age to have to do. But I admired her determination. She was the glue that held everything together.

And after the peer teaching he commented:

A number of people talked about Tracey and I think it opened a lot of people's eyes about the sort of person Tracey was...to show initiative and be responsible... leadership skills – Tracey's ability to do that really did surprise people.

Tracey surprised herself, too, even though she was self-critical. When asked how the peer teaching made her feel she said:

Powerful – because you feel like a real teacher... it was really good – it was valuable to learn. I'd give it nine out of ten only, because it just didn't work out the way I wanted it to. I had it all ready, but nerves just hit you... I wanted it to go really well.

She noted changes in herself and her behaviour – including in a serious conflict with another (Aboriginal) girl:

The other day I came in depressed, and when I was doing my [drama] I just forgot all about my depression and let this other character take control inside of me... now if I am angry I just change into someone else and forget my old self until I am happy again.

The teachers commented:

She'll think before she has her outburst, then if she's got something to be said she'll say it, but before with Tracey it would just be stomping, slamming, screaming...

Before, she would get a posse and a band behind her and she'd go and confront this girl no matter what colour or creed she is... and so the maturity and the coping mechanisms are changing.

By the end of term, Tracey was 'off report' [part of the school's behaviour management system for difficult students] and by 6 months later she had processed the experience most articulately and realistically:

I've learnt to be myself, to deal with my anger in different ways. DRACON taught me to stay calm, you know, take a few breaths and just think about things. I've improved out of sight. More confidence, my attitude, just my attitude towards schoolwork, towards my family, towards the teachers, everything's just changed. It's great. It's made me feel like I have got to listen to others and there are other ways to deal with conflict. Ever since I've been doing [DRACON] I haven't been getting into trouble at school lately. I love school now... they all tell me I've improved and they're proud of me all the time. My results have been really good and so I think it must have done something. It was my pleasure and thank you for helping me with my problems.

In Year 10, as part of the longitudinal study, we returned to interview Tracey and her mother, who was quite categorical about the impact of the Project:

She used to be... a lot of outbursts and then we'd just yell and scream at one another. Now she'll come home and tell me what's wrong and we'll sit down together.... From my child's point of view it's been wonderful and she's found a new interest too in drama and it's helping her, and I'm proud of the program and I'm proud of her.

A year on from that, the Principal informed us that she was a well-adjusted Year 11 student with a new boyfriend, and the intention to join the police as a career.

In some ways the Clifton year was a successful experiment; the data indicated that the students learned about conflict, and many of them either had or were ready to put to use what they had learned. The transformation of attitudes and behaviour that occurred in Tracey, Alexia and Katrina was particularly significant.

As indicated in the previous chapter, the DRACON research team was particularly exercised to discover the extent of transformative learning and real-life usefulness of the project, without which it would have had little residual value. As we have described above, some students' attitudes and approaches to conflict were indeed transformed, more emphatically than those we had identified in the data at Thistle High during the previous 3 years. However, the Clifton High school interviews did throw up a little data that ran counter to this. One year 11 Key class student wrote in her journal:

> I think drama is a good tool to inform people about conflict but I don't think that knowing will change anything. In a conflict you're not going to stop and think: 'This is the emerging stage and I can stop it'. You can identify 'the stages' after, when it's over and you're distanced from it. But it becomes cloudy when you're involved in it.

A Year 9 Focus class student wrote in the immediate post-project questionnaire:

> DRACON taught me about what to do and how sometimes people are different to each other in ways. But I still think if I ever become involved in a conflict none of this would come into my head until after everything is over, because I would be too angry.

These shrewd comments appear to contradict the clear evidence of change in Tracey and the others we have mentioned, However, because of the logistical difficulties and absenteeism, the program was far less consistently applied than we would have wished, particularly in terms of the learning reinforcement through peer teaching, and therefore it was not surprising that the results were equally inconsistent. We were not yet convinced, either, that we had found the right mix of drama techniques for all students. The next 2 years were to provide us with the opportunity and through participant help significantly to refine the drama techniques, and also to provide us, in most of the schools, with a more stable environment for peer teaching.

The impact of Cooling Conflict on Clifton High school as a whole was also hard to measure, and even more equivocal. It was not possible to identify the impact of the project on the multicultural ethos of the school – and whether the racism problems had been alleviated. The staff and principal remained strongly supportive, and complimentary about the program's effects. However, the logistical problems of timetabling and absenteeism were not addressed through any kind of forward planning, and the program was not continued in any formal way the following year.

4.5 2000–2002: Cooling Conflict in Sydney Schools

> Year 8 peer teacher: All conflict always comes down to the same thing in the end: people are different. Everyone is different.
> Year 6 student: If they weren't everything would be so boring.
> Year 8 peer teacher: Exactly, it would all be so boring if everyone was the same.

The outcomes of the research in Clifton High School led to a large Australian Research Council grant, still with the NSW Multicultural Programs Unit as our industry partner, which permitted us to implement the project during a 3-year action research program in a range of selected high schools in and around Sydney.

Now we were able to address several key controllable variables, by selecting schools that encompassed a range of new criteria. This was welcome in research terms after the extremes of our first two research sites: Thistle with its exceptionally high drama profile and generally effective conflict management structures, and its stable, middle-class population; and Clifton, with its low and unstable socio-economic setting, its very low drama profile and its exceptionally high and immediate experience of deep conflict.

Working officially under the aegis of the Multicultural Programs Unit, we could have had the choice of almost any school. However, as before, we limited the selection of schools through three pre-conditional criteria. First, the project High school must have access to at least one primary feeder school, so that the Focus class peer teaching could be continued downwards below Year 7. Second, the school needed to have a Principal who supported it, and saw the need for it. This latter part of the condition may seem unnecessary, but while scoping the schools both for this project and for its successor, *Acting Against Bullying* (See Chap. 6) we were struck by a number of school principals who flatly denied that their school had either conflict or bullying problems, and certainly not ones that were not being fully addressed by the school. (In one of these schools, we both separately noted that our trip through the school yard to the Administration building to meet the Principal was like walking through a war zone, with latent, emerging and manifest conflicts evident on all sides, among the students and with the staff). Third, the school needed to have a willing senior drama or English and drama teacher with enough status and influence to coordinate the project.

To these we added other criteria, to ensure that the schools gave us a reasonable cross-section, and would provide us with the opportunity to study particular factors if they emerged as significant.

- *Geography*: we wanted a mix of inner-city, suburban and outer-suburban or satellite city locations;
- *SES*: we wanted a range of socio-economic profiles and make-ups;
- *Gender*: NSW state schools offered the opportunity to visit single-sex and co-educational schools;
- *Multi-culture:* we wanted a range of cultural profiles, including schools with established multi-cultural populations, predominantly mono-cultural populations, and less established multicultural populations with more recent Australians and a diversity of first languages.

We finally chose 'Cardwell High', an inner-city co-educational school with a highly volatile population; 'Brighton Girls High', an inner-suburban mainly middle-class girls' school; 'Ellington High', a long-established co-educational school in an older predominantly working class outer suburb; and 'Connolly High', a fairly new school in a satellite city on the far western edges of Sydney.

In 2001, we added one more school, 'Camden High', a co-educational school in a socially disadvantaged country town – not unlike Clifton – about 400 km from Sydney, at the request of the Multicultural Programs Unit and the school's extremely enthusiastic Principal and Head of English and Drama.

4.6 2000: Action Research for Consolidation

The first year of this action research was primarily intended to consolidate our provisional findings from 1996 onward, and build on those from Clifton. It involved implementing and running the project in a number of schools, applying the strategies developed both at Thistle and at Clifton. In most of the schools the research team was able to withdraw from the teaching, as we had hoped to the previous year, to let the schools run the program for themselves. Occasionally the schools needed interventions, but none as serious or prolonged as at Clifton. In this first cycle we developed and formalised the in-service program. All the schools made a variety of arrangements so that feeder primary schools could be involved in the second round of Relay class peer teaching: some by taking the primary students to the high school, some by the high school students visiting the primary schools. We still used either process drama or forum theatre as the drama technique. The data that emerged during this year indicated that the program was having similar effects in the Sydney schools to its impact in both Thistle and Clifton, affirming the techniques as providing students with useful knowledge in an enjoyable and challenging project, and confirming that both of the key elements, the drama and the peer teaching, were crucial to its success.

There were a number of significant occurrences that are noteworthy in this account. In one of the West Sydney schools, the Project had its first (and only) failure, with a Year 8 Focus class. The students had a difficult and unhappy relationship with their new and inexperienced class teacher, who was herself confused and unsure about the project, and had not been able to prepare the class effectively for the visit of the Key class. This was exacerbated for her by the ambivalent attitude of the Key teacher, who, having taken on the project with apparent enthusiasm, appeared to us to be undermining its success. Neither teacher was able effectively to support the Key class, who were not surprisingly extremely tentative. The Focus students were resistant to the Key class teaching, and unwilling to take part in the drama activities. They were equally resistant to a 'rescue' visit from one of us. In the end, the plans for them to peer teach a primary class had to be abandoned.

By contrast, in the other West Sydney school, there was a notable success with an initially resistant Key class. Like Clifton, this small Year 11 group had a high absenteeism rate, including 'Kylie', who stayed in the first session long enough to announce that we need not expect to see her, as she was just waiting for an opportunity to leave school as soon as possible and thought the whole thing a waste of time. She was indeed absent for much of the preparatory work. However, she appeared to have learned the concepts and techniques despite her absences, perhaps partly by talking to her friends. She not only turned up for the Peer teaching, but took a lead, even explaining the three stages of conflict to the whole Focus class so confidently and articulately that we used the footage of her doing this in our training video of the project; it included the quote by Kylie included earlier in this chapter. By the end of the project, Kylie had decided to stay at school until the end of Year 12, principally, she explained, so that she could take a lead in Cooling Conflict next year.

On the whole the peer teaching by the Focus classes to the primary Relay classes was better prepared for and worked more successfully than at Clifton. There were at least some committed primary teachers around on all occasions. Interestingly, some Year 7 and Year 8 students seemed more confident and effective in the peer teaching and in the drama than their older peers – a fascinating phenomenon that we had no means of following up or confirming.

This phase of the action research also confirmed that the project could be successfully replicated in the younger years of primary school. Several of the Relay classes were Year 5 students, who proved quite capable of doing the drama and thoroughly grasping and remembering the concepts. One of the primary school class teachers was so excited by the project that he organised his Year 6 class to peer teach a Year 3/4 combined class, using slightly modified and simplified forum theatre techniques; he invited us in to watch and video it. The process worked effectively and the data we collected indicated that just as much thoughtful reflection and learning were taking place at this level as with significantly older students.

At the end of the year, we held a joint feedback day, inviting Key, Focus and Relay teachers and students from all the schools and classes involved. This was one of our richest and most informative data-gathering exercises. Overwhelmingly, but not uncritically, they endorsed the program and spoke eloquently of effects on particular classes or individuals they had experienced or noticed. This day's greatest and most lasting significance was in clarifying comprehensively the effectiveness and the limitations of the two central drama techniques: forum theatre and process drama.

The majority of the teachers and the students had found forum theatre by far the easier technique to master and use. The concept of devising and acting out an incident of conflict to an audience who are then invited to stop the action and intervene if they think they might resolve or de-escalate it is simple enough for even young children inexperienced in drama to understand. This proved still true even in the slightly elaborated form that we had put into operation, to help embed the basic conflict concepts, where the scenario was split into three scenes rather than one, depicting in turn the latent, emerging and manifest stages of the conflict. We had also already incorporated the modification from the 1998 Thistle performance that spect-actors could intervene in any role to de-escalate the conflict, not just the protagonist. This was because we were not specifically addressing oppression, but conflict, and two of the concepts we were teaching were that all parties in a conflict can have a role in resolving or de-escalating the conflict, and that making partisan judgments (automatically implied in the word 'oppression') is generally unhelpful in conflict management. That modification made the prospect of intervening much easier and freer for the spect-actors, too.

However, although they appreciated forum theatre's simplicity, many of the teachers and students felt it to be over-simplified. The feedback from many of them confirmed what the research team had already identified, that the learning and understanding about conflict which emerged from forum theatre was superficial, especially when compared to process drama. In addition, the research team had been concerned for some time that forum theatre might even be teaching bad conflict management practice. The central concept of encouraging a direct intervention in a manifest conflict, on which the whole technique depends, is in many instances of real-life conflict a practice to be avoided, not encouraged. The interventions were also based on far too little background knowledge to be convincing or reliable. Although it certainly highlighted the conflict concepts and engaged the students in animated discussion, the use of forum theatre, even structured in three scenes, instead of generating effective conflict resolution or management in practice, could be encouraging premature or ill-informed action.

On the other hand, process drama was seen by the teachers and students as providing much richer and more reliable information on which informed judgments for action could be made. Unfortunately, participants unfamiliar with it found it very much harder both to devise and manage. Some participants, both teachers and students, found it hard to grasp the idea of stepping into a make-believe situation and just behaving normally within that scenario as the character, without any audience, so that the understanding of the conflict is through direct and first-hand experience: 'stepping into the shoes' of the people in the situation. This is of course the central mode of dramatic play of young children, who do not think twice about stepping straight in and out of fictional roles. Perhaps because the research team members were all steeped in process drama, we had underestimated the difficulties for those who had left behind the spontaneous 'let's pretend' of their childhoods. These participants were more familiar and comfortable with the concept of actors performing a rehearsed story to an audience. This uncertainty was particularly significant in the planning, since for older children and adults, just stepping into role 'cold' is often self-conscious and difficult, so that quite sophisticated preliminary 'enrolling' activities are often necessary to scaffold the characters' identification with their roles. Many participants also found it difficult to conceptualise the combination of experiential ('living-through') role-play with the more distanced theatrical and rehearsal techniques that are incorporated in process drama for reflection, and so they found devising process drama scenarios very difficult.

4.7   2001–2002 Enhanced Forum Theatre in Sydney

As part of the second Sydney action research cycle we put together a dramatic structure that would retain the strengths of both forum theatre and process drama but overcome their limitations, and also embed better conflict management practices. This was a hybrid that we termed 'Enhanced Forum Theatre' (EFT). For this we used as a base the modified forum theatre that had originally been used in 1998 in the Thistle School TIE performance *As One Door Closes* (See Chap. 3). EFT retained the basic shape of our three-scene forum performance, but added two key elements of process drama, which also entailed repeating the forum performance once or twice more, and added a major new component. All of these additions provided food for more and deeper reflective discussion. The whole process there-fore became considerably longer.

In addition to these extensions to the performance itself, which are explained in more detail below, a number of more formalised approaches to generating the specimen conflict situation to be explored were also devised:

(a) to ensure that the scenario was powerful, authentic and complex enough to sustain the attention, provide a real challenge to the audience, and subsequent deep discussion;
(b) at the same time, it had to be safe enough not to result in any emotional distress from residual real conflict issues that the students had.

This process in itself provided a valuable part of the concept learning for each performing group as it prepared its piece of EFT to present to the audience.

Although it was possible, and occasionally advisable, to generate a situation of entirely fictional conflict very quickly and easily through dramatic exercises, wherever possible a more elaborate set of exercises was used, which were based on real conflicts that the students had experienced or were experiencing, a system that we termed 'Confessions'. This started with the students in pairs, each in turn relating to their partner a story of ongoing conflict that they had experienced, had observed, or were still experiencing, which had not finally, yet or ever been resolved, leaving at least residual elements of conflict. It was stressed in advance that this should not be one that was so traumatic that it would cause them personal distress to discuss or explore it. In turn, each of the students related this story to their partner, without interruption, until the end, when the partner was given 30 s for questions. Immediately, the partner had to relate the story, again uninterrupted, back to the teller, but in the first person, as if it had happened to them, not to their (now) listener. This was the first step in distancing this real conflict to make it safely usable for a performance. Then each pair chose one of their two stories, linked up with another two or three pairs, and shared in telling the story to this new audience, who were left to guess who the story had really happened to – another distancing step. Then one of the three or four stories was selected, to form the basis of the scenario for an EFT performance; to that basis everybody else was invited to add one fictional but possible background detail, on the authentic likelihood of which the whole group would need to agree – to distance it still further, and to give all members of the group some ownership of the dramatic piece. Then the group would improvise, background and rehearse the three scenes for performance, with two stipulations:

(a) that one member of the group would not act in the performance but take the position of the Host, to introduce the scenes and control the interventions;

(b) that the person who had provided the original story could act in the performance, but not as the character or in the role of their real life original, nor as the Host. This was to prevent the real-life memories of what was no longer their experience or exclusive property clouding the action or discussion of this group-owned piece of EFT.

For peer teachers preparing a piece of EFT as the introductory activity for the younger students they would be working with, the process was simpler. If possible, the group of peer teachers would be encouraged to meet the younger class in advance, and hold discussions with them, or alternatively send them simple questionnaires, inviting them to identify the kinds of conflict that were most prevalent and concerning to them at their age and in their circumstances, and perhaps retail some stories. Then these surveys or notes would form the basis for the peer teachers to develop an appropriate scenario – and if a real story was being used, to add fictional details as above.

The actual EFT performance began with the Host introducing the basic situation and the characters (necessary since no costumes or make-up were used, and the performers were often playing the opposite gender and a different age group). Following a straight performance of the three scenes, the Host invited the audience to choose two or three of the protagonists, to 'hot-seat' them (question them in role) one at a time, to find out why they were behaving as they were. This technique from process drama entailed much more thought and time being given in advance by the actors to fleshing out the whole background of the conflict and its characters. That not only ensured that the characters were properly and authentically backgrounded, but that they were all working off exactly the same story. Quite often in the earlier simpler forum theatre form, during the interventions the characters would become tangled in conflicting details of the characters' lives that they had not properly worked out, which sometimes derailed the whole drama. A further control that we added to assist the audience to get at the truth was the 'truth button', which any audience member, or the Host, could press if they felt that a character was not telling the truth, or was being evasive, after which the actor would have to reveal their character's real nature and motives. To further inform the audience, as the scenes were performed again, they could stop the action at any time in order to find out exactly what was in any character's head at that moment – another process drama technique known as 'thought-tracking'.

The effect of these additions meant that when the audience came to intervene in the dramatic action, they were very much better informed, and their interventions tended to provoke much more sophisticated reflective discussion, which was always one of the prime opportunities for learning. It changed the nature of the interventions and the discussion, with the audience much less likely to find glib solutions, as student audiences were able to identify in discussion:

> *This might be solving Jamie's conflict with his mum, but won't it increase the tension between mum and dad?*
>
> *Yes, and what will they do when the same situation arises in the future, when his sister isn't around to step in?*

This increased level of exploration and understanding of the complexities of conflict resulted in far fewer of the Enhanced Forum Theatre interventions being successful, and far more unfinished business (and consequently richer reflective discussion) emerging from the performances. Students of all ages were confronted with the difficulty of solving genuine conflict situations, and challenged to find real solutions.

The added difficulty of resolving the conflicts being portrayed in EFT also led to another adaptation of the technique as part of the action research. To address the problem of the forum theatre intervention modelling and encouraging premature and inappropriate direct intervention in conflicts, a further step was added – termed 'Scene Four'. The Host grouped the audience into smaller discussion groups, and asked them: If the conflict could not be resolved by direct interventions in any of the three scenes of latent, emerging and manifest conflict, what other place, time and possibly characters might provide an opportunity to resolve or de-escalate it? The Host invited the groups to identify such a place and time, and then, in turns, each group would either brief the actors and watch what happened, or, if they were confident enough, they would enact that fourth scene themselves. These Scene Fours were just as subject to the exigencies of 'magic' being called by the audience, who by this time were experts themselves in that particular conflict.

We implemented this Enhanced Forum Theatre in all five of the Sydney schools in 2001 and 2002, with extensive positive outcomes, and it was used as the central drama technique for the Acting Against Bullying project that followed (see Chap. 6), and in all successive iterations of Cooling Conflict in other countries and settings. Its efficacy is consistently demonstrated by the depth and authenticity of the drama work, perhaps even more so by the level of deep reflective discussion generated by the end of the process, and the resulting increased understanding.

To give an example of the structure and how the process worked itself out, here is a précis of one piece of EFT that conformed almost exactly to the model – it was a 'specimen' that was created and used as a guide and template to Key teachers preparing for their Cooling Conflict program – not by senior students, as it happened but by first year university students – whose work could be formally and professionally videoed; this EFT was also selected because its conflict was quite ordinary and not melodramatic. Most of the teachers and student peer teachers stuck pretty closely, structurally anyway, to this model, though of course sometimes they changed the techniques for generating the fictionalised conflict, if there were particular conditions in the class group making a more distanced approach necessary. With children younger than Years 5 or 6, the performance would be simpler and more schematic, using freeze-frames rather than extensive action sequences or hot-seating.

In this specimen, the situation and scenario were devised using a slight variation on the Confessions technique that allowed the group to share common elements from their own real-life conflicts. From there on it ran exactly according to the model. Trevor is an unassertive youth with parents separated, living with his mother and younger sister; the father has re-partnered a former work-mate called Sally. Father gives Trevor some money, that he decides he will put away towards buying a car, and his controlling mother persuades him to put it into her bank account (latent conflict). Trevor's father invites Trevor for a weekend camping holiday with him and Sally, to the disappointment of the younger sister, who is adjudged 'too young' – and the mother sides with her (emerging conflict). The father asks Trevor to provide some of the money he has given Trevor, to help him pay his way on the weekend. Mother refuses to release the money, on the grounds that Trevor himself has vowed to put the money away towards a car; and the scene ends in a four-way confrontation when Trevor makes a lame explanation in front of both his parents, with his sister gloating at Trevor's discomfiture, and the parents furious with each other (manifest conflict).

During the hot-seating, the audience first chooses to question closely the little sister, who is frank about her perceptions of all the family, particularly her ambivalent feelings towards her father's new partner; she plays the 10-year old beautifully. Then they question the mother, who again role-plays with complete conviction, and is a difficult nut to crack; so much so that the audience calls on the Host to 'press the truth button' after which the real depth of the mother's controlling nature is revealed, and her resentments, particularly against Sally and the father's unwitting insensitivity, but also her deep care for both her children. There is no time to hot-seat other characters, but some further insights come out in the second performance, which follows immediately, where the audience stop the performance at several key moments to 'thought-track' some of the characters.

Three 'spect-actor' interventions are tried by the audience, one in each scene: Rachel steps in to take the place of Trevor, to demonstrate how much of the conflict could have been avoided if Trevor had stood up to his mother in the first place, and set about finding out how banks worked. The audience inevitably calls 'magic' and a brief but thoughtful discussion notes with admiration that this is exactly what Trevor should have done, but that it is not true to his compliant and timid nature; so Rachel, laughing in acknowledgment, retakes her seat in the audience. Hannah interrupts the second scene to take the place of Sally, and suggests to Dad that he and Trevor go away together camping for a male bonding weekend, while she and Trevor's sister spend the weekend together. This proposal is accepted with alacrity by both in their roles, and is greeted by the audience with a round of spontaneous applause for its insight and clever strategic thinking. However, in an equally insightful discussion, several audience members point out that while this would certainly resolve the lesser conflicts between Trevor and his sister, and between her and Sally, it would be likely to have exactly the opposite effect on the mother, who will more than likely see it as a direct challenge, and escalate the main conflict. So Hannah too re-takes her place in the audience. Josh's intervention in Scene 3 as the mother ends in some hilarity as his well-meaning and entirely in-character efforts immediately escalate the conflict all-round.

That immediately leads naturally to Scene Four, with the host dividing the audience into two groups. Each group must come up with an alternative time and place, and possibly people, who might help to de-escalate or resolve ('cool') the conflict – for instance a colleague of the mother and Trevor's friend have been briefly seen in the performance – both backing out. After 15 min of intent discussion, one group is still divided and unable to agree on a strategy. The other suggests that Trevor's father is the person with the biggest stake and also the most influence for change, and perhaps has appeared flexible and calm enough – as they explain in detail –to be able to appeal to his ex-wife's pride in their son. Deftly and sensitively, and with entirely realistic lack of sentimentality, the actors take this direction and play out a tough and tense scene, where finally the mother reluctantly and ungraciously gives in… resolving the trigger for the conflict. The relieved and triumphant audience cheers, but in the ensuing discussion out of role with the actors, acknowledge that the play has left them with salutary residual reminders that some conflicts, like this one, can't be solved, though they can and should be 'cooled' (de-escalated and managed).

A noticeable feature of many of the EFT presentations in all the schools and at all levels, particularly the better – i.e. more authentically complex – examples, was that interest in the play gradually gave way to the kind of intent and reflective discussion illustrated above; often the drama would recede in import and the Scene Fours not be played out at all. Frequently there was no resolution found satisfactory to audience and players. However the research team grew to realise that this was entirely healthy, indicating that the interest was now focusing on the learning concepts that were the objective of the whole program. Students were grappling, fully engaged, with the mechanics and consequences of conflict, not the dramatic fiction in which it had been clothed, and acquiring the tools for a deeper understanding of conflict and how to manage it in real life.

Cooling Conflicts continues, often in modified form, in a number of NSW schools, frequently incorporated into the schools' behaviour management plans. The Multicultural Programs Unit continued to support it for over a decade, using one of our Key teachers (who was also writing his own PhD on it) to conduct the in-services for the selected schools each year.

During the 3 years of the action research in Sydney, the four research questions were addressed and partially answered, coalescing into a refinement of Question 4.

> Can drama and peer teaching strategies assist in developing whole-school improvement in conflict management?

Over the 3 years of the two Cooling Conflict projects there were positive indications from the research and extensive anecdotal feedback from students and teachers, that the combination of drama and peer teaching techniques were in fact effective in empowering students to manage conflict in their lives:

> *We had a lot of them actually starting to form friendships that they hadn't otherwise done, and I think DRACON reinforced that process. (Key teacher)*
> *From the staff point of view, at the end of the project I think they were flabbergasted in terms of some of the things that the kids were saying. Some of the kids that assumed leadership roles that you would not have expected to… well, if we could keep that going so they internalise those skills – we might see a turnaround in perhaps some of the suspensions and that sort of stuff that are associated with those kids… there was immersion in the success – in the celebration of this. (Principal)*

The evidence from the students themselves, more than in the Thistle or Clifton schools projects, indicated their assured and sophisticated understanding, and their confidence in what they had learned being useful. This was consistent from the eldest to the youngest, as this representative selection of anonymous comments from the post-project questionnaires of Sydney Year 5 students:

Before, I didn't know the three stages of conflict, but now I know how to stop a fight if it's started.

I have learned to manage my conflicts better because my fighting has gone down

I have learned, by me trying to stop the fight instead of making it worse

I don't have any conflicts - but just in case I have one... It's good!

It was fun and interesting so I learned more.

However we lacked much substantive evidence of the sustained effectiveness of our Cooling Conflict strategy at a whole-school level, especially since, in some of the schools, Cooling Conflict did not survive our departure. In terms of long-term transformation or residual and usable individual learning, too, we did not have the longitudinal capacity in the Sydney schools that we had briefly had in Clifton, of following students over a period of months or years.

Nevertheless, anecdotal data analysed as evidence emerged (and continues to) of long-term benefits; none more strikingly than from the last school to join the Project, *Camden High*, the country town school whose enthusiasm did survive the end of the project and our leaving. The Cooling Conflicts program was incorporated in the school's behaviour management plan, and sustained at least for several years, which allowed at least one remarkable instance of the project's lasting power to surface. The Head of English and Drama, who had been the Cooling Conflict progenitor in her school, reported to us that 1 day a Year 8 student had knocked on her staff room door at morning recess, announcing: *'Miss, I think there's a fight on down at the swimming pool – you'd better come.'* A little flustered, she hastily started to get herself organised, when the boy calmly advised her: *'There's no big hurry Miss – it's only emerging – hasn't yet got to manifest'*. She accurately identified his use of the Cooling Conflict terminology as a very sage piece of decision-making by a student who had weighed up a real-life situation in terms of the conflict structures he had internalised well enough to deliver considered advice to an adult. As the Year 8 students had at that time not yet started on their internal Cooling Conflict program, and some of the Year 7 students had missed the project the previous year, she sought out the student again (when she had sorted out the fight) to find how he was familiar with the language and concepts. It turned out that 3 years earlier he had been a Year 5 recipient of the High school's Cooling Conflict Year 8 peer teaching visits to his primary school, and had also remembered her from then. He was understandably keen to take part as a Year 8 student in the forthcoming exercise.

In 2003 a major new project, Acting Against Bullying, was commenced in Queensland with another large Australian Research Council grant, this time to implement the strategies, and collect extensive quantitative and qualitative data to identify just how effective the approach could be in dealing specifically with bullying. This gave us an opportunity to extend the frame of reference of the research, to consolidate our drama and peer teaching structures, and test them out in a new setting. It was to provide us with interesting new challenges, and the opportunity to follow the progress of the project for several years in one school as it changed its own nature, and played its part in changing the relationships and conflict patterns in the whole school. The project is evaluated in depth on Chap. 6, but before that, further confirmatory evidence of the effectiveness of the strategies that had evolved had emerged from the UK, in research conducted at Cambridge University, and this forms the substance of Chap. 5.

References

Bharucha, R. (1996). Negotiating the river. In J. O'Toole & K. Donelan (Eds.), *Drama, culture and empowerment: The IDEA dialogues* (pp. 159–166). Brisbane: IDEA Publications.

Briggs, D. (1998). *A class of their own: When children teach children.* Connecticut: Bergin and Garvey.

Dodgson, E. (1982). Working in a South London school. In M. Wootton (Ed.), *New directions in drama teaching* (pp. 9–34). London: Heinemann.

Fyfe, H. (1996). Drama in the context of a divided society. In J. O'Toole & K. Donelan (Eds.), *The IDEA dialogues* (pp. 61–69). Brisbane: IDEA Publications.

Grady, S. (2000). *Drama and diversity: A pluralistic perspective for educational drama.* Portsmouth: Heinemann.

Manley, A., & O'Neill, C. (Eds.). (1997). *Dreamseekers: Creative approaches to the African American heritage.* Portsmouth: Heinemann.

New South Wales Bureau of Crime Statistics and Research. (1998). NSW recorded crime statistics January – December 1998. Sydney: NSW Government.

Plunkett, A. (2002). *The art of cooling conflict: Using educational drama and peer teaching to empower students to understand conflict.* Ph.D thesis, Griffith University, Brisbane.

Schonmann, S. (1996). The drama and theatre class battlefield. In J. O'Toole & K. Donelan (Eds.), *The IDEA dialogues* (pp. 70–76). Brisbane: IDEA Publications.

Chapter 5
Negative Leaders in School: Extending Ideas from the DRACON Project

5.1 Introduction

The findings of the initial DRACON research in schools provided clear evidence of the power of peer teaching as a means of exploring conflict. However, it also emerged that this experiential approach to concept learning had significant possibilities for wider personal and interpersonal learning on a number of levels. This chapter investigates how another related project evolved through exploring the potential of the pedagogy itself, i.e. peer teaching in the service of re-engaging negative leaders in school. It also marked the extension of DRACON-related work into the United Kingdom. Morag Morrison, initially engaged as a teacher-participant in the very early stages of DRACON work, developed her involvement as a doctoral student, and following her appointment as a Lecturer in Education at the University of Cambridge, extended her research with adolescents in a British education context. The project described here was funded through the Wallenberg Foundation. The guiding principles of the foundation are to conduct research for the improvement of education; to formulate dynamic learning systems based upon research, and promote good practice in education. The Faculty of Education in Cambridge had a strong history of involvement with the foundation through research into 'pupil voice', spear-headed by Professor Jean Rudduck. When Morag was approached by Professor Rudduck to work with a team exploring how peer teaching the Arts might be able to play a role in re-engaging negative leaders, the stage was set – a perfect opportunity to explore how ideas developed through DRACON research could be focussed in a new, but related direction.

5.2 Background

Disengagement in school can be identified in a number of ways, ranging from behaviour that represents a lack of motivation, through boredom or general disinterest in learning, to active disruption and challenge within the school system and truancy.

© Springer International Publishing Switzerland 2015
B. Burton et al., *Acting to Manage Conflict and Bullying
Through Evidence-Based Strategies*, DOI 10.1007/978-3-319-17882-0_5

A range of studies have identified many of these behaviours in research which has sought to discover what might lie behind such negative and disaffected engagement (Osler et al. 2002; Bigger 2006; Jackson 2006a; Kendall and Kinder 2005).

In some cases, challenging pupils can become leaders within their school context and their negative behaviour a source of admiration or inspiration for other pupils harbouring a desire to 'buck the system' (Finney et al. 2005). These 'negative leaders' often do have the respect of their peers, though their teachers struggle to engage them positively in the classroom context. Disaffected pupils are not always disruptive; some are passively disinterested and do not challenge the system but move through it silently, never really articulating their lack of connection, exhibiting behaviour best described as 'dispirited' (Bigger 2006). In all cases it would seem that these pupils do not find that school is stimulating their interest or meeting their needs. It was necessary to find out why these pupils might have become disengaged in school, in order to see how both passive and negative attitudes and behaviour could be changed.

Throughout the developed world, the task of supporting students in the process of change is a major issue in education (Collins and Laurensen 1995, p. 216) and this research, it was hoped, would shed some fresh light on how engagement could be viewed within this process. Research suggested disengaged pupils did not necessarily give voice to their dissatisfaction (Schultz and Cook-Sather 2001; Osler et al. 2002). The voices of negative leaders are sometimes misheard or ignored (Brown 2005, p. 60). In current school systems, disaffected and disruptive students find it hard to break free of negative stereotypes (Finney and Tymoczko 2003; Finney et al. 2005), whilst more passively disengaged pupils may simply slip through the system unnoticed and unvalued (Gilligan and Brown 1992, p. 6).

Peer teaching, or peer-tutoring as it is also called, requires pupils to undertake responsibilities which usually reside with the teacher (Flutter and Rudduck 2004, p. 188). Generally, schemes in schools have tended to focus on how effective peer teaching is for the acquisition of skills for tutees, e.g. how younger pupils might be supported in Literacy and Maths by older pupils. In this study peer teaching was to be considered in terms of its impact on the tutors – the peer teachers themselves.

Peer teaching could be considered as one strategy that might offer young people an authentic opportunity to take responsibility. Current research suggests that effective teaching and learning may need to involve risk-taking, and for both teachers and young people to feel comfortable with risk, a more democratic educational environment is vital – one where students are empowered, through the offer of real opportunities, to take responsibility. It needed to be considered how classrooms might become more democratic places, and identify what problems and possibilities might emerge through looking closely at contemporary classrooms.

Professor Rudduck was keen to gather together a team of colleagues from the Arts areas within the Faculty of Education to look at the impact peer teaching of the Arts might have on what she called, 'Negative Leaders', i.e. those students in school who are confident, though disruptive in class, and appear to have power and respect within their peer group – though this power may not be directed toward positive learning goals. These students might variously be called disaffected, disruptive or disengaged; students dissatisfied with school to the point where they 'buck the system', either removing themselves from it entirely (through absenteeism) or challenging it (through disruption.) Morag's academic interest in becoming involved in the Wallenberg research was immediately sparked because DRACON research had indicated that peer teaching might have a significant role to play in affective learning. Involvement in the Wallenberg project offered the opportunity to extend research into possible links between peer teaching and personal, transformative learning.

5.3   The Research: DRACON Connections and Departures

The DRACON research analysed in Chap. 2 had focused on exploring the impact of a set of research questions to do with teaching Conflict Management through Drama – peer teaching being just one of the strategies utilised to this end. The Wallenberg project had peer-teaching, from the outset, as a focus and by employing a case study approach, it sought to explore how this strategy might work to re-engage a specific group of pre-selected students. Clearly the focus on peer teaching was a strong link between the projects, but other elements also resonated in both. In terms of structure and approach, both DRACON and Wallenberg sought to offer students decision making opportunities within the research process, as collabora-tors, and encourage further collaboration with their own 'peer pupils'. Both projects valued what participants could offer as research partners, though there was possibly even more autonomy offered in the Wallenberg project. Whereas the DRACON project had pre-selected the group the peer teachers were to work with, even this decision was left up to the Wallenberg peer teachers themselves.

As well as similarities, there were key differences between the projects that impacted on the way data emerged. Morag's Morrison's role in earlier incarnations of DRACON was as either participant or insider researcher, e.g. the class teacher. In the Wallenberg project she was an outsider, part of a team of researchers each considering a role for peer teaching in relation to a particular art form – Drama, Visual Art, Design and Technology and Music. Other differences included the fact that she was the sole researcher working with the Drama student participants; the timescale of the Wallenberg project was much shorter and activities within this time frame more consolidated.

Central to the Wallenberg project were key principles of democratic teaching and learning, so a good deal of autonomy was handed to the participants in terms of shaping decision-making related to such things as the content of their teaching and the strategies they chose to use in the work with their class. The focus for this project was the impact of the *process* on participants, i.e. the impact on them through their role as a peer-teacher of others. Although these negative leaders were in conflict with others, and certainly at odds with school as a cultural environment, there was not an expectation that they would be learning a conceptual understanding of conflict as such.

5.4   The Context

The Wallenberg project involved working with two negative leaders – the two young women selected were 15 years old at the start of the project – and a small group of pupils in their last year of primary school (in the U.K., around 11 years old.)

The first phase of this project involved the selection of a school with a Drama teacher who would be interested in working as a research partner. Contact was made with the Drama co-ordinator of a local urban Secondary school, Ridgefield. This was a school which had for some time been struggling to improve its profile locally. The Drama Department, however, had enjoyed, for a sustained period, a very positive reputation and its long-serving Drama teacher, Ellen, had considerable experience of working with challenging adolescent pupils. Ellen had a pivotal role in selecting the students and in interpreting and monitoring the impact of the project on the two girls involved.

Ridgefield Community College was one of the partnership schools used by the Faculty of Education in Morag's university for teacher training. Ridgefield College was a government-supported mixed comprehensive school. It was set in an area where there was a significant density of social housing which, in the United Kingdom, tends to mean a less affluent, less socially advantaged community. Ridgefield was relatively small (under 1,000 pupils at the time of the research), and also had the reputation of being a very challenging school in which to work because of the poor behaviour and attendance records of many of its pupils. Nonetheless, the school had a core of very committed staff, and a number of its teachers had worked there for a considerable time. Some years before the research commenced in the school, Ridgefield was threatened with closure by the local government authority because of falling standards and enrolment. The local community and its teachers battled hard to ensure this did not happen and until recently, when the school was amalgamated with another small local secondary school, it maintained its own very proud identity.

5.5   Key Participants: Two 'Naughty Girls'

The criteria for selecting the pupil teachers was straightforward. The Wallenberg research goal required work with between one and four pupils who were not consistently committed to the school's learning process; who were perhaps disruptive or disaffected from school, but who were nonetheless 'negative leaders' in the sense that they had the respect of peers. Though these pupils might not be positively engaged with most aspects of schooling, there was required to be at least one area where they were working and motivated, i.e. in the Arts (Finney et al. 2005). In the case of the Drama students, it was Ellen, the key teacher contact in the school, who was asked to identify students who enjoyed, and were working effectively in, this subject – but who appeared disengaged and uncommitted to work elsewhere.

Ellen quickly identified two pupils in Year 9 who seemed very appropriate, Ashley and Kayleigh. Though they worked well in Drama, these two girls were disengaged and uncommitted to school generally, and they were often disruptive in other subjects. However, both were looked up to by their peers and were socially confident and popular. Both enjoyed Drama and were generally strong in performance components of the course as they particularly enjoyed acting.

Kayleigh was often absent from school, and Ashley's disengagement often took the form of aggressive and disrespectful behaviour in class. Both were in Ellen's Year 9 Drama class, and also good friends and it was hoped this would mean they would be able to work compatibly and collaboratively as co-tutors. Anna, their Science teacher, confirmed that both girls were clearly negative leaders:

> They are both quite different, but they have a very big sort of face in the classroom if you like and will often lead quite disruptive behaviour, because the other kids look up to them. They're well respected. (Anna)

Both girls, when approached by Ellen and asked if they would like to teach acting skills to a group of younger pupils, were pleased and keen to help. It is worth noting that this very first step, asking the girls if they would share something that they were good at, seemed to have a very positive impact. They were keen to be involved from the outset.

5.5.1   Ashley

Ashley's behavioural history, which emerged in conversation with teachers and with Ashley herself throughout the project, reinforced perspectives that she was a disruptive pupil and a challenging individual in many of her subjects outside Drama as well as outside the classroom. In an interview with Ashley's English teacher, Linda, she made the following observation,

> Ashley is well respected I think because she is scary. You know, she can scare kids and she is from a family that can scare people and you know, it's better to get on with Ashley than not get on with Ashley. She was involved in fights, and she wouldn't be able to talk her way out of anything, or reason with anybody. It would be fight first, talk later. (Linda)

It seemed Ashley could also be "argumentative and verbally aggressive" with teachers (Anna). Ashley admitted this herself when she reflected after the project on how she had treated some teachers.

> Walking out of the classroom, not aggressive as in like I'd punch the teacher, but my tone of voice and stuff. But I'm not being horrible, but teachers can wind you up. Certain things can trigger you off and set your hormones going. (Ashley)

Comments by teachers in her Year Eight reports suggested Ashley was not very engaged in classroom learning: *"Ashley must maintain focus and attention in class"; "Ashley needs to always come to class ready to work and with a positive attitude'"; "Ashley's target is not to let silly pupils drag her into arguments."* (Year 8 Reports).

Ashley's school attendance record was generally good, and though she did not seem to be very productively engaged in many of her classes, she was at least committed enough to come. She also enjoyed Drama and was working in this subject, and this seemed in large part due to her respect for Ellen. Ashley described the difference between this teacher and others with whom she was misbehaving:

> With the Drama teacher, when she talks to you, like other teachers, if you're not listening to them they'll shout. But she'll just stop. She just looks at you and you know. She's not strict. She says, "If you don't want to be here then you know where the door is" and you don't want to go so you just sit there, and go all quiet. (Ashley).

Ashley was certainly not afraid to be very open and honest whenever she disagreed with a decision, or wanted her ideas to be used.

As is the case with many challenging students, she was aware she had a reputation and had acquired various labels and she was also aware that teachers, and other pupils, had certain expectations of her behaviour as a result: *"Like when someone is loud and mouthy, they go "Oh, that's just Ashley"* (Ashley). Whether justified or not, it was clear was that Ashley did not like having this negative label, *"I've like this reputation hanging over me and I don't really want it"* (Ashley).

5.5.2   Kayleigh

Kayleigh's teachers seemed unified in their opinion that she was a bright girl, but hampered by a lack of commitment in class. Although not as volatile as Ashley, it seemed she was also very selective in who she respected within the school. Anna described her in the following way,

> Kayleigh is funny because she is very bright, so you can have a good conversation with her. She can get rude though. I mean there are certain teachers that she will be rude to. (Anna)

Kayleigh, it seemed, was recognised as a young woman who had potential but was not pushing herself. The well-worn phrase *"can do better"* appeared regularly on her reports, and comments included, *"making satisfactory progress, but could work harder to achieve her potential"; "Has the ability to do better".* Teachers also commented on her lack of focus: *"Kayleigh is a lively if chatty student who generally produces good quality work, but she needs to focus more clearly on her work to develop her ability in English"* and *"Kayleigh must maintain a good attitude and put effort in lessons."* It seemed teachers recognised in Kayleigh a student who could be, and should be, achieving more highly. In comparing the girls, Linda made the following observation.

> Kayleigh's not really as aggressive, they're quite different that way, but they both can be quite disruptive. I think she's a very attractive girl, they're both attractive, but you know, she's got a lot going for, Kayleigh. But she is, you know, kicking the system a little bit, or

she was anyway. Never as much as Ashley. Ashley's been the one most difficult to manage.
(Linda)

Kayleigh's teachers had commented that she was well-liked by her peers, and her physical ease suggested she also may have been admired for her appearance. Linda's comment, "She's got a lot going for her" suggested that she hoped Kayleigh would make as much of her personal ability as her physical appearance.

As well as Kayleigh's lack of wholehearted commitment in lessons, her disengagement from school was also manifest in chronic absenteeism. Numerous reports commented that one of Kayleigh's targets should be to "improve attendance". Although Anna had commented that Kayleigh's home life was stable and secure, she suggested that education was not a high priority in the family, evidenced in the fact that her parents seemed to sanction the numerous days she had away. Family holidays or extended weekends were often planned with little regard to school term time or assessment commitments. Kayleigh's absences from school cannot have helped support her academic performance, though she seemed unconcerned as, similarly to Ashley, the social aspect of school – relationships, good or bad, with peers and teachers – was of more importance.

Kayleigh's contribution of ideas showed she was thoughtful and realistic, and her easy confidence from the outset, suggested she would be 'up' for a challenge!

5.6   The Drama Class: Year 6 Pupils

When it was suggested to Ashley and Kayleigh that they would be peer-teaching others, they expressed a strong desire to work with younger pupils. It was Ashley and Kayleigh who selected the school, and the age group, for the work. Meadowbank Primary School was the obvious choice. The school was next door to Ridgefield so, logistically, travel would be very easy. Meadowbank was only a small school, and at the time the research was undertaken there was only one cohort of pupils in each year level though each was in excess of 30 children. When Ashley and Kayleigh developed a survey for all students in Year 6 this was, in effect, delivered to just one class.

The students were selected on the basis of their responses to a questionnaire their peer-teachers hoped would reveal some insights into personalities and interests. They selected eight pupils – four boys and four girls. Although not all pupils proved to be as Ashley and Kayleigh had anticipated – e.g. one pupil who had described himself as 'shy' ended up a great deal more lively than expected – they did, nonetheless, have quite a representative sample. There were equal numbers of each gender; three of the pupils, one girl and two of the boys, were not from Anglo-Celtic backgrounds; and pupils had a mixture of Drama experience that ranged from very little to one girl who was attending Drama classes outside school.

The Year 6 pupils who were selected by Ashley and Kayleigh were approached by their class teacher and asked if they were happy to be involved; they were then provided with a permission letter to take home.

As Ashley and Kayleigh were the focus of this study, no further background knowledge of the Year 6 group beyond their questionnaire responses was required. Personalities did, of course, emerge during the lessons but this is best revealed in the context of discussing the lessons themselves; they were a lively group of 1 who provided plenty of challenge!

5.7   Teachers: Ellen, Linda and Anna

As stated previously, Ridgefield was a challenging school, but like many such schools, it had a small core of teachers who were very committed to its pupils. Whilst this type of school often has very transitory staffing, there are usually a number of teachers who find working with challenging pupils satisfying and vocationally rewarding. These teachers often find that the role of subject teacher is secondary to the important pastoral role they can play. Of course, the longer they stay in the school, the more background and experience they gain of local families too. Pupils value continuity, and the fact that they might end up with same teacher as their older brother or sister had for a particular subject does appear to communicate that certain teachers do have a commitment to their school. Ellen, Anna and Linda were three such teachers at Ridgefield, and a comment by Anna reflected what all three felt about their pupils and the context in which they worked,

> ..you have to look at outside influences in their life as well. All the work we do here will definitely make a difference but it is forever being pushed back." (Anna)

Linda was Ashley and Kayleigh's English teacher and she had taught at Ridgefield for a number of years. She was particularly familiar with Ashley because she had also taught her in Year 7 but, as Form Tutor for both the girls, she had a perspective on their progress and behaviour that extended more broadly across the school. Similarly, Anna also had a very strong background history to draw upon in her opinion of both girls. Anna had not only taught both girls Science in Year 8, but as Head of Year for Year 9, she also was aware of their wider reputation in the school. Anna also had extensive background knowledge of Ashley's family and she had taught both an older sister and a brother. She demonstrated considerable knowledge of Ashley's home situation and, although sympathetic rather than judgemental, she did comment that one of Ashley's brothers was in jail and an older sister had recently become a teenage mother. Although she acknowledged that Ashley could be difficult, she was also quick to point out the challenges Ashley faced: "she's got, there's a lot of chaos you know, it's a chaotic home." (Anna).

Both Anna and Linda wanted Ashley and Kayleigh to succeed and did see that the project could be valuable, but they were also sceptical about change. Linda reflected on the value placed on academic achievement within a narrow range of subjects and, as this limited view of the system suggests, held little hope:

> *I wish it didn't matter because, as I have said to you before, in an ideal world we could develop whatever skills they have and not just judge them by a written exam. (Linda)*

5.7.1   Ellen

Ellen was a very experienced Drama teacher and Head of Performing Arts in the school. Ellen's 'no nonsense' approach and down-to-earth manner appealed to students. She was firm, but scrupulously fair, allowing students to speak as well as listen; respecting her pupils and expecting respect in return. It was clear that she liked Ashley and Kayleigh as young women and had faith in their ability in Drama; in return they seemed to want to please her. Ellen had established a very warm and personal rapport with the girls.

All three teachers offered invaluable insights, both in terms of feedback and comment on the research and in terms of their own reflections on how best to manage challenging pupils generally.

> *They get along with teachers who will still listen to them and treat them with respect, and that's common for all kids in this school. Some (teachers) will just stand up at the front and think, you know, it's my right to teach you, you sit there and shut up. You know that's not going to work with kids, not with these kids. (Anna)*

5.8   The Structure of the Project

The exact structure of the project was not pre-determined beyond the fact that it would involve participants engaging in some form of peer teaching of Drama. The reason for this was that the project was designed to give the pupil teachers some sense of responsibility and power in shaping their experience. For instance, Ashley and Kayleigh had been directly involved in selecting the students they would work with, in planning the material they would teach and then of course in actually doing the teaching. The demands on them were considerable, and with limited background knowledge of their class, it was unclear how much time they would both need with, and be able to request of, their group. There were effectively three key phases.

5.8.1   Background Research and Decision Making

In this phase it was decided exactly what aspect of Drama the peer teachers would like to teach, and which group they felt they would like to work with to share their skills. Along with Ellen, it was decided that, as acting was a strength Ashley and

Kayleigh shared, they could teach acting skills. The peer teachers also decided they would like to work with a younger age group, Year Six (pupils in their last year of Primary school in the U.K.), and that they would work with just a small group of 6 to 8 pupils to make up their 'Drama class.' The local Primary school, Meadowbank, was approached and it was agreed that a group of pupils could be withdrawn from a regular class twice a week for 3 weeks to work with their peer teachers and then for one final lesson to perform for the rest of their Year 6 peers.

Ashley and Kayleigh needed background information on their pupils in order to help decide specifically what they would teach, and how. They decided to design a questionnaire which would go to all the Year 6 students at Meadowbank Primary School. They anticipated the questionnaire returns would give them information about the interests of Year 6 pupils so that they could select what to teach. The questionnaires would also help identify the degree of confidence that the Year 6 pupils had in acting, and thus help inform the selection of pupils for their Drama class.

5.8.2   Planning the Teaching Episodes

Using the data gathered from the questionnaires, a number of decisions were made. Firstly, they wanted to have pupils who were variously more and less confident in Drama, as they wanted to work with a mixed group. They hoped their teaching might make a difference, particularly to those pupils who had started out feeling less confident about acting.

The peer teachers decided acting skills could be taught through preparing their Drama class for the performance of a play. It was decided, based on the interests expressed in Year 6 questionnaires, that this play would have a 'spooky' theme. The play could not be too lengthy and would have to have equal parts for each member of the group. Ashley and Kayleigh decided they would need to write their own play to ensure it met these needs and that 2 weeks' planning would be required before going into the Primary school. To ensure as little disruption to other subjects as possible, meetings were consolidated into two one-and-a-half hour planning meetings per week, but times rotated. The script would also need to be written outside these times, as well as refined within them.

Six lessons needed to be planned for Meadowbank, plus one lesson allocated for the performance. The peer teachers decided the first two lessons would be skills lessons, with some time for the group to become familiar with the script, and the final four lessons devoted to rehearsal, with the peer teachers acting as directors to develop Drama skills.

5.8.3   The Teaching Episodes

Six lessons, each of one-and-a-quarter hours, two mornings per week for 3 weeks were conducted, with the first lesson shaped around getting to know the group and distributing scripts, and the second lesson devoted to selecting the cast and reading through the play. The following four lessons were rehearsals, each to begin with a 'warm up' and a short introduction to a 'target' skill (e.g. characterisation, focus etc.). Following each lesson there was a short amount of time over morning break to discuss how things went and make any decisions needed for the subsequent lesson. Ashley and Kayleigh were also able to discuss ideas with Ellen during the week between their teaching periods.

5.9   Methodology and Data Collection

This particular research used a Case study approach in that it focused very specifically on the experiences of two young women in the bounded context of a school environment. In educational research, 'case study' is the term used for a research strategy that focuses enquiry around the detailed study of a particular teaching and/or learning phenomenon. There are several definitions in the literature, spanning a range of different emphases and approaches, but for the purposes of this study the following brief definition provided by Yin served as an appropriate starting-point:

> A case study is an empirical inquiry that investigates a contemporary phenomenon within its real-life context especially when the boundaries between the phenomenon and context are not clearly evident. (Yin 2003, p. 13)

Instrumental Case study (Stake 2000, p. 437), aims to look very closely at an instance in order that broader conclusions might be drawn. All classroom contexts have subtle differences and certainly no two adolescent girls are the same. However the research did reveal common experiences and thus issues for consideration in wider contexts. Case Study Research in this project could be considered more theory-building than theory-testing (Layder, cited in Denscombe 2002, p. 33), for new insights were generated as a result of the research.

5.10   Methods

5.10.1   Observation Notes

Observation notes were written throughout all 'action phases' of each project, i.e. during classroom activities.

Observation did not employ a structured schedule of pre-determined categories as a checklist, or systematically record events against a scale for future numerical assessment. More important was acknowledging "critical incidents" (Booth 1997; Bell 2002; Cohen et al. 2007); that is, noting particular events and moments that seem to "typify or illuminate very starkly" (Cohen et al. 2007, p. 404) a particular behaviour or issue, observing individual response and reflecting, in the moment, on the significance of this in relation to the research question.

Observation notes were only taken during the 6 peer teaching episodes.

5.10.2   Reflective Journals

A reflective journal, kept by the researcher, recorded thoughts and reflections about what had been observed with the benefit of hindsight. Some journal entries were quick jottings of things to think about. At other times, more significantly, they contained extra detail. Bell describes one method of recording events as a "critical incidents" approach, where rather than a detailed description of all events, the diarist notes selectively those events which stood out for some reason (Bell 2002, p. 151). Notes seemed to evolve organically to take the form of a log of reflections on critical incidents and it soon became apparent that key incidents were often the most revealing sources of information.

There were also occasions when the researcher received feedback from the girls' class teacher about what they had said to her immediately after they had returned from teaching. Often full of either enthusiasm – or disappointment – the girls would return to school eager to tell their Drama teacher what had happened. These post-lesson discussions were relayed back to the researcher. The Drama teacher would often offer her own analysis of their stories as she retold them, and her insight, particularly at the beginning of the research, as someone closer to the girls, did influence reflections.

Rather than compromising the research, numerous theorists support the view that research can be validated in dialogue with participants (Elliot 1991; Grumet 1997; Cohen et al. 2007).

5.10.3   Interviews

Structured, semi-structured and unstructured interviews were used and, over the course of the research, it was the latter two approaches that were employed more often and found most useful. Given that critical incidents emerge during the course of research, the flexibility of unstructured interviews allowed responsiveness.

Although it is relatively easy to define what is meant by a 'structured' interview, the latter two forms have more fluid boundaries. As Denscombe (2002) points out, semi-structured and non-structured interviews are really on a continuum and can slide back and forth along a scale (p. 113).

Because the research was interested in the thoughts and feelings of individual interviewees, the researcher needed to be less obtrusive to allow participants to feel comfortable about offering their ideas and following their own trains of thought. Rather like Foley and Valenzuela (2005), a more conversational or "dialogic style" of interviewing was sought which encouraged interviewees to share more of themselves (p. 223).

It was intended that students would be interviewed four times, first with their drama teacher at the initial meeting, twice during the planning and peer teaching phases of this project, and then finally following the final teaching episode. Although the researcher was able to interview one of the girls the fourth time, the other was not at school. Two of the girls' other teachers were also interviewed, and following the final peer-teaching episode, the Year 6 pupils were also interviewed, as a group.

5.11 Findings and Analysis

The project was a tale of challenges and risks – and risks which did not always pay off. But these risks did nonetheless yield important insights – both for the researcher and also, in this case, for the two young women themselves. From the start, the girls were engaged and enthusiastic. They attended all the planning meetings – despite their reputations as unreliable – and took their roles as co-planners very seriously, showing great maturity of attitude. Already they were warming to a certain sense of power and of being able to shape events in school. Their commitment confirms Patti Lather's (1991) assertion that there should be more reciprocity in our interaction with students towards mutual negotiation of meaning and power.

From the perspective of co-planner, it was important to "let go" in order for the girls to assume responsibility, even though on some occasions decisions were made that were not always ideal. For example, the decision to write an original script for the performance took a good deal of time and compromised the big picture objectives of teaching the Year 6 pupils acting skills. But Ashley and Kayleigh were keen to honour the interest of the Year 6 pupils in performing. The pupils had communicated in the questionnaire responses they wanted "a scary story" that they could act out, so Ashley and Kayleigh were prepared to devise this for them. As Goodlad and Hirst (1998) has said, one of the key features of peer tutoring is the handing over of responsibility, that usually resides with the teacher, to the pupils.

What was particularly interesting was evidence that Ashley and Kayleigh were starting to use a "teacherly" language from an early stage in the project. Kayleigh spoke about "knowing what it feels like" and the need to "break things down" and to use terms that the Year 6 pupils would be able to understand. It was apparent that empathy was going to be a key feature of their relationships with the Year 6 pupils – and also that they were drawing on their own experience of what made for good pupil teacher relationships in lessons.

The girls also seemed to enjoy, from the comments they made, the fact that other teachers knew they were engaged in the project, were asking them about it, and were giving them encouragement – and attention. Moreover, a letter was sent home informing their parents what they were doing. Ashley described her amusement at seeing her mother open a letter from the school which, for a change, was telling her something good that Ashley was doing!

5.12   The First Two Lessons

After several weeks of planning, the time came to meet the Year 6 students in the local primary school. Ashley and Kayleigh were aware that they would have to assume control once they were in the classroom and they were prepared to rise to the challenge.

After a slow start the first lesson went very well. Interestingly, Kayleigh, usually the quieter of the two, took control and Ashley stood at her side smiling support-ively but nervously. The Year 6 pupils were on their best behaviour. A lively Drama game set the tone and the Year 6 pupils quickly accepted Ashley and Kayleigh as "their teachers". Once the pupils were introduced to the scripts, Ashley sensitively took two pupils who were not involved in the first scene aside and worked with them on her own. This seemed to build her confidence and when she returned to the rest of the group, she shared in the leadership – although usually as a reinforcement for Kayleigh's role rather than working on her own initiative.

The second lesson went relatively smoothly. By now the pupils and their 2 Year 9 teachers were comfortable enough with each other to engage in some playful chat. Forgetting there was another adult in the room (Morag) one of the boys was confident enough to start fooling around – giving a bit of cheek to his "teachers" and encouraging his mates to join in. Kayleigh, no doubt all too familiar with the routine, pulled him gently but firmly into line, reminding him where the boundaries were and his responsibility to the group and its ultimate performance. It was clear that this incident was significant moment, a point when Kayleigh could look from the perspective of a *teacher*, at how her own behaviour might be experienced by a teacher.

At this time, some of the Year 6 pupils came to the high school to attend the Orientation Day. Ashley was pleased when some came up to her with their peers, said hello and introduced her as "my Drama teacher". This was evidence, it seemed, that an authentic relationship based on mutual respect had been established.

5.13   The Third Lesson

Kayleigh demonstrated an innate ability to think on her feet, to sense when something wasn't quite working and to move on. Ashley was ready to "go with the flow" but was less secure in taking initiative. The degree to which Kayleigh had really led the class only became evident in lesson 3 – when she didn't turn up. Kayleigh went on a last minute family holiday leaving Ashley to cope on her own. Ashley was under-prepared for the lesson and in her fluster forgot what she had intended to do. Things went from bad to worse as she struggled. The class soon realised her uncertainty and decided to test her. At one point she froze and said to the class, *"Er.. what shall we do next?"* A student, aware that Ashley was speaking in desperation rather than in a spirit of democracy shot back, *"Well, you're the teacher!"*. The 'tough girl' image had gone and Ashley's vulnerability was exposed. It is in these situations that the role of the researcher is a particularly difficult one; while the role requires ethical 'distance', it is difficult not to intervene to save greater humiliation for the participant. The lesson was a disaster: the Year 6 pupils needed structure and they needed to feel they were going somewhere in the lesson. The boys in the class particularly were unfocussed and disruptive, and they made it impossible for Ashley to teach effectively at all. This incident was a significant moment; one of those 'critical incidents' that provide develop deeper understanding. Morag was very worried that Ashley might have returned to the school upset after her lesson, but talking to Ellen after the school, an interesting perspective was offered on the event. Ellen stated that Ashley was indeed upset but that it should be seen as a *"...good thing."* Somewhat mystified by this response, Morag was relieved when Ellen elaborated…

> *Can't you see? It's a good sign. It means she cares, she cares about the project and what she is doing…it matters to her. (Ellen)*

The lesson was indeed a turning point for Ashley. In the past she might well have made excuses, blamed someone else or just walked away and pretended that she didn't care. This time she actually admitted that she was frightened – she had actually allowed herself to engage with the project and it mattered to her. In an interview later in the project Ashley reflected on what had happened and how she had felt,

> *I was all nervous and a bit frightened as well because I didn't want to muck up, but I did - so I felt gutted. (Ashley)*

5.14   The Fourth Lesson

There was only 1 day between Lesson 3 and the next and Morag feared Ashley would decide not to come back. Furthermore, Kayleigh would not be there to support her in that lesson either. But Ashley arrived the next morning determined, smiling, ready to go. She outlined what she intended to do and bravely stepped back into the lions' den. The Year 6 group were ready to challenge her again but she didn't give them a chance. She had planned every step and took complete control. The class responded and once she started to relax they all enjoyed themselves. If someone forgot a line, they laughed then got straight back to the task. The look of exhilaration on her face at the end of the lesson revealed a young woman genuinely proud of what she had achieved. Later, Ashley tried to explain how exciting it had felt:

> *I took control of them.. I felt more confident, just bubbling.. it made me really proud. Like the end of the session I thought to myself, 'you've done it, well done, you've proved everyone wrong.' I've even proved myself wrong, so it made me happy. (Ashley)*

Ashley had managed to create what Brown and Gilligan (1992) identify as an authentic connection i.e. an experience that provides a genuine sense of being valued: people were actually listening to her and she seemed to have taken control of her own self-doubt.

5.15   The Final Performance

By the final session, Kayleigh had returned. Together they conducted the final rehearsal with the Year 6 pupils. Ashley and Kayleigh's students worked with nervous and excited energy to pull things together in time for the arrival of their audience – the rest of the year group. Kayleigh stood for no nonsense and directed her actors not to giggle. In no uncertain terms they were told to remain *"focussed and professional"* !

In the end it was not the most polished production ever staged (there were still a few giggles despite the earnest "shushing" backstage!) and the acting skills of the group still needed a little work too, but everyone seemed proud of what they had achieved. The audience did seem to take pleasure seeing their peers and, though not exactly convinced by the "scariness" of the story, did enjoy the entertainment. All considered the performance a success.

5.16   Outcomes

Back in school, Ashley and Kayleigh's Year 9 reports were distributed. Their Drama teacher was keen to highlight the comments that had come from other teachers who were finding evidence of an improvement in the attitude and behaviour of both the girls. This improvement seemed to coincide with their involvement in the peer-teaching project. Comments on Ashley's reports included *"…sound progress.. particularly pleased with the improvement I have seen in her behaviour" "… a lot more settled" "..improved attitude to work"*. Her drama teacher said that one clear development was that Ashley had started asking about the marks she had received – before, Ashley had never tried to understand what levels meant and seemed not to care. Ashley seemed to be becoming interested in the business of learning. Teachers also reported a visible improvement in Kayleigh's behaviour and, although attendance was still an issue, her reports seemed to indicate more engagement in school, *"..good attitude and effort" ".. marked improvement in skills" "Kayleigh has worked on some tasks with great enthusiasm"*.

There was clear evidence that the process of peer-teaching had a positive impact on academic motivation for both girls, however it would appear it may have also had an influence on Ashley's emotional development. It was her Science teacher (Anna) who made a noteworthy comment. This teacher said that in Ashley's family the older siblings had become increasingly disengaged and negative about school from year to year and she was excited to see that Ashley seemed able to break the pattern. Ashley's teacher noted that in a particular Science lesson, she had overheard Ashley talking with her peers about a serious book that she was reading:

> She was reading bits of it out to others and she was talking about how emotional it made her feel, which I don't think she would have talked about before.. I think she has made a huge journey in a short time. (Anna)

This was an important observation as it illustrated that Ashley was not only developing empathy, but was feeling brave enough to share her feelings with others. This enabled Ashley to make closer connections with others and attach implications, for herself and others, when considering behaviour. This was a significant step towards helping her to break the negative behaviour patterns that were often hurting her as much as others. It was hoped that being able to share her feelings would enable Ashley to form more honest and authentic relationships.

Although Kayleigh had missed some crucial lessons in the middle of the project, she had returned with commitment and determination. Kayleigh could have easily seen picking up again as too difficult and terminated her involvement. She could have given up – as she had with other things in the past. But she did feel a responsibility to her year 6 pupils, and her delight when they greeted her return was obvious. It might be hoped that this positive experience proved to Kayleigh that she is valued and respected.

There seems to be a close and complex relationship between academic performance and engagement in the classroom, and engagement appears to be strongly influenced by social and emotional factors. At the heart of disengagement and negative leadership are issues of power. Although Ashley and Kayleigh had always appeared to be strong young women, with the confidence to be vocal and assertive, their transgressive behaviour had worked against them ever being able to realize any constructive power within the school system. Jackson (2006) describes this behaviour as 'self-handicapping' and asserts that individuals often behave in ways likely to jeopardize their performance in exams as a way of providing an excuse for failure (p. 86) Jennings (2003) suggests that much research on academic performance seems to neglect the influence of social and emotional variables (p. 43), and how pupils themselves feel about school. It would appear that the role of peer teacher offered Ashley and Kayleigh the opportunity to redraw power relationships and develop personal insights to support their social and emotional development.

Some very significant insights emerged from the research. As Goodlad and Hirst (1989) had noted, peer teachers particularly value the feeling of "being needed'. Researchers have also underlined the significance of the peer tutor actually becoming personally engaged with the task. However risky the situation, Ashley and Kayleigh felt that their teaching mattered. For education to be an enriching experience, meanings must become personal – only then will they be incorporated into experience and tried out in everyday living. The positive experiences of giving and of being accepted filtered back into Ashley and Kayleigh's general sense of self-worth and their attitude to other areas of the curriculum.

5.17 Conclusions and Reflections: The Role of Drama

As stated above, the process of peer teaching offered significant social and emotional development for the two young women in the study, but there are strong links to draw back to the role of Drama in this project. Drama, as a discipline, played a significant role in the peer-teaching project in question, and it is worth considering this for several reasons. Firstly, Drama as a subject, was one of the few subjects in which the girls in this study were achieving. In understanding the reasons for this, there are implications for how we might understand the nature of effective *learning* more generally. Secondly, Drama was used by the young peer teachers as a teaching pedagogy, and Ashley and Kayleigh had the *real-life role* of a teacher for the duration of the project. They also utilized improvisation and roleplay when working with their pupils. Deconstructing the nature of role and role-play, and how these operate as learning experiences in drama, also has implications for how we might understand the nature of effective *teaching* more broadly.

Sarason (1999) explores teaching as a Performing Art and aligns the role of teacher with that of actor and curriculum with script. While Ackroyd (2004) explores this notion of teacher as performer in her research on the use of teacher-in-role in the classroom, Sarason holds all teaching as performance. While one might have some strong reservations regarding how far he takes this comparison "… teacher is chief actor, the 'star', the actor that gets top billing." (1999, p. 3), he does offer a useful definition of how role might operate, "Becoming and sustaining a role is an artistic process of identification and imagination.." (p. 4) Certainly in this project Ashley and Kayleigh had to use their imaginations as they entered into the 'what if ' context of their own classroom and took on the role of teacher. At the start of the project Ashley and Kayleigh were not supportive of many of their teachers and had little respect for most. The process of peer teaching resulted in their acknowledgement of how difficult the job of could be – clearly they could now identify with a role previously unfathomable to them O'Hanlon quoted in Ackroyd (2004) states that the act of teaching 'confers professional identity' (p. 9); I would suggest that while the act of teaching did allow these young women an insight into the professional challenges of teaching, it also fostered a sense of identity in a broader sense – it gave them an opportunity to been seen as something other than 'naughty girl.

Philip Taylor (2000) reminds us that transformation does not happen in a vacuum, and needs the careful structuring of strategies to facilitate a 'wide-awakeness' in participants (p. 8) He refers to the work of arts philosopher Maxine Greene and democratic education theorist and educator Paolo Freire in defining this concept as a heightened conscious where young people can consciously reflect on their actions and change as a result of their discoveries: " Such transformation is a praxis: action-reflection- transformation."(p. 9)

Although Taylor is exploring the nature of Applied theatre in this discussion, some of the key issues he raises in terms of transformational processes can be applied more broadly. Although Ashley and Kayleigh were using drama strategies in their teaching, the process of peer teaching was, of itself, a 'carefully structured strategy' that offered students positive experiences outside their lived experience. Maxine Greene (1995) is discussing the nature and potential of aesthetic experience to release the imagination and offer young people new possibilities through dialogues that stir them to 'reach out on their own initiatives' so apathy and indifference can give way to 'images of what might be' (p. 5)

Researchers have underlined the significance of the peer tutor actually becoming personally engaged with the task. Morrison et al. (2006, p. 148) offer the following overview of the connections between empathy, engagement and peer teaching:

- Empathy and engagement are key to learning through peer teaching.
- Reflective opportunities offered through peer teaching can be personally empowering and emotionally developmental
- Opportunities to reflect from another perspective, e.g. students as teachers, can foster more democratic relationships in the classroom.
- Personal insight offered through reflection can encourage disengaged students to redirect negative behavior into more positive behavior
- Improved academic achievement as well as improved self-esteem is possible when students are motivated and engaged – practical opportunities for reflection are key.
- Reversing roles can provide new insights into practice

The insight we have into practice is that engaging pupils in a wholistic sense means acknowledging the vital role of the affective realm in addressing educational issues. Returning to lessons learnt in earlier DRACON research, the importance of collaboration, engaging empathy, the role of risk and the challenges of peer teaching were all identified as significant issues. Conclusions drawn from the Wallenberg Case Study reinforce the importance of these issues, and highlight how important it is to consider them as central in any educational initiative working to improve academic achievement through fostering engagement and motivation.

References

Ackroyd, J. (2004). *Role reconsidered. Stoke on trent.* Sterling: Trentham.

Bell, J. (2002). *Doing your research project* (3rd ed.). Buckingham: Open University Press.

Bigger, S. (2006). *Tranquility, guided visualisation and personal discovery for disengaged 'dispirited' pupils.* In: BERA paper, Warwick, 6 Sept 2006.

Booth, D. (1997). Research and practice from the inside out. In J. Saxton & C. Miller (Eds.), *The research of practice, the practice of research* (pp. 12–20). Victoria: IDEA Publications.

Brown, L. (2005). 'Violent girls': Similar or different from 'other' girls? In G. Lloyd (Ed.), *Problem girls* (pp. 63–76). New York: Routledge Falmer.

Brown, L., & Gillian, C. (1992). *Meeting at the crossroads – Women's psychology and girl's development.* Cambridge, MA: Harvard Press.

Cohen, A., Manion, L., & Morrison, K. (2007). *Research methods in education* (6th ed.). Abingdon: Routledge.

Collins, W., & Laurensen, B. (1995). Conflict relationships during adolescence. In C. Shantz Uhlinger & W. Hartup (Eds.), *Conflict in child and adolescent development.* Cambridge: Cambridge University Press.

Denscombe, M. (2002). *The good qualitative research guide.* Buckingham: Open University Press.

Elliot, J. (1991). What is action research in school? *Journal of Curriculum Studies, 10*(4), 355–7.

Finney, J., & Tymoczko, M. (2003). Secondary school students as leaders: Examining the potential for transforming music education. *Music Education International, 2,* 36–50. ISME.

Finney, F., Hickman, R., Morrison, M., Nicholl, B., & Rudduck, J. (2005). *Rebuilding engagement through the arts*. Cambridge: Pearson Publishing.

Flutter, J., & Rudduck, J. (2004). *Consulting pupils: What's in it for schools?* London: Routledge.

Foley, D., & Valenzuela, A. (2005). The politics of collaboration. In N. K. Denzin & Y. Lincoln (Eds.), *The sage handbook of qualitative research* (3rd ed.). London: Sage.

Gilligan, C., & Brown, L. M. (1992). *Meeting at the crossroads*. Cambridge, MA: Harvard University Press.

Goodlad, S., & Hirst, B. (1989). *Peer tutoring: a guide to learning by teaching*. London: Kogan Page.

Goodlad, S., & Hirst, B. (Eds.). (1998). *Mentoring and tutoring by students*. London: Kogan Page.

Greene, M. (1995). *Releasing the imagination: Essays on education, the arts and social change*. San Francisco: Jossey-Bass.

Grumet, M. (1997). Research conversations: Visible pedagogies/generous pedagogies. In J. Saxton & C. Miller (Eds.), *The research of practice, the practice of research* (pp. 7–11). Victoria: IDEA Publications.

Jackson, C. (2006a). *Lads and ladettes in school: Gender and fear of failure*. Berkshire: Open University Press.

Jackson, C. (2006b). 'Wild' girls? An exploration of 'ladette' cultures in secondary schools. *Gender and Education 18*(4), 339–360. London: Routledge.

Jennings, G. (2003). Meaningful participation and caring relationships as contexts for school engagement. *Californian School Psychologist, 8*, 7–27. Sacremento: USC.

Kendall, S., & Kinder, K. (2005). Engaging the disengaged: Messages from across Europe. NFER National Foundation for Education Research.

Lather, P. (1991). *Getting smart: Feminist research and pedagogy within the post-modern*. London: Routledge.

Osler, A., Street, C., Lall, M., & Vincent, K. (2002). Not a problem? Girls exclusion from School. *New Policy Institute and Centre for Citizenship Studies in Education*. University of Leicester.

Sarason, S. (1999). *Teaching as performing art*. New York: Teachers College Press.

Schultz, J., & Cook-Sather, A. (2001). *In our own words – Students' perspectives on school*. Lanham: Rowan & Littlefield.

Stake, R. (2000). Case studies. In N. K. Denzin & Y. S. Lincoln (Eds.), *Handbook of qualitative research* (2nd ed., pp. 435–454). London: Sage.

Taylor, P. (2000). *The drama classroom: Action, reflection, transformation*. London: Routledge.

Yin, R. (2003). *Case study research: Design and methods* (3rd ed.). London: Sage.

Chapter 6
Acting Against Bullying in Schools

6.1 Introduction

Following the extensive positive outcomes of the Cooling Conflicts research reported in Chap. 4, the researchers decided to investigate whether the research model and techniques developed for conflict management in schools could be applied to address bullying. Education Queensland, the government authority responsible for all state schools in Queensland, was approached, and agreed to become a research partner in a major grant application to the Australian Research Council. The application was successful, and a 3 year action research project followed, using essentially the same structure as Cooling Conflict (Chap. 4), with year-long action research cycles involving explicit teaching about the nature of bullying combined with improvisation, role and process drama to explore approaches to bullying management. As with the conflict management research, peer teaching about bullying using Enhanced Forum Theatre performances was the vehicle for enhancing the students' understanding, and for disseminating the project throughout each school in the research (O'Toole et al. 2005). At different times over the 3 years 18 schools were involved in the project.

This chapter provides a detailed evaluation of the success of the use of drama and peer teaching to empower adolescent students to deal with bullying in a range of secondary schools. The research is reported in linked case studies of three large secondary schools where the Acting Against Bullying project was implemented over the 3 year period, making it possible to collect detailed, longitudinal data. There is an analysis of the modifications and adaptations that were required to the original model of conflict management in schools developed in previous research to specifically address the issue of bullying, and the chapter also identifies the most significant problems and constraints encountered in the research.

© Springer International Publishing Switzerland 2015
B. Burton et al., *Acting to Manage Conflict and Bullying Through Evidence-Based Strategies*, DOI 10.1007/978-3-319-17882-0_6

6.2 Bullying in Schools

Surveys and overviews conducted during the past decade in the UK, Europe, Canada, Australia and NZ have consistently identified bullying as a major concern in schools. A meta-evaluation of anti-bullying programs, undertaken by Rigby (2002), suggests that one child in six is bullied on a weekly basis. Whitted and Dupper (2005) assert that bullying is the most prevalent form of low-level violence in schools today and, if left unchecked, can lead to more serious forms of violence. In their overview of bullying, Smokowski and Kopasz (2005) found that it affected approximately one in three children in US schools A national survey in Australia found that parents give anti-bullying policies a higher priority than academic standards when deciding on a secondary school for their children. Almost 75 % stated that it was essential for a high school to have an anti-bullying policy, whilst only 45 % placed the same emphasis on high academic standards and 43 % on outstanding final year results (Survey of Parental Priorities in Deciding Schooling 2008).

Bullying is most prevalent in adolescence: "Teens in grade sixth through 10th grade are most likely to be involved in activities related to bullying. About 30 % of students in the United States are involved in bullying on a regular basis" (Bullying Statistics 2010). The figure for the United Kingdom is 46 %, with students aged 11–15 years being the ones most concerned in bullying (NSPCC 2013). The Acting Against Bullying research was therefore structured with the aim of having every student in the target secondary schools involved in the project. The program was also extended into primary schools through peer teaching conducted by the students from the research secondary schools.

An international survey of attempts to deal with bullying in schools over two decades (Smith et al. 2004) identifies only limited success, and this is confirmed by research in the United Kingdom (Sullivan et al. 2004) and the United States of America (Roberts 2006), which continues to indicate that bullying is the most significant behavioural problem confronting schools. The most recent international data indicates that bullying in schools continues to escalate (NSPCC 2013; Bullying Statistics 2010) and it has even argued that bullying is increasing because it is an evolutionary adaptation that benefits some adolescents in dealing with their school environment (Volk et al. 2012).

Key conceptual understanding about the nature of bullying drawn from the literature formed the content of the formal teaching which was conducted at the beginning of the program at each year level. This essential knowledge differed from the set of concepts used in the DRACON and Cooling Conflicts programs (Chap. 2), especially in its focus on bullying's negative impact on children and the harm it causes. Rigby (2007) defines bullying as: "repeated oppression, psychological or physical, of a less powerful person by a more powerful person or groups of persons" (p. 15), and this was the definition taught at every level to the research participants, but increasingly simplified in terminology with the younger children.

Extensive studies of all forms of bullying have shown that frequent acts of aggression toward victims are related to increased loneliness for the victim, peer rejection, anxiety and depression and low self-esteem. Approximately 15 % of victims are distressed or even traumatised as a result of encounters with bullies. In some rare but highly publicized cases, relentless bullying can result in a victim committing suicide (Björkqvist et al. 2001; Storch and Masia-Warner 2004; Underwood 2003). Research has also revealed that bullies suffer similar long-term negative consequences. During their school years, bullies are more likely to be disengaged and exhibit problem behaviour, have juvenile records and achieve poorly in their studies, and these behaviours remain remarkably constant. They are less likely than their peers to have achieved success academically, professionally or socially and are more likely to have children who are bullies (Roberts 2006, pp. 59–60). Merrell et al. (2008) found that "bullies also tend to be at heightened risk for substance use and later criminal behaviour, are likely to become increasingly unpopular with peers as they get older" (p. 26). Again, this information about the impact of bullying on those involved was taught to the students at each phase of the research.

The extensive research in bullying prevention clearly demonstrates that of the three parties involved in bullying: the bully, the victim and the bystander, it is the bystander who has the most agency in preventing bullying from continuing (Healy 1998), and this evidence-based knowledge is one of the crucial concepts central to the *Acting Against Bullying* program. Recent Canadian research indicates that only 11 % of children intervene when someone is being bullied, and yet: "bullying stops within 10 s 57 % of the time when a child intervenes and confronts the bully" (Canadians Against Bullying 2013). Oh and Hazler (2009) argue that the: "bystanders' potential for breaking the cycles of school bullying is substantial considering the fact that they are usually the majority of participants" (p. 293). This is confirmed by (Cassidy and Watts 2000, p. 213), who state that: "the nature of the audience as bystanders or witnesses to bullying [is] crucial since it is this group of people who have the power to act when they witness or suspect an act of bullying". In research focusing specifically on the role of the bystander in bullying amongst school children, Johnson and Rigby (2006) found that "once a child has acted as a positive bystander he or she is more likely to do so on subsequent occasions. Establishing this habit is important. This can be encouraged through practising the use of intervention skills in role play situations and reinforcing attempts to do so in real situations" (p. 8).

A range of dramatic techniques have in fact been used in international anti-bullying research and in school based programs to allow students to explore bullying in a safe, fictional environment. There is compelling evidence that dramatic enactment can be effective in enabling students of all ages to understand and deal with bullying (Smith and Ananiadou 2003; Parsons 2005; Belliveau 2007; Zins et al. 2007). There is also some evidence that students themselves prefer the use of drama to other approaches in anti-bullying programs (Crothers et al. 2006).

6.3   Peer Teaching and Bullying: A Neglected Strategy

There is clear and extensive evidence in educational literature over more than two decades that peer teaching is extremely effective in both enhancing learning and empowering students (Falchikov 2001; Goodlad and Hirst 1989; Gordon 2005; Hall et al. 2013; Sturdivant and Souhan 2011; Svinicki 1991). Both the Cooling Conflicts research (Chap. 3) and wider research (Burton 2012; Morrison 2004; Morrison et al. 2005), have demonstrated its effectiveness in enhancing conflict management in schools.

However, peer teaching has been a neglected strategy in the field of bullying. In particular, there is very little evidence in the current literature on bullying nationally or internationally that peer teaching has been empirically tested as a mechanism to address bullying. Instead, the use of school students as peer mediators has become widespread internationally, particularly in primary schools. In most cases upper primary students are trained in simple mediation techniques and then encouraged to act as mediators outside the classroom.

Some earlier studies claimed outstanding success in reducing conflicts in primary schools through the use of peer mediation, using selected students as peer mediators or bullying prefects (Johnson et al. 1994). However, a major review of nine peer mediation programs carried out in four states in the United States at the time (Powell et al. 1994) questioned the validity of most of the findings, especially in relation to adolescents. Whilst reported incidents of conflict declined in many the primary schools that adopted peer mediation, there was very little evidence to show that the students at those schools had actually learned to manage their conflicts better, or that conflicts were genuinely de-escalated by the peer mediators. In a number of projects the mediators wore special sashes or belts, and appeared to function as mediation police, breaking up fights and preventing bullying, but not necessarily addressing the causes or empowering the protagonists to handle bullying themselves.

Most importantly, the survey by Powell et al. (1994), found that in the high schools where peer mediation was introduced, there appeared to be little change in behaviour, and in one school the number of suspensions and the incidence of weapons carrying was actually higher after the program than in a neighbouring school. The researchers concluded that teenagers are far less likely to accept being policed by their peers than primary children, and in the case of bullying far less likely to respond to peer intervention. Whilst peer mediators develop a valuable understanding of conflict management themselves, there is very little evidence at all that the rest of the students in the school are similarly empowered Rigby (2010, p. 62) concludes "It is generally accepted that mediation is difficult, if not impossible, to achieve if there is a notable imbalance of power between the bully and the victim".

When all the students in a school were actually taught about conflict management, and then taught others in the Cooling Conflicts research, there was extensive data to indicate that conflict, including bullying, was significantly reduced (Chap. 4). The AAB research reported in this chapter offers compelling evidence that all school students, especially secondary school students, are able to become competent at dealing with bullying in their own lives if they empowered to do so by confronting it through drama (Jackson 1993) and then teaching what they have learned to their peers.

6.4 The Acting Against Bullying (AAB) Project

The 3 year research project was conducted in partnership with the state education authority, Education Queensland, by Bruce Burton, John O'Toole and PhD researcher Maureen Owen. The research was designed to de-escalate bullying in schools and to alter the prevailing culture that perceives bullying as simply an acceptable part of growing up. The AAB project was aimed at empowering students to manage bullying more effectively as part of a whole school approach to the problem. The project also experimented with approaches to professional development for teachers to equip them to deal with bullying successfully through drama in their own classrooms, and this was the focus of Maureen Owen's thesis. A total of 18 schools in Brisbane and regional Queensland were involved at different stages over the 3 years of the action research. Schools became part of the project by applying to be research sites and appointing Key teachers who undertook in-service training on the structure of the project and were responsible for its implementation in the school.

A series of action research cycles were used to develop strategies to deal specifically with bullying whilst also continuing to refine the drama and peer teaching system that had been successful in the DRACON and Cooling Conflicts research reported in Chaps. 3 and 4 of this book. The bullying research was conducted over all 3 years of the project in schools that represented a range of demographic and educational settings.

Like Cooling Conflicts, the Acting Against Bullying project aimed to develop a whole-school anti-bullying program that was disseminated within the standard school curriculum. The first stage of the action research began in each school with the researchers and a senior secondary class teacher introducing the students to a set of concepts and definitions about the nature and consequences of bullying, using drama to investigate and apply this learning in practice. This cognitive understanding and a range of bullying management techniques were further explored through Enhanced Forum Theatre (Chap. 4). Once the senior secondary class had acquired a clear understanding of the nature of bullying and had experimented through drama with identifying and managing its causes and consequences, the second stage followed with groups of senior students teaching a number of younger classes in their school, using the same conceptual framework and enactment strategies.

This peer teaching took place across a range of curriculum areas, so that the program was perceived as cross-curricular (Forsyth and McMillan 1991). With the assistance of their classroom teachers and the older students, the younger secondary school classes reinforced their understanding of bullying and the use of drama to explore strategies to deal with it. In stage three they relayed what they had learned to classes in the local primary schools. Stage four followed with those students in the primary schools continuing the same process throughout their schools.

6.5 The Case Studies

To obtain more extensive and longitudinal data about the impact of the project on the adolescents who are most involved in bullying behaviour (Bullying Statistics 2010; NSPCC 2013), three large secondary schools were selected as the sites of detailed case studies. The schools were chosen on the basis of their long-term commitment to the research, especially through the Key Teacher in each school, and for the diversity of contexts and students they offered.

Once three appropriate research sites had been chosen, the data gathering began with a scoping of the particular context of the school with special reference to its behaviour management plans and incidence of bullying profiles. This proved difficult and in places unsatisfactory, owing to the scarcity and erratic nature of the available base-line data. For instance, Queensland schools have varying methods of identifying and recording bullying incidents, and varying confidentiality procedures.

However sufficient base-line data on the incidence and nature of bullying in the case study schools was provided by the pre-questionnaires which were administered to all the 18 schools involved in the project. Similarly, the post-questionnaires provided extensive data on the students' learning and their changes in attitudes and behaviours. These questionnaires were similar in format to those used in the Cooling Conflicts research (Chap. 3) but focused specifically on questions related to bullying.

As well as the 216 questionnaires completed by students in the research schools, surveys were also administered to participant teachers. Interviews were conducted with focus groups of students from all year levels in each school, and summative one-on-one interviews were conducted with selected students and their class teachers. Observation notes were written by the researchers, and a number of students, especially in the high schools, wrote reflective journals. These data sets were collected during each of the 3 years of the Acting Against Bullying research in the three high schools and their neighbourhood primary schools.

6.6 The Case Study Schools

Westside State High School is located in Ipswich, a neighbouring town to Brisbane, and services the town's retail, industrial and residential communities and those of surrounding rural areas. A school planning document noted that many of their students experienced substantial socio-economic disadvantage, and youth unemployment in their area was high.

The overall impact of the Acting Against Bullying program on Westside was diverse. Whilst the participating students identified increased awareness of methods for dealing with bullying, the rest of the school was not involved in the program except as a supportive mechanism and did not therefore receive the same benefits as the participants. Participating teachers identified greater confidence and skills in dealing with bullying as a result of their involvement and acknowledged the benefits of the peer teaching and drama components on their students. However, they were reticent to identify demonstrated leadership in themselves or their colleagues as a whole. Also, due to changes in staff it was difficult to determine if any cultural changes could occur at Westside at the time of writing.

At Westside a number of changes occurred during the Acting Against Bullying Program. A number of the participating teachers, including the Key Teacher, were transferred to other schools during the first year of the program and this meant the project had to be re- established with new teachers. This delayed the dissemination of the program in the school. Despite this constraint, the data at Westside identified significant development in teacher confidence and student empowerment when dealing with bullying as a result of participation in the program.

The students at Westside demonstrated a significant development in their understanding of the nature of Bullying by the end of their participation in the research. The data indicates that on completion of the program the students were more aware of the power of the bystander to de-escalate bullying, they could identify subtle and insidious forms of covert bullying, and they had a greater understanding of why people become bullies. At the very beginning of the AAB program at Westside, year 12 students were asked what they believed was the definition of bullying, and their responses indicated that the students had some knowledge of bullying but only in general terms. In interviews at the completion of the program these students had become proficient in giving more detailed and often more sophisticated definitions and explanations for bullying:

It could be continuous, unwanted harassment and then there're so many different areas – physical, emotional, anything that can make a person feel less of a person than they actually are. I think the main key is that it is continuous.

The Key Informants in the summative interviews demonstrated that they were also more aware of the nuances and subtleties of bullying that are not always evident to teachers or students. Importantly, they demonstrated an ability to see bullying situations while at the latent stage, and were able to explore strategies for de-escalating bullying by dealing with it outside of the immediate conflict and through calm communication. The students clearly indicated that they were now more confident in intervening if they were to encounter a bullying situation, and that they had not only developed greater understanding of the pervasive nature of bullying, but also how it could be managed in schools. On the summative questionnaire, two students observed:

I think they'll never stop bullying at all, but just de-escalate it, by just having groups of people telling them what to do if they are in that situation, like walk away is better than listening to what they have to say about you.

It's going to be, like, it's a matter of cutting it off at the latent stage. Like you can see it starting to happen so you have to cut it off there, like more of a preventative thing - you're never going to stop it because people don't know any other way.

The post- project questionnaire also revealed significant increases in understanding about bullying management amongst the students at Westside. When asked after the project had finished who they thought was the person most likely to change a bullying situation, 56.5 % of students identified the bystander. A Johnson and Rigby (2006) study revealed that only 28 % of secondary students would support the victim in a verbal bullying scenario and 30 % in a physical bullying scenario. These figures are significantly lower than the 56.5 % of Westside secondary students who indicated that bystanders could intervene to change the bullying situation after participating in the *Acting Against Bullying* program.

When Westside students were asked if they thought differently about any people in bullying situations as a result of participating in the *Acting Against Bullying* program, 36 % of students said they were more aware of the power that a bystander has to change a bullying situation and 27 % said they now understood that all parties (bully, bullied, bystander) play a role in preventing or stopping bullying.

You might be going along and you might see something happening and you might just go up and say "guys just cool it down a notch". I've had one instance where a girl came up to me and said "I'm not sure what to do." I said "Would you remember how we learnt it and …what do you think you should do?" and she says "I think I should tell someone" and so she did.

Both the peer teaching and the drama components helped teachers and students become more confident and empowered to become leaders during the program. Despite some initial concerns over the drama component of the program due to the fact that they weren't drama trained teachers, the key teachers eventually recognised the benefits of its use with students. One teacher observed:

I think that they enjoyed exploring bullying and solving it under an alias. I know some of them had experienced bullying. I know it was empowering for them.

This teacher not only became very confident at facilitating the drama and the peer teaching, she also became very skilled at it. During the second year of the project she was transferred to another school, but remained involved in the project by training other teachers in her new school and acting as a supporting mentor in her district.

A group of 3 students who had been the Key Class in the first implementation of AAB in the school expressed their enthusiasm for the project in interviews that indicated their sense of achievement and confidence.

I just loved it. I loved teaching the kids and I just loved the feeling that I was helping them in some way and possibly helping the community.

It's great to feel that you make a difference to the way that they look at different aspects of schooling.

It was good too to make it fun for them to learn. Not too boring for them.

One of the teachers identified the positive outcomes from this experience for the students in terms of bullying management in the school.

They recognise it more themselves, that bullying occurs and that some of them were bullies, but they didn't realise… so now, even in the playground, they tell me about themselves.

Some of them will go up to kids and say "what's going on here?" They're trying to be proactive themselves – I think it's been really good in opening their eyes.

The staff of the school who were directly involved in the project also developed both understanding and expertise in bullying management. In interview, these participating teachers identified greater confidence and skills in dealing with bullying as a result of their involvement, and acknowledged the benefits of the peer teaching and drama components on their students. Furthermore, 85.7 % of them indicated on a questionnaire that they felt more confident in dealing with bullying among students other than their own, and more confident in dealing with bullying at an adult level in the school community as a result of participating in the program. However, they were reticent to identify demonstrated leadership in themselves or in their colleagues as a whole as a result of the project.

The key teacher who replaced the original facilitator of the program in the school emphasised the need for real engagement by the whole school to continue on with the project for an extended period of time and to enlarge its anti- bullying involvement with the local feeder primary schools. Unfortunately, her attempt to teach all the year classes with only her students as peer teachers meant there were some logistical problems, and by the third year of the action research the program had still not been fully implemented.

I think the previous two years were done extremely well, but I don't think it impacted on the school because it was only a small number of classes that were being taught, which is what I tried to do differently.

The overall impact of the AAB program on Westside therefore varied according to the level of involvement of students and teachers. The administration of the school was supportive of the project and gave flexibility to the teachers, but it was only implemented at the level of individual classes because of the changes in staffing and the difficulty of engaging replacement teachers in the research. Whilst participating students identified increased awareness of methods for dealing with bullying, the rest of the school was not involved in the program except as a supportive mechanism and did not therefore receive the same benefits as the participants.

North Beachside State High School is a regional seaside school with a large number of students coming from a transiting population. Although the project had not been designed to move into rural areas until year 3 of the research, the guidance counsellor at this school was very proactive and the school was allowed to participate from the beginning of the second year of the research.

A key finding that emerged from the data at North Beachside was that there was a general increase in understanding of bullying and confidence in dealing with it among both teachers and students after participating in the project. Sharp and Smith (cited in Rigby 2002, p. 27) suggest that the first step in establishing an anti-bullying policy is raising awareness of its existence in a school. The participating teachers at North Beachside indicated they had acquired useful knowledge about bullying, including recognising the differences in bullying behaviour between the genders and the nature of different forms of bullying. They also believed they were more competent at dealing with bullying in general. Teachers indicated after completing the program that they believed there should be a whole school anti-bullying program in place at their school.

One of the drama teachers became more aware of the bullying issue in his school by observing how much the students could relate to bullying during their participation in the program. He was also impressed by how quickly they learnt to deal with bullying through enhanced forum theatre.

> I was astounded at how much my kids knew inherently about how bullying takes place and the sort of things bullies do...and they were quite good at trying to use the forum process to try and alleviate that bullying.

Students indicated they were more aware of bullying situations around school as a result of being in the program and were more confident in dealing with bullying situations. When asked if they could explain what bullying was, 100 % of students responded positively and all could name the three stages of bullying. Of those students, 89 % could also write down the three types of people in a bullying situation.

The following response from a year 11 boy was reflected in the interviews with many of the other students when asked what they understood about bullying from the project,

> I learned its consequences and how far it does get and how much it upsets people.

When asked on the questionnaire if they felt differently toward people involved in bullying after participating in the project, 56 % of students replied they felt differently toward the bully, the bullied and the bystander, and 64 % of students replied that they were more likely to do something in response to a bullying situation in order to de-escalate or end it. Not one respondent replied 'no'. Asked if they had learnt how to manage bullying situations better, 66 % of students responded 'yes', 11 % responded 'no', and 23 % said they were unsure. One year 12 student observed:

> If you were in a bullying situation and you didn't know what you could do, you could, like, flash back and remember 'oh this is what they did in the activities'.

One student confessed to being a bully in the past and remarked that she no longer bullied others as a result of the program.

> My attitude to everything's changed now, but I used to be a bit of a bully. I used to bully the younger kids who were in a group, but now I understand that 'hey, it's not right-I shouldn't be doing this". I've played the bully, I've played the bullied person, I know how they feel. So I try to be nicer to those people and generally we're getting along really good now.

Significant understanding relating to bullying management emerged from the data at North Beachside School. Students maintained that they realised, after participating in the program, that they had the power to intervene, and 56 % believed that the person most likely to change a bullying situation was the bystander. North Beachside students also felt they had the option of soliciting the help of bystanders if they were being bullied. When asked if they were more likely to intervene as bystanders to try and de-escalate a bullying situation, 78 % said 'yes', and of these 56 % replied they would report to someone in authority. Nobody answered that they would walk away or participate in the bullying even though those alternatives were given as choices on the questionnaire.

Some students at North Beachside stated that doing nothing at all when bullying was occurring was not appropriate and that the bystander had the power, if not some kind of responsibility, to de-escalate a bullying situation. The students also indicated that as bystanders, they would not support a bully, but would look for solutions to de-escalate the bullying.

Whenever I see people being bullied I always think to myself, 'oh, they could do this to stop it or they could do that to stop it' whereas usually I would probably want to get involved and see what was happening and take sides...so I think it's really helped me.

The teachers confirmed that a new awareness of the power of the bystander had emerged amongst their students as a result of the program. One remarked that his students felt guilty that they had not used this power by objecting to the bullying being observed in the past:

I've had a lot of discussion about whether the bystander would go in and break it up...A lot of the people who had been bullied let them in on the real world and said basically, "this does happen and people don't step in and why didn't you about two years ago?.." It's really put a positive spin on the class. While they've been sort of challenging one another, they've all in a way felt horrible about the situation because they realised that it was happening and they did nothing about it.

The results from the data of the program showed that the peer teaching benefited both the younger and the older students (Simmons et al. 1995). Once the older students were prepared and had some experience teaching the younger students, they quickly developed confidence and skills in passing on the anti-bullying message. The older students commented on the fact that they felt satisfied that they could make a difference as a result of the peer teaching;

I really like the fact that we can teach them-and even though there may be a teacher there, the students were more relaxed and more willing to open up and stuff like that and I really liked that fact. I just liked the fact that we could really make a change even though we're just students- that we could go out there and make a change for the next students coming into the High School.

The older students also found that their confidence and self-esteem improved as a result of the peer teaching experience and that by teaching younger students their own knowledge of bullying increased:

It makes you feel good and gives you self-esteem and you get more confidence while you're doing it, and the more you do it the better you know about it and get more experience and as you get more experience you can use that and pass it on to younger people, and then they'll start learning and they'll pass it on. It is like a snowball effect and will keep going on.

The improvement in self-esteem and peer relations experienced by these students is significant. Adolescents appear to develop a significant amount of maturation as a result of peer teaching. Maskell (2002) found that "in many evaluative studies it has been seen that their personal development is accelerated... one of their greatest rewards is that of working alongside adults in an equal and responsible relationship" (p. 107).

There was a similar positive development in both attitude and behaviour observed amongst the younger students when they became peer teachers in turn. Goodlad and

Hirst (1989) found that "having been helped by older children acting as tutors, the younger children started to adopt a helping relationship towards other people- a sort of transfer of tutor role to the tutees who extended this role to their peers" (p. 39).

One of the teachers stated during an interview that she really saw the benefits of letting go of the teaching reins in her classroom. The students who had normally been classified as 'troublesome' became effective leaders and teachers when given the chance:

> *Like I said what didn't work well was probably that initially the kids were a little bit shy. But what worked really well was when my Year 9 class became the key class for the younger Grade 6 class and they actually really surprised me. I thought "I wonder how this is going to go" and I just handed it over to them to sink or swim and they were really good – real troublesome boys in the class took over, they were getting up and explaining things and instructing all the kids.*

However one constraint became apparent at North Beachside in relation to the peer teaching, and this was the lack of teaching skills amongst the participating students. It was evident that the older students needed some training from their own teachers before they too could benefit from the process. The Key Teacher observed:

> *While I don't think it's important that we teach them how to teach, personally I think it is better to give them a few little hints before they go into the class. That wasn't discussed – not that I can remember – at the in-service and it is probably something I would probably do next time is teach the kids a little bit, just very, very basic structures around teaching, focus, the class and that type of thing – which they should pick up from me and my style.*

The data from the two other case studies confirmed that older students needed some basic teaching strategies before they peer-taught younger students. Although this had not initially been an element of the program, it became evident that teachers needed to ensure that their students had some basic teaching strategies and skills before they functioned as peer-teachers.

Southside State High School is an established school located in a southern suburb of Brisbane and services families at the higher end of the socio-economic scale. It is recognised for its performing arts and has a strong academic record. However, at the beginning of the research, the school had been identified as having a serious bullying problem that had been publicised in the press. Because of these issues, Southside was the first school involved with the *Acting Against Bullying* program, and was the longest participating school in the project, since its collaboration lasted from the pilot stage in 2002 until the end of the project in 2005. Furthermore, *Southside* continues to run *Acting Against Bullying* to the present day as an integral part of its overall behaviour management program.

Straight after the program, 66.7 % of the students surveyed said they were able to notice bullying more easily after their participation in the project. On being asked, "Who do you think is the person most likely to change a bullying situation?" 63 % of students answered 'the bystander' after they completed the program. Of those students, 73 % said the bystander could intervene and attempt to negotiate or mediate between the bully and the bullied. The remaining 7 % suggested the bystanders could make the bullying situation known to a teacher or someone in authority. When the students at Southside were asked if they were more likely to do something in response to a bullying situation in order to de-escalate or end it, 77.8 % responded 'yes', 14.8 % responded 'no' and 7.4 % felt 'unsure'. Asked if they felt they could now manage bullying situations more effectively, 80 % of students agreed.

In an interview at the half way point of the research, the Key Teacher noted:

> *A lot of the students who have been involved in this project have generally been those who have not participated in this sort of thing before and that's absolutely delighted me to see how some of them have grown.*

Almost 2 years later, in her summative interview, she reflected that: "Student awareness about the process and stages of bullying has been heightened" as a result of participating in the program. She added that "we now have a language to use to describe bullying and tools to decode situations" as a result of the students' participation in the program.

An indication of the success of the project at Southside was the fact that the School won a $10,000 grant to apply anti-bullying strategies in its district as a result of its application to 'Safe Schools' and because of its success in developing anti-bullying strategies.

> *We received funding through the National Safe Schools Framework to put into place a program that uses drama and the arts to look at the social issue of bullying. We now have established a school policy framework for anti-bullying and developed a dynamic anti-bullying curriculum unit for all year 8 students which incorporates the Acting Against Bullying program.*

By framing the *Acting Against Bullying* project within the Behaviour Management Policy of the school, the Key Teacher succeeded where other teachers were unable to sustain the project in their schools, particularly in their primary schools. She was given a part in formulating that policy by her principal, so that the program became integral to the school. Most importantly, she was willing to both change her own previous practices and accept responsibility for organising the project in her school, and in particular, the peer teaching, which she recognised as particularly valuable for her students.

> *The change that I have probably noticed the most is how well they have stepped into a leadership role, doing their mentoring, their peer teaching. In many ways it has been wonderful to see how some of them have grown and in fact are great little teachers, with relatively little training on our behalf, just from the few sessions that we ran. I have been very impressed by the way a number of them have just stepped into taking over that leadership role. That's from the Year 11 point of view.*

During the implementation of that *Acting Against Bullying* program at Southside, the school began to keep accurate records of the incidence and seriousness of bullying behaviour throughout the school. In the 2 years following the conclusion of the research, the school records indicated a significant decline in reported bullying, and the disappearance of major bullying incidents as a behaviour problem.

6.7 Results of the Research

The research findings from each action research phase, from the case studies, and from the summative data collection clearly and consistently revealed significant impacts on major manifestations of bullying in the subject schools. These impacts involved an increase in awareness about bullying itself, and positive changes in the attitudes and behaviours of bullies, those being bullied, and bystanders.

Over 90 % of the 216 secondary school students involved in *Acting Against Bullying* who were surveyed during the final stages of the program were able to define bullying, identify the three types of people involved in bullying and list the stages. In the final surveys and questionnaires, 87.2 % of all students involved in the project stated that they were more able to recognise when bullying was taking place, and 87.1 % believed that bullying could be de-escalated or stopped. Asked if they were more likely to do something in response to a bullying situation in order to de-escalate or end it, 64 % of all students involved in the program replied yes and 33 % said they were not sure; only 3 % responded negatively. Questioned whether they had learned how to manage bullying situations better, 70.3 % students replied yes, 19.3 % stated they were unsure and only 10.4 % responded no.

Furthermore, the majority of students involved in the *Acting Against Bullying* program over the 3 years identified the role of the bystander as crucial in a bullying situation, and in Enhanced Forum performances students intervened more often as bystanders than as bullies or bullied combined. In the final surveys and questionnaires, 87.2 % of all students involved in the project stated that they were more able to recognise when bullying was taking place, and 87.1 % believed that bullying could be de-escalated or stopped. Asked if they were more likely to do something in response to a bullying situation in order to de-escalate or end it, 64 % of all students involved in the program replied yes and 33 % said they were not sure, whilst only 3 % responded negatively. Questioned whether they had learned how to manage bullying situations better, 70.3 % students replied yes, 19.3 % stated they were unsure and only 10.4 % responded no.

As students developed an understanding of the nature and causes of bullying, their awareness of consequences and of their own role in these increased significantly. This was particularly true of students who had been responsible for bullying behaviour.

Some students indicated that their increased awareness of the consequences of bullying as well as empathy for how others feel in a bullying situation, helped them to deal with their own conflicts when they arose. A year 9 student explained in detail how her involvement in the program had transformed her attitude and her behaviour:

> *Before I did Acting Against Bullying, I didn't know how to deal with a situation when I got into it...I didn't think about what I was doing and about the consequences of what I was doing and about how it would make other people feel. But since doing the Acting Against Bullying project, people have said that whenever I get into fights and stuff- which I sometimes do - that I've dealt with it in a more mature way and it hasn't got me into as much trouble.*

Perhaps the most potent experience for those students who were bullies when the program began was the role reversal that occurred when they portrayed the characters of students being bullied, both in improvisations and in the Enhanced Forum Theatre plays. A teacher of year 10 students reported:

The interesting thing that we come across is the students who tend to be bullies, when they are acting out the scenarios - have taken sometimes the role of the bullied and it's very interesting to then speak to them about that role afterwards and they say 'yeah I think I know now, miss, how they feel and I know that it probably isn't a real cool thing to do.

Having a conceptual understanding of the nature of bullying and the experience of experimenting with managing bullying situations also proved to be effective in empowering students who were being bullied to take more responsibility for their own situations. Both teachers and students identified this empowerment in children who were being bullied. One teacher of year 9 students observed:

By understanding the process of bullying, the bullied students were empowered to keep resisting the bullies and to seek support from bystanders. The other students realize their power position as a bystander and this also empowered them. I have seen a few cases of extreme bullying turn around through this.

A year 9 student who had been involved in drama activities that included role reversal described the effect on bullying she had been experiencing:

It's definitely made my relationships stronger with the people in my class doing the project with me. Like, this one girl I felt very intimidated by her and we actually had to do a play together and she would bully me and then we had to swap the role around so we both know where each other stood then and now we're actually friends.

When interviewed, a majority of teachers indicated that they had been empowered by their participation on the program, and were able to recognise bullying much more clearly, including the different types of bullying behaviour and the differences between genders. Over 80 % of teachers believed that the program should be a part of a whole school anti-bullying program in their schools, because of its positive impact. One year 9 teacher believed that there had been a change of culture in regard to bullying in her school

The bully no longer holds the balance of power and by simply reminding the groups about the power of the bystander they continue to deny the bully that power and that opportunity.

Teachers generally agreed they saw positive changes in the more problematic students' attitudes towards bullying after they had participated in the program. Interestingly, students who had previously displayed bullying tendencies often became the leading advocates of the program during the peer teaching sessions.

In a number of the primary schools where the *Acting Against Bullying* program was successfully implemented from the neighbourhood high school, teachers were able to identify a greater awareness in their students of the nature of bullying and their greater confidence in being able deal with it. One primary teacher explained:

I think all students got to identify what constitutes a bullying situation and the different phases of bullying. For them to actually identify these phases and realise what bullying is, they realised they had been bullied in the past and maybe if they can catch it at a certain stage that they have been empowered with the ability to do something about it other than just taking it.

6.8   Limitations and Constraints

Base-Line Data The lack of reliable statistical information on bullying within individual schools was a fundamental problem throughout the research in measuring the impact of the use of the drama and peer teaching. Only one of the high schools involved kept comprehensive records of the incidence of reported bullying, and this only commenced after the research had begun. However, the numerous questionnaires provided extensive information about behaviour related to bullying, and confirmed the wealth of overwhelmingly corroborative anecdotal evidence provided by the other data, such as the interviews and focus-groups of both students and teachers, and the field-notes and journals of the researchers and teachers.

Systemic Support At a systems level, a lack of continuity in management within the participating State Education Department made effective communications and the provision of on-going support for the schools and teachers involved in the research very difficult to sustain. The transfer of teachers actively involved in the project in their schools became a major issue during the research and in one school seriously delayed the implementation of the action research. It also became clear by the end of the first annual cycle that teachers needed more of the in-service support which the research coordinator provided to give them understanding, confidence, basic drama skills and ownership of the program, and a level of stability that transcended the endemic staffing upheavals which disrupted the research. A sustained level of in-service support and on-going assistance also proved essential to maintain the program once the research phase was over.

The Master Teacher Program Some initiatives to expand and build on the program were tried, but were not found to be sustainable within the time and financial scale of the project, particularly with the lack of systemic support noted above. After 2 years, we had identified five highly committed and now experienced Key Teachers, all of whom were interested in building the program more widely, both in their school and by creating a cluster of neighbouring schools, as a formal support network, where they could take over our role in running the in-service and taking the responsibility for the management of the program in those schools. In Year 3 of the program (2004) we structured this initiative as a means of ensuring the sustainment and expansion of the program beyond the end of the *Acting Against Bullying* project funding. We held a master-teachers' training program for them and, using Project funds, created a structure for them to work towards, and a checklist of tasks and responsibilities, and monitored their progress, including two formal interviews and an end-of year feedback session. Although all of them remained (and several have remained ever since) committed to the program in their own school, their work schedules did not permit them to do the necessary preliminary work to establish ongoing links in other schools, and after some brave short-term efforts, the master-teacher program was discontinued at the end of the Project. This was to us a clear case where systemic support, in the form at least of teacher release and facilitation of the inter-school liaison, was demonstrated to be essential, and without it even those super-keen teachers could not augment or sustain their efforts.

Implementing the Program Across Schools Another prospective development that appeared at first to have great promise, was actually initiated by the participants themselves. At the suggestion of a focus group comprising participating primary school principals, in the second cycle the program was implemented directly in five schools, without receiving any peer teaching from the neighbourhood secondary schools. This was partly because they were eagerly anticipating implementing the program, but were forced to wait until it had worked its way down through the secondary school towards the end of the year. However, it proved difficult to establish the program in primary schools using this model. The experiment was not expanded in the third cycle, and by the time the research finished, none of the five schools was still running the program. The data revealed that many primary teachers lacked confidence in using the drama techniques, and a number were also wary of overtly addressing bullying in their classrooms. The administrators, teachers and students in the primary schools surveyed all acknowledged that they were more motivated and felt more competent to engage in the program when it was introduced by a high school.

Time Constraints Many of the participating teachers had very heavy workloads, and found that time pressures eventually forced them to take short cuts or to look for solutions outside of the curriculum in implementing the program. As an example, one of the teachers found that she could only participate in the program at the end of the year when assessment was over and the school schedule was less restricted by using some of the rooms left spare by the older students. Other teachers found that they simply could not participate at all, despite their interest in the program, due to timetable constraints. One teacher who had completed the in-service was then very disappointed that she could not participate in the program, due specifically to her timetable restrictions and not being able to match up her classes with the key drama students.

6.9 Conclusions

The summative evidence from the research clearly indicates that the combination of learning about bullying, exploring it through drama and then peer teaching it, can significantly assist school students to deal more effectively with bullying in their own lives.

The questionnaires administered during the 3 years of the research recorded a consistent rate of 99 % in students' ability to remember and define the three stages of bullying and identify these stages in their own drama work. As a result, a clear outcome of the research has been that almost all participating students recognised the need to intervene in bullying before it became manifest, and students were able to articulate a valid understanding of the nature and implications of bullying.

The majority of students surveyed also identified the bystander as being the party most able to intervene to change a bullying situation.

The data from the action research conducted with a number of primary schools consistently indicated that students as young as 8 years old found no difficulty in remembering the parties to bullying and the terminology of 'latent, emerging and manifest.' Early primary students involved in the research were also able to describe the nature of each party to bullying and the key features of each of the three stages, and could discuss their representation in specific scenes in improvised plays they created or watched.

At *North Beachside* and *Westside* schools, the evidence demonstrates that adolescents in classes that participated in the program were successful in developing effective bullying management skills and there were significant changes in the attitudes and behaviour of the students. However, to keep the momentum going, it is evident from the data that every teacher and student in a school needs to be involved in the program, and it must be embedded in a whole school behaviour management structure that provides the school staff and students with effective knowledge and strategies for dealing with bullying (Glasl 1999).

The evidence from the case study of *Southside School* clearly shows that when this occurs, it can have a major and lasting positive impact on bullying in a school. During a 5 year period that lasted well beyond the research project, *Acting Against Bullying* was established in *Southside School* as the centre of their behaviour management program. During these years, the same teachers were actively involved in the program throughout; the whole school embraced the program as part of its anti-bullying policy; and even the local community and feeder primary schools were invited to participate in demonstrations and information giving sessions. As a result, the school which had been the site of serious, publicised bullying when the research began did not record a single serious incident of bullying during the 2 years after the research concluded. This outcome indicates that a cultural shift in regard to bullying can occur in a school if an anti-bullying program is maintained and cultivated, although it can take some years for the results to be evident.

Finally, confirmatory evidence is supplied by the longitudinal data collected in Sydney as part of an on-going evaluation of the outcomes of the earlier *Cooling Conflict* project (Chap. 4). This data indicates significant positive changes in the whole culture of some schools running the program for 5 years or more, with improved student relationships and a decline in the incidence of conflict in schools.

References

Australian Schools Directory. (2008). Survey of parental priorities in deciding schooling. www. australianschoolsdirectory.com. Accessed 28 Aug 2013.

Belliveau, G. (2007). An alternative practicum model for teaching and learning. *Canadian Journal of Education, 30*, 47–67.

Björkqvist, K., Oesterman, K., Lagerspetz, K. M. J., Landau, S. F., Caprara, G. V., & Fraczek, A. (2001). Aggression, victimization, and sociometric status: Findings from Finland, Israel, Italy, and Poland. In J. M. Ramirez & D. S. Richardson (Eds.), *Cross-cultural approaches to research on aggression and reconciliation*. New York: Nova.

Bullying Statistics. (2010). Stop bullying harassment and violence. http://www.bullyingstatistics. org/content/bullying-statistics-2010.html. Accessed 9 Sept 2013.

Burton, B. (2012). Peer teaching as a strategy schools for conflict management. *Australian Educational Researcher, 39*(1), 45–58.

Canadians Against Bullying. (2013). Response ability project. http://www.raproject.org/video/ entry/bullying-bystanders. Accessed 5 Oct 2013.

Cassidy, H., & Watts, V. (2000). Using drama to relieve the oppression of school bullying. *Queensland Journal of Educational Research, 16*(2), 207–223.

Crothers, L. M., Kolbert, J. B., & Barker, W. F. (2006). Middle school students' preferences for anti-bullying interventions. *Psychology International, 27*(4), 475–478.

Falchikov, N. (2001). *Learning together: Peer tutoring in higher education*. London: Routledge Falmer.

Forsyth, D., & McMillan, J. (1991). Practical proposals for motivating students. *New Directions for Teaching and Learning, 45*, 53–65.

Glasl, F. (1999). *Confronting conflict – a first aid kit for handling conflict*. Stroud: Hawthorn.

Goodlad, S., & Hirst, B. (1989). *Peer tutoring – a guide to learning by teaching*. London: Kogan Page.

Gordon, E. E. (2005). *Peer tutoring: A teacher's resource guide*. Lanham: Scarecrow Education.

Hall, S., Lewis, M., Border, S., & Powell, M. (2013). Near-peer teaching in clinical neuroanatomy. *The Clinical Teacher, 10*(4), 230–235.

Healy, K. (Ed.). (1998). *Bullying and peer pressure*. Balmain: The Spinney Press.

Jackson, T. (Ed.). (1993). *Learning through theatre: New perspectives on theatre in education*. London: Routledge.

Johnson, B., & Rigby, K. (2006). Bystander behaviour of South Australian schoolchildren observing bullying and sexual coercion. *Educational Psychology, 26*(3), 1–10.

Johnson, D. W., Johnson, R., & Johnson, F. (1994). Effects of conflict resolution training on elementary school. *The Journal of Social Psychology, 134*(6), 803–817.

Maskell, P. (2002). Peer mentoring: What is it. In U. M. Elliott (Ed.), *Bullying – A practical guide to coping for schools* (pp. 104–114). London: Pearson Education.

Merrell, K. W., Gueldren, B. A., Ross, S. W., & Isava, D. M. (2008). How effective are school bullying intervention programs? A meta-analysis of intervention research. *School Psychology Quarterly, 23*(1), 26–42.

Morrison, M. (2004). Risk and responsibility: The potential of peer teaching to address negative leadership. *Improving Schools, 7*(3), 217–226. Sage.

Morrison, M., Burton, B., & O'Toole, J. (2005). Re-engagement through peer teaching drama: Insights into practice. In P. Burnard & S. Hennessy (Eds.), *Reflective practices in arts education* (pp. 139–149). Dordrecht: Springer.

Oh, I., & Hazler, R. J. (2009). Contributions of personal and situational factors to bystanders 'reactions to school bullying. *School Psychology International, 30*, 291–310.

O'Toole, J., Burton, B., & Plunkett, A. (2005). *Cooling conflicts: A new approach to conflict and bullying in schools*. Sydney: Pearson Education.

Parsons, L. (2005). *Bullied teacher, bullied student: How to recognize the bullying culture in your school and what to do about it*. Markham: Pembroke.

Powell, K., et al. (1994). A review of selected school-based conflict resolution and peer mediation projects. *Journal of Social Health, 65*(10), 426–431.

Rigby, K. (2002). *A meta-evaluation of methods and approaches to reducing bullying in preschools and early primary schools in Australia*. Canberra: Commonwealth Attorney-General.

Rigby, K. (2007). *Bullying in schools and what to do about it*. Camberwell: ACER Press.

Rigby, K. (2010). *Bullying interventions in schools: Six basic approaches*. Camberwell: ACER Press.

Roberts, W. B., Jr. (2006). *Bullying from both sides: Strategic interventions for working with bullies and victims*. California: Corwin Press.

Simmons, D., Fuchs, L., Fuchs, D., Mathes, P., & Hodge, J. (1995). Effects of explicit teaching and peer tutoring on the reading achievement of learning-disabled and low-performing students in regular classrooms. *The Elementary School Journal, 95*(5), 387.

Smith, P., & Ananiadou, K. (2003). The nature of school bullying and the effectiveness of school-based interventions. *Journal of Applied Psychoanalytic Studies, 5*(2), 189–209.

Smith, P., Pepler, D., & Rigby, K. (Eds.). (2004). *Bullying in schools: How successful can interventions be?* Cambridge: Cambridge University Press.

Smokowski, P. R., & Kopasz, K. H. (2005). Bullying in school: An overview of types, effects, family characteristics, and intervention strategies. *Children and Schools, 27*(2), 101–110.

Statistics on Bullying. (2013). National Society for the Prevention of Cruelty to Children. http://www.nspcc.org.uk/inform/resourcesforprofessionals/bullying/bullying_statistics_wda85732.html. Accessed 30 Sept 2013.

Storch, E. A., & Masia-Warner, C. (2004). The relationship of peer victimization to social anxiety and loneliness in adolescent females. *Journal of Adolescence, 27*, 351–362.

Sturdivant, R., & Souhan, B. (2011). Peer-to-peer teaching using multi-disciplinary applications as topics. *Primus: Problems, Resources, and Issues in Mathematics Undergraduate Studies, 21*(3), 283–293.

Sullivan, K., Cleary, M., & Sullivan, G. (2004). *Bullying in secondary schools: What it looks like and how to manage it*. London: Paul Chapman Publishing.

Svinicki, M. (1991). Practical implications of cognitive theories. *New Directions for Teaching and Learning, 45*, 27–37.

Underwood, M. K. (2003). *Social aggression among girls*. New York: The Guilford Press.

Volk, A. A., Camilleri, J. A., Dane, A. V., & Marini, Z. A. (2012). Is adolescent bullying and evolutionary adaptation? *Aggressive Behaviour, 38*(3), 222–238.

Whitted, S., & Dupper, R. (2005). Best practices for preventing or reducing bullying in schools. *Children and Schools, 2*(3), 167–175.

Zins, J. E., Elias, M. J., & Maher, C. A. (2007). *Bullying, victimization, and peer harassment: A handbook of prevention and intervention*. New York: Haworth Pres.

Chapter 7
Moving On from the Trauma
of Childhood Abuse

7.1 Introduction

The first decade of experiment and research reported in the previous chapters focused on the use of improvised drama, forum theatre and peer teaching in schools in the search for effective approaches to address bullying and conflict. As extensive evidence of the success of these strategies continued to emerge from the DRACON, Cooling Conflicts and Acting Against Bullying data, a range of initiatives were implemented by the authors, applying these strategies in a number of adult and professional contexts including nursing education, teacher training and professional development in a number of different countries. These projects are explored in Chaps. 8 and 9. However, another, completely different application of the strategies was developed in the Moving On project, a 3 year action research project using drama processes and theatre performance with the adult survivors of childhood abuse, and that research is the subject of this chapter.

7.2 The Research Project: Moving On

During the 1990s, an increasing volume of evidence emerged world-wide about serious physical, sexual and psychological abuse of children in church and state orphanages going back 50 years or more. Evidence of this abuse, and the consequences of it, continue to be revealed in a number of countries today. A report by the UN committee on the Rights of the Child stated that the Catholic Church worldwide: '…has not acknowledged the extent of the crimes committed, has not taken the necessary measures to address cases of child sexual abuse and to protect children, and has adopted policies and practices which have led to the continuation of the abuse by and the impunity of the perpetrators.' (Cyprus Mail 14th February 2014). In Australia, a federal commission into abuse in orphanages was established by the government in 2014 to investigate the on-going evidence that continues to

© Springer International Publishing Switzerland 2015   99
B. Burton et al., *Acting to Manage Conflict and Bullying*
Through Evidence-Based Strategies, DOI 10.1007/978-3-319-17882-0_7

emerge. However, the first formal investigation of this issue in Australia was a Commission of Inquiry into the Abuse of Children in Institutions that examined the nature and extent of this abuse in the state of Queensland, and published a detailed account – The Forde Report, released in 1999. A counselling service, the Aftercare Resource Centre, was established with the purpose of assisting adults who had suffered abuse as children. Despite extensive counselling over a number of years, many of these ex-residents of homes and orphanages, some in their 50s and 60s, continued to suffer from severe post-traumatic stress, and were unable to function effectively in their daily lives.

Following the successful outcomes of the DRACON and Cooling Conflicts research in schools, and the emerging positive data from the Acting Against Bullying research, Bruce Burton was approached by a colleague at Griffith University in the field of counselling and criminal justice, Dr. Merrelyn Bates, A researcher on the DRACON Project (Chap. 3) she was a member of the Management Board of the Aftercare Resource Centre. She proposed extending the use of the effective strategies developed in the previous projects into the field of psychological damage and post-traumatic stress suffered by adults who had been abused as children in orphanages and homes and who were clients of the counselling service.

For these survivors of childhood abuse, conflict was at the centre of their psychological disorganisation. They were in conflict with the society that had failed to protect them or heal them, and in conflict with themselves, unable to move beyond the anger and grief caused by the trauma they had suffered. Herman (1997: 1) argues: 'Remembering and telling the truth about terrible events are prerequisites both for the restoration of the social order and for the healing of individual victims'.

A 3 year Australian Research Council Grant was obtained in partnership with the Aftercare Resource Centre by a team of academics composed of Bruce Burton, Merrelyn Bates, Penny Bundy, with a Masters student, Sarah Woodland, and an honours degree student, Allira Power, also part of the research team. A number of the experienced counsellors at the Aftercare Resource Centre were aware that traditional approaches to counselling were inadequate to redress the ongoing problems experienced by this particular client group, and willingly joined this team as expert advisors and to provide support to the participants. As the research developed, some of the counsellors became actively involved in the drama workshops, participating in activities and even leading some of the work. One counsellor commenced a doctorate as part of her engagement in the project.

All the clients of the Aftercare Resource Centre were informed of the research and invited to participate. Twenty-five attended the initial meeting, but a number of them felt threatened by the idea of exploring their traumatic childhood experiences through drama. As the project evolved, a core group of 12 participants emerged who remained with the research throughout. Although some were absent at different times, this cohort remained engaged for the 3 years and were involved in some capacity in the final, public performances. Most of this core group were between 40 and 60 years of age, so the abuse they had suffered had occurred in the 1960s and 1970s. However, there were two older members of the group, and younger participants as well, in their 20s and 30s.

7.3   The Impact of Childhood Abuse in Institutions on the Adult Survivors

The participants in the Moving On project had suffered extensive abuse as children in church and state orphanages or foster homes. Crossley (2000: 57) states that: 'traumatic events in a person's life can lead to a radical sense of disorientation and the breakdown of a coherent life story', and many of the participants either suppressed memories of the abuse they had suffered as children or were obsessed by their experiences. Hudgins (2002: 11) observes: 'When trauma hits, the self becomes psychologically disorganised. The patterns and structures of self-organisation that were there, whether in childhood or as an adult, become frozen in time'. A number of the participants were being treated by their counsellors for severe Post-Traumatic Stress (PTSD), despite the fact that in some cases the abuse had occurred 30–40 years ago.

Psychotherapists identify a number of major long-term consequences of childhood abuse, and the Moving On participants exhibited many of these traits. Briere (2002: 2–6) lists negative relationships, highly-emotional responses to experiences and the inability to regulate emotions, disassociation and substance abuse, whilst Margolin (1999: 5–6) includes sexual dysfunction, self-harm, learning difficulties and impaired parenting.

Recent clinical trials and studies have confirmed the impact of childhood abuse on the lives of adults. In their clinical research, Castellini et al. (2012) found that physical and sexual abuse in childhood was a significant risk factor in the development of eating disorders and was associated with impulsive behaviour. Wu et al. (2010) discovered that: ' substance abuse and mental disorders were up to nine times higher amongst the adult survivors of childhood traumatic events than the general population.' There was a 1.2–1.5-fold increased risk for PTSD, current tobacco use, alcohol dependence, injection drug use, sex work, sexually transmitted diseases, homelessness, and myriad physical health problems, as well as reduced overall quality of life' (Wu et al. 2010: 71) In their research with adult women who had suffered childhood sexual abuse, Robinaugh and McNally (2011: 486) found that; "Individuals who appraise a traumatic event as a turning point in their life story, a central part of their identity, and a reference point for generating expectations about the future exhibit greater psychological distress. Our results suggest that individuals who appraise a traumatic event as a reference point for their future maybe especially at risk for PTSD."

Cattanach (1992: 123) explains why childhood abuse has such a negative effect on the adult lives of the victims. 'Body boundaries have been so violated by aggression or through the emotional or sexual gratification of others that it becomes hard to value the self as a person with rights and needs'. The adult survivors of abuse tend to blame themselves for all the negative experiences that happen to them, believing that it must be their own fault. They are unable to trust others and suffer intense sensations of worthlessness, hopelessness and powerlessness. As well as the intentional abuse experienced by children in orphanages and state institutions, they also suffered from forms of neglect that impact significantly on their adult lives. These included inadequate schooling, poor health care and little or no vocational training. At the commencement of the Moving On project only one of the participants was in a stable relationship, although a number of them had been married; a number of them had on-going health issues; none of them was currently employed.

7.4   The Use of Drama with Adult Survivors

One form of psychotherapy that attempts to assist patients suffering from Post-Traumatic Stress and the consequences of abuse uses narrative. Draucker and Martsolf (2006: 146) state : 'The key to narrative therapy is that life stories that are hurtful or limiting can be changed by discourse that introduces alternate meanings to storied events or highlights previously un-storied events.' The aim is for the patients to construct dramatic autobiographies that transform the story of the trauma. 'The fundamental premise of the psychotherapeutic work is a belief in the restorative power of storytelling.' Herman (1997: 181). In narrative therapy, patients engage in the process of recreating themselves (Crossley 2000), and this takes place most effectively within a therapeutic group where the participants create and recreate their narrative autobiographies in interaction with others (Nicholson 2005). The group becomes: 'a microcosm of the patients' larger relationship with the world' (Emunah and Johnson 1983: 235) and Herman argues that the therapeutic group is a powerful antidote to traumatic experience and actually assists patients in restoring their humanity (1997: 214).

The key features of narrative therapy are closely related to the processes of drama and in particular to the nature of group-devised theatre performance, and the use of drama as a therapeutic tool has become increasingly widespread since Moreno's pioneering work in the field of Psychodrama (Moreno 1977). Jennings (1998: 33) defines drama therapy as: 'the term used for the application of theatre art in special situations, with the intention that it will be therapeutic, healing or beneficial to the participants.' Theorists and practitioners (Emunah 1994; Landy 2001; Pendzik 2006) argue that drama allows patients to externalise and validate their internal worlds, and to find strategies to deal with psychological disorientation and the disorganisation of their lives.

Through the practice of drama therapy, participants can also experience powerful emotions and understand them at the same time.' Landy (1994: 113–4) explains: 'one is able to simultaneously play the role of the actor, who relives the past, and the observer, who remembers the past.' This dramatic balancing of reality and fiction was identified by Boal (1995) as metaxis, and it occurs when the participants in drama function as both actor and audience at the same time. This was also an important feature of the forms of learning through drama exploited by both the Cooling Conflicts and Acting Against Bullying programs. Briere (2002: 10) argues that this experience of distancing, of metaxis, provides a therapeutic window: 'a psychological location between overwhelming exposure and excessive avoidance.'

The intention of the Moving On project was first of all to investigate whether the use of drama strategies developed in the Cooling Conflicts research could be adapted to assist the adult survivors of child hood abuse to deal with the unresolved psychological conflict in their lives. The second aim of the research was discover if it was possible to empower the participants to make conscious use of theatre performance to generate an effective therapeutic experience.

7.5   The Structure of the Moving On Project

The overall organisation of the project remained constant during the 3 years of the research, and there were three action research cycles implemented during this period with the group of participants who were engaged for the whole period of the research. The timing of the cycles was flexible, with a short pilot project at the beginning, a year-long second cycle, and an 18-month final cycle focused on the rehearsal and performance of a play. Whilst the overall structure, research methodology and participation remained largely unchanged, the nature of the project altered considerably during the 3 years in response to the needs of the participants and the outcomes of each research cycle.

The attendance at each workshop fluctuated throughout the life of the project. Individual participants were often physically ill, suffering anxiety or depression, or unable to attend due to personal issues in their lives, Members of the research team were also sometimes absent due to other commitments, whilst one counsellor withdrew because she found it difficult to engage in the research. The imaginative, cooperative, interactive and physical nature of the drama process was in complete opposition to the private, face-to face, therapeutic conversations she practised. Two other counsellors left to take other jobs and were replaced eventually by other counsellors. Numbers in the workshops therefore ranged from as low as six up to 16. Once the rehearsals of the play commenced, the attendance of the participants was consistently very high.

From the beginning of the project, a number of the participants were determined to stage a play to make the public aware of the abuse they had suffered as children and its consequences for them as adults. The reason most of them gave for participating in the research was this opportunity to tell their stories in public. They were adamant that their mistreatment as children had been concealed by the institutions where it occurred, and continued to be denied and ignored by the churches and state organisations that administered these institutions, as well as by governments and law enforcement agencies. Throughout the life of the project their anger and frustration at the abuse they had suffered and the neglect they continued to experience was a dominant thread in the drama work and the discussions. Meekums (1999: 256) notes : 'The need to speak and be heard appears in many ways to be central to the survivor's therapy, since abuse is so often marked by secrecy, disbelief and even judgements on the victim.' The Moving On participants were determined to speak, and be heard, through the agency of theatre performance.

Whilst previous projects explored in this book had used Enhanced Forum Theatre as a major strategy to deal with conflict and bullying, the public staging of a group-devised play as an act of therapy represented a new approach. However, both the applied theatre researchers and the counsellors believed that before this could happen, a pilot project and an action research cycle exploring the use of improvised drama activities were needed. This was planned to be followed by a second cycle which would enable the participants to develop the performance skills and the confidence and self-esteem necessary to stage a play. The implementation of this second cycle was also seen as experimental, because the counsellors were concerned that their clients lacked the communication skills and confidence to perform for an audience, and they believed that to revisit childhood abuse in perfor-mance could trigger major re-traumatisation. The research team discussed these concerns with the participants, and they agreed that Moving On would begin with a pilot phase experimenting with a wide range of drama activities which would then be refined and developed in the first full cycle of the research.

7.6   The Action Research

Participatory Action Research (Zuber-Skerritt et al. 2009) was chosen as the specific methodology because of the need to empower the participants, as it did in many of the projects analysed in this book. The research team, the counsellors and the participants were searching for new strategies for moving on from the trauma of childhood abuse. In participatory action research researchers and subjects actively collaborate throughout to find solutions to problems (Choudry 2010). The Moving On participants were able to draw on their own experiences, to identify where particular drama strategies were effective, and to choose the nature and content of the theatre performance they wished to create. The research team provided the research structure and theoretical knowledge and expertise in drama processes and theatre, whilst the counsellors contributed therapeutic expertise and valuable input into the planning of the activities. Data was gathered by both the researchers and the counsellors.

The collection of data was extensive, and focused on amassing a significant range of evidence related to the impact of the improvised drama and performance on the participants. Every workshop and debrief was filmed, and the discussions, planning and debriefing conducted by the research team were audio recorded. The rehearsals and performances of the play were filmed. The counsellor who was researching the project for her doctorate also conducted follow-up telephone inter-views with participants each week, and these were also recorded. She kept a detailed research journal, as did the masters and honours candidates. Extensive observation notes were written by the applied theatre researchers, and the counsellors made clinical notes when counselling related to the research was required. A number of documents were also generated, including project guidelines, lists of participant goals and their written narratives of their experiences, and observation notes kept by the research team.

Through the use of action research, the research team searched for effective techniques to address the issues confronting the group of Moving On participants. Beyond this, it was hoped that some of the discoveries might provide worthwhile responses to a major international social and health problem – the difficult and previously hidden issue of the damage caused to adults by their abuse as children in institutions and foster homes.

7.6.1 Cycle One: The Pilot Phase

This cycle began with a series of meetings with the counsellors from the Aftercare Resource Centre and involved eight drama workshops with the Moving On participants.

The project group met once a week, on a Wednesday, for the 3 h drama workshops and discussion. There were also meetings and planning sessions each week among the researchers, and a debriefing was held immediately after each workshop involving both the research team and the participants. In the first phase of the research, these meetings took place in a building opposite the Aftercare Resource Centre office, and participants often sought individual counselling immediately after a workshop. It was also a regular occurrence for participants to need counselling during the workshops.

This first phase of the Moving On project was tentative and experimental. The members of the research team came from two very different fields and paradigms – applied theatre academics on the one hand and professional counsellors on the other. The initial meetings and exchanges of emails that led to the establishment of the project revealed radical differences in the approaches to the challenge of the research. The applied theatre researchers were focused on experimenting with a range of drama strategies with the participants as a group to discover the most effective techniques to assist them to move on in their lives. The counsellors were most concerned with the therapeutic treatment of their individual clients, and wished to avoid any form of re-traumatisation. When asked what were the therapeutic issues facing the participants, one of the counsellors replied:

> Primarily I guess it is a couple of things, mainly trust related issues I guess but that is what I see is the main issue as far as interacting with others and being able to function day to day, on top of the post-traumatic stress response of course... Basically, post-traumatic stress rules every part of your life. That impedes their ability to function, because of the hyper-vigilance they experience, so always on edge or always re-experiencing in some ways, nightmares, flashbacks or actually feeling like they are going through it again... (Tammy)

For the participants, the initial workshops were particularly challenging. Given the nature of the damage done to them by their childhood experiences, they found it difficult to structure and articulate ideas and responses in discussion and in the drama activities. Due to a lack of social and communication skills, some members of the group dominated every activity and refused to listen to other ideas, whilst other participants did not contribute at all. Margolin (1999: 5) identifies lack of control as a cognitive effect of childhood abuse and the inability to interact socially and personally as a long term outcome. The pilot phase therefore focused intensely on providing safety and building trust in the group. The group negotiated their agreement with guidelines about respect, safety, confidentiality, participation and ownership. The research team and the counsellors all agreed to work within these guidelines. Even so, the workshops often had a traumatic impact on participants.

Sometimes the drama session left us raw inside, then debriefing and counselling helped, though the effect of counselling was not always instant and sometimes we carried stress and pain home with us. (Sarah)

Most of the group also had no experience of improvised drama, and no skill in structuring an improvisation or representing a character, and they struggled to form even the simplest of dramas either in discussion or in improvisation. Honours student Allira Power noted (2004: 35) 'For a number of the participants who had had no previous experience working in a drama group, there were issues concerning communication and control'. The counsellors noted that some of the participants tended to wait for assistance from the facilitators rather than initiate action, and the nature of the dramas was entirely focused on content. The researchers became aware that others restricted themselves to playing only high – status roles, often the same role over and over, regardless of its appropriateness to the drama being improvised. As a result, the improvised dramas that were developed at this stage tended to be very brief and often unfocussed. O'Neill insists: 'if art is to be created or apprehended, there must be an awareness of the presence of form'.

The participants were also reluctant to dramatise situations and characters where there were conflict and anger involved. They tended to act out scenarios representing only positive behaviour and situations. However, in discussion and debrief at the beginning and end of the workshops they would often refer to their traumatic experiences as children. For the applied theatre researchers, exposure to some of these stories was quite disturbing, and the counsellors would often provide informal counselling to the researchers after these sessions. There was a clear disjunction between what the participants wanted to discuss and what they were representing in the drama.

Given these complex constraints, the workshop sessions on the Wednesday mornings for the first 4 months were largely dominated by discussion and debriefing, and the drama activities tended to be very brief group improvisations focusing on the development of social and communication skills such as acting out ordering a meal in a restaurant or returning a faulty item to a shop. For some of the participants even these scenarios were difficult to enact, as they found them too stressful to do in their daily lives.

One workshop at this stage involving the scenario of taking a train ride to go on holiday clearly demonstrated both the level of development, and the limits, of the participants' skills and engagement with drama techniques. Each member of the group chose a character and a scenario related to the train trip and they then began improvising. There was very little evidence of the creation of different roles, and most of the participants represented characters with the same attitudes and behaviour as their own. Two rows of pairs of chairs had been set up to represent the train, and the participants used these as train seats throughout the drama, but there was no sense of them actually boarding the train at a station or travelling on a train. The members of the group appeared to accept the fiction and continued to improvise in role, but there was no clear overall narrative established, even when different facilitators intervened to try and provide a focus. There was also very limited character interaction and communication, and a few of the other participants in the train improvisation only functioned at a minimal level in role, and contributed little action or communication to the drama.

One intervention by a facilitator in role as the train driver stating the train had broken down did reveal indicators of emerging abilities to create effective roles and generate tension and action. Two of the participants in role responded to the suggested breakdown of the train by challenging the suggestion that it had actually stopped working, arguing that the driver had stopped the train on purpose. One the other participants, Donna, took the role of a government official who supported the train driver. She later intervened in role again in an attempt to sustain the thread of the train breakdown when one of the other participants attempted, in role, to get the train started. This was the first time Donna had actively intervened in a drama or taken on a high status role, so it was a significant breakthrough for her, one that was generally sustained in the workshops from then on.

These indicators of the increasingly effective use of dramatic elements to enhance the improvisations were also reflected in discussions by the participants about the drama. In her honours dissertation, Allira Power observed that by the end of this cycle, there had been a shift in their understanding and appreciation of drama. She noted that in the debriefs at the end of each workshop: 'The responses have become less about the participants' feelings towards the content of the workshop and have focused on the style of drama that was presented' (Power 2004: 41). The research team decided it was time to encourage the participants to consciously use drama as a strategy to explore complex situations, relationships and emotional states.

7.6.2   Cycle Two: Improvised Drama as Empathy

At the beginning of the next cycle, a drama activity which generated much higher levels of focus, commitment and effective improvisation marked a shift in the research. The research team structured a complex drama that challenged the participants to take on roles very different from themselves, to address a social and political issue that was controversial and contained elements of aggression and conflict. The Refugee Workshop was carefully structured by the applied theatre facilitators in a number of stages, with the participants first enrolled as journalists reporting on the fictional situation of a group of refugees to establish some information and understanding about refugees. Then half the group remained in role as journalists and interviewed the other half who were in role as refugees. One of the counsellors then took on the role as a refugee and the participants out of role interviewed her. Finally, the participants were divided into two groups, with each group creating a different piece of improvised performance about the experiences of immigrants and refugees in Australia.

The purpose of this workshop was partly diagnostic: to determine the level of development and application of drama skills the participants had achieved and discover what further training was necessary. It also aimed at discovering how effectively they would be able to use these skills and strategies for the first time to investigate an issue that resonated with conflict and suffering, and required a certain level of empathy and understanding. The workshop was also designed to confirm the shift from improvised drama to structured performance that was planned for the second cycle of the research. Insistent on telling their stories to the world through theatre, the participants had been demanding this shift for some months.

The most significant outcomes of this workshop were related to the ability of most of the participants to take on roles very different from themselves and to manipulate these roles to explore fictional experiences that dealt with conflict without being traumatised by this exploration. David, the participant with the some theatre experience, was able to create and sustain an extremely aggressive character as an Italian migrant. At the same time, one of the counsellors noted that he consciously reduced the level of aggression in his performance when other participants in the drama were finding it threatening. David acknowledged that he had been aware of the responses of the other participants and had modified his performance, and he also noted that he had taken on the challenge of portraying an aggressive and dominant character even though he found it uncomfortable to do so

> My real life story was of sadness dealing with my illness of asthma, isolation and identity...
> My working with the Moving On Project may allow me to deal with this more effectively.
> (David)

Mary, another participant in this drama, was deeply disturbed by the aggression and conflict being enacted, because it triggered traumatic memories. However, rather than withdraw from the drama, and from the workshop altogether, which she had done on a number of occasions in the past, she remained in role. She was able to distance herself from the impact of the conflict through her understanding that she was engaged in a constructed fiction. Landy (2001) describes this as aesthetic distancing, where the participant is able reflect upon and appreciate the impact of a performance by clarifying their own emotional responses rather than being impacted by them.

This workshop allowed the participants to actually explore new forms of behaviour and aspects of themselves they had previously rejected or suppressed. As Emunah (1994) notes, drama provides the opportunity to express facets of a person's personality that have been concealed, even from themselves. As a result, some of the Moving On participants were able to develop insights into themselves and their relationships with others.

Four of the other participants accepted the challenge to portray characters different from themselves and to explore the emotional impact of the conflict associated with those roles. Three of the women in particular gave convincing and strong performances in roles that were very different from their own personalities and their own belief systems. One of the men, Pete, was unable to sustain the level of aggression he had intended for his character, but in discussion and reflection he was able to identify and discuss the traumatic experiences that some refugees have suffered and continue to suffer, and to demonstrate empathy for them. He also indicated his determination to take on more demanding roles because he could see the positive outcome for himself.

The refugee drama also had a significant impact on Donna, who had only attended the workshops infrequently. She was disturbed by the improvisation because it triggered traumatic memories but she did not break role, choosing to remain in character but silent. Some weeks later during a debrief, Power () observed: 'she was able to discuss the difference between reality and drama, and identify how this allowed her to explore issues and emotions that were otherwise too threatening In summing up the progress of Moving On at this stage, and in particular the outcomes of the refugee drama, the researchers concluded that the use of improvised drama was allowing some participants to increase their self-knowledge and to develop strategies to deal with their trauma.

A workshop towards the end of this cycle provided further evidence that the participants were increasingly able to utilise improvised drama to explore real and imaginary experiences and to manipulate them to achieve personal outcomes. Groups of participants were encouraged to act out the performance of a job or hobby that they enjoyed and that made them feel really competent. Each member of the group took it in turns to enrol the rest of their group in their activity. Stephen, one of the quietest and most passive of the participants, was encouraged to dramatise work he had done as a chef. He enrolled the rest of the group as workers in his kitchen. As the improvisation progressed, Stephen became increasingly active and assertive, and totally involved in the drama. The other participants responded to his energy and commitment, and the rest of the groups stopped their improvisations to watch. Despite their previous reluctance to perform for an audience in earlier workshops, Stephens's group continued to improvise for some time, despite being aware of being observed. This was partly due to the fact that Stephen was intense and assertive in role as a chef, and had them working extremely hard in his imaginary kitchen; and partly it was due to the commitment of the group to the fictional world they were creating. At the conclusion of the drama, there was a lively discussion, with Stephen answering questions about cooking and his various jobs as a chef, with the other group members discussing their experiences of the roles that they had taken. A number of them made overt connections with jobs they had done. When the other groups resumed their improvisations, there were much higher levels of energy, enthusiasm and effective dramatisation in the space.

Despite the difficulties and challenges encountered in this second action research cycle, the interviews, observations, films and journals all demonstrated that the participants had acquired sufficient performance skills to represent a range of roles and scenarios successfully, and they had increasingly felt competent to do this. Drama had also significantly empowered the participants to investigate and communicate a range of experiences and emotional states that they had previously avoided or suppressed. There was far less evidence of them being disturbed by moments of conflict or traumatic memory than in cycle one. The honours candidate Allira Power observed 'There was a significant decrease in this tendency in time. This has come with an acceptance and appreciation of the difference between the fictional and real worlds. Similar, their understanding and acceptance of the human context has also increased.'

In terms of socialisation and communication, all the members of the group reported being much more confident and able to engage in social and interpersonal interactions. The extensive observations of the nature of their group interactions in the workshops had revealed significant advances in their ability to co-operate, interact and function as members of an effective group. Simone identified how the use of drama had assisted some of the participants to relate more effectively to others.

We moved on in various ways. But moving on encompasses many things. We had to be willing to be vulnerable but the power to heal is enormous. Drama like writing and painting is helpful to those who can't speak easily or find it difficult to be helped.

The interviews and discussions at this stage in the research also revealed that as a result of their involvement in the drama workshops, a number of the participants now felt able to operate in the outside world in ways previously too difficult to attempt. These included enrolling in adult education courses, making contact with family and friends they had not seen for years, and applying for jobs. Bundy in her evaluation of the first part of Moving On notes: … We have found that engaging in drama has offered opportunities for participants to develop insight into their relationship to themselves, to others and to their own social/political environment differently'.

7.6.3   Cycle Three: Memoirs of the Forgotten Ones

By the time the final phase of the project commenced, the research had been on-going for almost 2 years. This final cycle was focused on the creation and performance of the play Memoirs of the Forgotten Ones. However, before this process could begin, the entire research team believed there was essential preliminary work that needed to be done. The applied theatre researchers were aware that only one of the participants had any experience of working with written play texts, and he was also the only member of the group who had any knowledge of theatrical form. The counsellors were concerned that there was a high risk of re-traumatisation once the participants began to tell and dramatise their stories of abuse.

The cycle therefore began with some work with existing texts that were not connected in any way with abuse or trauma. Participants working in small groups chose to be either actors or directors for each piece of text, and the interpretation and performance of the dialogue was negotiated within the group. Initially, the participants struggled with the language and the meaning of the texts, but all of them demonstrated high levels of interest and engagement and there was a rapid development in their ability to speak the lines and express themselves through the language. A number of other participants also began to involve themselves in theatre activities outside the project, attending the performance of plays, and in the case of Suzie, joining an amateur theatre company.

A number of positive outcomes emerged from the script work for the participants. In interview, David described how he had used the romantic and intimate nature of the script extract he performed to revisit a strongly positive emotion.

I haven't been in love for a long time, so I tried to imagine that intimate feeling...I was tired of playing angry roles...I wanted to be something passionate...I remembered that feeling and held that feeling.

David was able to recognise that his constant choice of roles involving anger in the drama workshops was counter-productive. These roles reflected his unresolved trauma from the abuse he had suffered and his sense of conflict with the society that refused to acknowledge, but they had not provided a solution. The experience of performing a character from a play gave him the opportunity to experiment with positive emotions he had felt in the past whilst still being safely protected by the fiction of the play from real emotional disturbance. This experience of distancing, of metaxis, identified by Briere (2002: 10) provided '.. a therapeutic window' for David.

By way of contrast, Suzie and Cath chose to perform scenes involving high levels of interpersonal conflict because they felt empowered by the use of scripts to explore situations they would have avoided in the past. Their counsellor Jenny observed that both these women had become more assertive in their daily lives as a result of the drama workshops, and their willingness to take on aggressive roles and enact them was a clear indication of this growing confidence and sense of self.

Another participant, Dee, had initially found interactions with males in the group extremely difficult, and this was identified by her counsellor as a consequence of the sexual abuse she had suffered as a child. Margolin (1999: 10) lists inability to trust and establish intimacy among the long term consequence of child abuse. In the workshops in the second cycle, Dee had tentatively commenced to interact with the males and to assist in the creation of improvisations that explored family life, marriage and friendships. Working with the play texts, she chose a role involving intense interactions with a male character, and she performed the text with confidence. Again her counsellor commented that this was evidence of the increasing confidence and ability to interact with males that had emerged during the first two cycles of the research.

Following their explorations of texts, the participants then began creating, rehearsing and performing dramas that dealt with aspects of the experiences of children in institutions, sometimes exploring unhappiness and abuse, but also dramatising experiences and occasions that were remembered as positive and enjoyable. The central aim of all this work was to discover if it was possible for the participants to use the art form of theatre to tell their stories without being re-traumatised. At this stage, it was still unclear what the final shape of the play would be, and whether public performances would be possible.

The creation and refinement *of Memoirs of the Forgotten Ones* took almost a year, and this part of the cycle finished with a performance of the play as a work in progress to a small, invited audience at the end of the third year of the project. Sarah Woodland was the facilitator of this process and the director of the play, and the other researchers increasingly withdrew from an active part in the workshops and concentrated on the collection and analysis of data. The process was challenging and participants were often deeply disturbed by their exploration of painful memories. Dee discovered that she was unable to perform in the scenes being created, and decided she did not want to contribute a story of her own. She withdrew from the project, but returned a few weeks alter stating that she still wanted to be part of the group, and this was achieved by her singing in the final performances.

Jack, a male in his thirties, joined the group during this phase. He was the most recent victim of child abuse amongst the participants, and exhibited the impulsive behaviour identified by Castellini et al. (2012) as a significant outcome of physical and sexual abuse in childhood. Whilst narrating and acting out incidents of the abuse he had suffered, he often became extremely angry and his behaviour became uncontrolled and bizarre. After only 3 months involvement in this phase he withdrew from the project because he felt re-traumatised by the emotions he was exploring. It is difficult to assess whether Jack might have been able to deal more effectively with re-visiting his experiences if he had experienced the first two cycles, however, it seems significant that all the participants who had been continuously engaged in the research from the beginning, even Dee, did complete the project and felt that they had been transformed by their involvement.

A key challenge that emerged in this phase was the need to balance the dramatic structure of the play with the demand by the participants that their memories and their stories be conveyed honestly and authentically. Meekums (1999: 256) notes : 'The need to speak and be heard appears in many ways to be central to the survivor's therapy, since abuse is so often marked by secrecy, disbelief and even judgements on the victim.' When the script of June's story of the sexual abuse she suffered was read to the group, there were protests that it was too confronting. June argued furiously that it should be performed as written because it was the truth

> *And then when I was reading the stuff out, what actually happened, she said "Oh no, no, you can't say that, you can't say that, people will walk out they won't be able to handle it" .... Well, I had to handle it.*

This clash between the need to tell their truths and the form of the play occurred a number of times, but increasingly the director, Sarah Woodland, was able to negotiate with the participants and to assist them to see that the construction of aesthetic form was essential if they were to have the impact on an audience that they wanted so intensely. In an interview, Gwynne triumphantly claimed that she had ben able to retain a scene she was passionate about. However, she also acknowledged to Sarah that she when she watched the scene as an audience member she recognised the importance of the aesthetic in offering a different, important insight on the experience.

> *Gwynne: You know, you were trying to take that last bit away from me. That's when I came down to the what's-a –name that you were trying to change into a different scene and I don't want that – I wanted it back the way it was. And I got my way!*

Sarah: So did it help for you to be taken out to watch it as an audience member.
Gwynne: It does take... because you're seeing it from another perspective, you know, and if
*   you don't get that other perspective, you're not going to know.*

A significant debate about performance style occurred when Pete wanted to represent the abuse he had suffered as a small child. The scene that had been developed showed a priest coming into a boys' dormitory in an orphanage at night and choosing which boy he would take away to abuse. Pete wanted to portray his younger self in the performance of the play, or at least have another actor do it. Steve argued that that this would not work effectively with a large adult trying to represent a small child. He also argued that puppets would allow the confronting action to be distanced from the actors and would not trigger re-traumatisation. Both Briere (2002) and Pendzik (2006) note that the use of drama techniques allows participants to externalise and distance their experiences in order to find strategies to cope with the psychological disorder in their lives.

Steve: I prefer it... it allows you to remove yourself one step form it so that you're telling the
*   story but its' not personalising the emotions so much.*
Pete: Well look at it this way – the performance has got to be real, see. We're real people,
*   not puppets.*
Steve: Yeah, but puppets can make it more real for the audience. They can tell the story
*   better.*
Pete: In my opinion, I think if you're going to perform live, you've got to have somebody
*   who's live like us, you know?*

This discussion was revisited a number of times, with Pete determined to have live performers depict the abuse as it really happened. For Pete, the experience of the abuse he wished to portray in this scene appeared to be perceived as a turning point in his life and a central part of his identity, the kind of crucial reference point identified by Robinaugh and McNally (2011) that generates expectations that can lead to greater psychological distress. However, when the use of puppets was experimented with in rehearsals using rag dolls, the dramatic power of the technique which transformed the doll into a small child had a powerful impact on all the participants, but especially Pete. Not only did he fully accept this technique, but he altered the dialogue and action of the scene to make the puppetry work more effective.

The impact Moving On had on Pete was profound. As the project progressed, he began to wear more feminine clothes and to put on make-up. For some time he argued that this was a fashion preference and not an indicator of his sexual preference. However, during the rehearsal period in the final cycle, he "came out" as gay, and admitted that he had wanted to be a girl from an early age. He actually incorporated this revelation into another scene he created, where he did depict himself on stage openly revealing his sexuality.

.. .. the first part was the most important to me because it tells the story of me when I was a
kid. I wanted to be a girl and while I'm an adult, I still feel that way myself. But because of
ill health and everything like that, I can't do it...,

Pete received an extraordinary level of affirmation from the rest of the group for his courage and honesty in acknowledging his sexuality both to them and on stage. He responded with increased confidence and commitment to the play and in his everyday life, and is one of the participants who have continued to be involved in action groups and performances related to the institutional abuse of children.

It is interesting to note that Pete identifies ill health as a major restriction on his life. Wu et al. (2010: 71) note that '… myriad physical health problems, as well as reduced overall quality of life ..', are characteristic consequences of childhood abuse, but the research team and the counsellors observed an apparent and significant improvement in Pete's health and well-being during the research. In a conversation during a rehearsal on his birthday, Pete revealed surprising optimism and resilience in his view of the future.

> Pete: I'm sixty-six today.
> David: do you still know who you are yet? Still searching? Like, you know what I mean?
> Pete: Well suppose you could say I am. .. Yeah, I'm still searching.

David also found improvised theatre performance telling a life story to be a valuable technique to address his lifelong conflict with the memory of his mother. She had placed him in an orphanage as a child and left him there for a number of years, despite promises to take him back on a number of occasions. David was both unable to forgive her, or express his anger about this traumatic turning point in his life.

> I wanted a play on that stage that told a true story…It was something I've never told anyone. Through all my treatment, my therapeutic treatment… I had to cover up many times, until one day I had to tell the truth. .. And by letting it out in that play, let out my story, it helped me inside and it gave me… I forgave my mother you know…

As Draucker and Martsolf (2006: 146) note: 'The key to narrative therapy is that life stories that are hurtful or limiting can be changed by discourse that introduces alternate meanings to storied events or highlights previously un-storied events.' Through the use of performance David was able both to portray for the first time his perception of his relationship with his mother, and also to effectively change his understanding of the nature of that relationship and move on from its consequences. Like Pete, David has continued his involvement with groups and performance work related to child abuse.

Another participant who found the use of improvised theatre performance extremely valuable in confronting the consequences of childhood abuse was June, a woman in her fifties. She was sent from an orphanage to a foster home as a child, and suffered physical abuse from her foster mother and sexual abuse from her foster father. Because of her defiant and rebellious behaviour as a response to this abuse, she was returned to the orphanage, but then sent back to the same home to be abused until she was fifteen. As Crossley (2000) and Hudgins (2002) found, traumatic abuse can cause the long-term breakdown of a coherent life story and the self becomes psychologically disorganised. In her opening monologue to the audience in her scene depicting the abuse she suffered in the foster home, June perceptively describes the breakdown of her life story as a mother and the emotional disorientation she feels.

> I feel I am not a complete woman. The happiest moments of my life were giving birth to my children. I was filled with the desire to love and protect them. But how do you show love? Why don't I know how to give the love I feel?

Cattanach (1992: 123) explains that the violation of the individual's body boundaries by sexual abuse makes it difficult for that individual to value herself as a person. This was certainly true for June, but she was determined to tell her story to an audience and confront the sense of anger and helplessness she had experienced for her entire adult life.

This is what somebody did to somebody...To innocent children you know and I want the truth, that's' it ... you want the truth out there.

Like Pete, June had initially wanted to represent her younger self on stage in the scene she had created about the abuse she had suffered in the foster home. However, in rehearsal she found it impossible to actually re-enact the events, and in terms of theatrical impact on an audience the scene did not work with a mature woman with no acting experience portraying herself as a child. Bianca, one of our university's applied theatre students involved in work-integrated learning on the project volunteered to act the role, and this transformed the scene, and June's experience of it. June was able to direct Bianca to enact the actual events convincingly and to convey the vulnerability and innocence of a child. This scene had a significant impact on all the participants and on audiences when it was performed. Sarah Woodland, the director, believes that this scene was:'.. Possibly the most successful in bringing the therapeutic and aesthetic imperatives of the project together on stage.'

A key moment in the scene involved June as herself today talking to her younger self, played by Bianca, and giving her advice. June indicated that this moment created a revelation for her. As an adult now she had the wisdom and experience to understand the abuse that had happened. As an innocent young girl, she did not understand, or know how to cope, and therefore the abuse was not her fault, nor a result of who she was as a child. However, this knowledge was not easily acquired. In interview at the end of the project, June described her struggle to cope with watching and taking part in the first performance:

I had to hold myself together on that first night... you know I couldn't let myself fall to pieces... but when it was actually happening, yeah, and I could see it... I just wanted to... I wanted to tum away but I couldn't. It had to be done.

As with the majority of the other participants, it was the driving need to tell her story of abuse that enabled June to create and perform the scene on stage, despite the difficulty and challenge it represented. For June, the 3 years of involvement in the research and the final outcome of public performances actually achieved for her the aim of finally moving on from the trauma of childhood abuse.

I'm taking it all away and putting something new into it now. Whatever it was I don't know how it all happened really... It's like I got a new... a new... well just like a new spirit – a spirit came into me. An enlightened spirit.

Interviewer: Do you think that spirit is still with you now?
June: Yes. I know that spirit is with me all the time.

7.7 Conclusion

Despite their struggle with the memories and emotions triggered by the material they improvised, created and performed, the majority of the participants in the Moving On project succeeded in achieving their aim of developing and performing a play about the abuse they had suffered as children in institutions. In the process of achieving this aim, they developed a range of skills and new and effective behaviours through the drama workshops. Allira Power, the member of the research team whose honours research focused on the use of improvised drama in the project identified this outcome 'From this research I conclude that although it is a long path, it is possible for participants who have experienced abuse and trauma, to engage in dramatic activity, develop continual understanding of dramatic skill, and process these skills into their own lives, which may contribute to their ability to deal with their experiences.'

The participants were driven throughout the more than 3 years of the project by their determination to tell their stories and be heard, which Herman (1997) identifies as crucial for the healing of individual victims of childhood abuse. Woodland describes how: '... certain Moving On participants engaged with the process of dramatically rendering their autobiographies in order to move them from the internal world of their subjective experiences to the world outside.' This process exploited the healing power of drama identified by Emunah (1994), Landy (2001), Pendzik (2006) and others, the power to externalise and validate the internal worlds of the participants, allowing them deal with the psychological disorientation and the disorganisation of their lives.

The measure of the achievement that the Moving On participants themselves felt was summed up in Simone's final reflection a month after the project finished with the public performances of Memoirs of the Forgotten Ones

> *Finally there were not just one but three performances in 2007 and a standing ovation. We had moved out of an oppressive atmosphere of painful memories into the bright lights and connections of the stage ... In the children's homes they had tried to crush our spirits and yet here we were. Standing up and speaking out, survivors, people who do not give up. Our stories, now historically woven into a pattern and design for change and perhaps for a different, better society*

Afterword

More detailed description and analysis of this project may be found in the following publication and unpublished dissertations, from which some of the researchers' observations in the text are drawn:

Bundy, P. (2006). Using drama in the counselling process: The Moving On project. *Research in Drama Education 11*(1): 7–18.

Power, A. (2004). *Moving On through drama: A study of the developing dramatic skills of trauma victims.* Unpublished honours thesis, Griffith University.

Woodland, S. (2008). *Memoirs of the forgotten ones: The dramatic rendering of autobiography with the survivors of childhood trauma and abuse.* Unpublished masters thesis, Griffith University.

References

Boal, A.(1995). *The rainbow of desire*. New York: Routledge Press.

Briere, J. (2002). Treating adult survivors of severe childhood abuse and neglect: Further development of an integrative model. In J. E. B. Myers, L. Berliner, J. Briere, C. T. Hendrix, T. Reid, & C. Jenny (Eds.), *The APSAC handbook on child maltreatment* (2nd ed.). Newbury Park: Sage.

Castellini, G., Lo Lelli, L., Sauro, C., Vignozzi, L. M., Faravelli, C., & Ricca, V. (2012). Childhood abuse, sexual function and cortisol levels in eating disorders. *Psychotherapy and Psychosomatics, 81*, 380–382.

Cattanach, A. (1992). *Play therapy with abused children*. London: Jessica Kinglsey.

Choudry, A. (2010). Education, participatory action research, and social change: international perspectives. *International Education, 39*(2), 72–76.

Crossley, M. (2000). *Introducing narrative psychology: Self, trauma and the construction of meaning*. Buckingham: Open University Press.

Cyprus Mail. (2014). Scathing UN report demands Vatican act against child sex abuse. http://search.proquest.com.libraryproxy.griffith.edu.au/docview/1494558579?accountid=14543 Nicosia Al Bawaba.

Draucker, C. B., & Martsolf, D. (2006). *Counselling survivors of childhood sexual abuse*. London: Sage.

Emunah, R. (1994). *Acting for real: Drama therapy process, technique, and performance*. New York: Brunner/Mazel.

Emunah, R., & Johnson, D. R. (1983). The impact of theatrical performance on the self-images of psychiatric patients. *The Arts in Psychotherapy, 10*(4), 233–239.

Herman, J. (1997). *Trauma and recovery: The aftermath of violence – from domestic abuse to political terror*. New York: Basic Books.

Hudgins, M. (2002). *Experiential treatment for PTSD: The therapeutic spiral model*. New York: Springer.

Jennings, S. (1998). *Introduction to drama therapy and healing: Ariadne's ball of string*. London: Jessica Kinglsey.

Landy, R. (1994). *Drama therapy: Concepts, theories and practices*. Springfield: Charles C Thomas.

Landy, R. (2001). *New essays in drama therapy: Unfinished business*. Springfield: Charles Thompson.

Margolin, J. (1999). *Breaking the silence: Group therapy for childhood sexual abuse*. New York: Hawthorne Press.

Meekums, B. (1999). A creative model for recovery from childhood sexual abuse and trauma. *The Arts in Psychotherapy, 26*(4), 247–259.

Moreno, J. L. (1977). *Psychodrama* (4th ed.). New York: Beacon House.

Nicholson, H. (2005). *Applied drama: The gift of theatre*. Basingstoke: Palgrave Macmillan.

Ortrun Zuber-Skerritt and Associates. (2009). *Action learning and action research: Songlines through interviews*. Rotterdam: Sense Publishers.

Pendzik, S. (2006). On dramatic reality and its therapeutic function in drama therapy. *The Arts in Psychotherapy, 33*(4), 271–280.

Robinaugh, D. J., & McNally, J. (2011). Trauma centrality and PTSD symptom severity in adult survivors of childhood sexual abuse. *Journal of Traumatic Stress, 24*(4), 483–486. C 2011.

Wu, N. S., Laura, C., Schairer, L. C., Elinam Dellor, E., & Grella, C. (2010). Childhood trauma and health outcomes in adults with comorbid substance abuse and mental health disorders. *Addictive Behaviours, 35*(1), 68–71.

Chapter 8
Drama for Learning in Professional Development Contexts: A Global Perspective

8.1 Introduction

Until the Moving On project, the use of the strategies that had been developed had focused on young people in school learning contexts. The lessons learned from the earlier research clearly illustrated that drama was a powerful tool for transformative learning, and in conjunction with the outcomes of Moving On, indicated that other learning environments could be considered, including professional training and development contexts. This chapter explores several examples of how applied drama as a learning medium has been used for the development of professional relational skills, including conflict management. Four explorations and context are presented; the first is a research study which focused on trainee teachers in the U.K., the second is a study using applied drama in Nursing Education in Germany, Jordan and Sweden, the third outlines how drama strategies drawn from DRACON work have been utilized in teacher development work in Kazakhstan, and the last one is a research study which focused on patients with dementia and their caregivers.

8.2 Background to the Explorations

Many professional practitioners including teachers and nurses, depend heavily on an ability to understand the personal nature of interactions in order to work effectively. These professions engage in what can be called 'relational practices' (Grossman et al. 2007). Therefore, effective pre-service preparation for such careers preferably should include support to develop relational skills, including conflict management techniques. Professionals do need conflict competence to be able to direct power relationships in school and health care contexts. Yet little training in either nursing or teaching focuses on the development of this critical skill. In teacher and nursing pre-service training internationally, young professionals are not adequately prepared

© Springer International Publishing Switzerland 2015   119
B. Burton et al., *Acting to Manage Conflict and Bullying*
Through Evidence-Based Strategies, DOI 10.1007/978-3-319-17882-0_8

to deal with the often complex interpersonal environment of a school or health care context, and professional development and in-service programs rarely focus on relational or interpersonal skills.

A teacher is required to meet, negotiate and interact within a wide range of relationships with colleagues, senior managers, pupils and parents. This is the same with a nurse, although the focus here is on the patient and their families. There is the potential for interpersonal misunderstanding and conflict in all these contexts. Professionals have to navigate an often complex range of power relationships and conflicting personal perspectives. Being able to manage conflict is a core competence required for functioning as a professional where differences of opinion and perspective can get in the way of core objectives i.e. effective teaching and health care (Morrison et al. 2013). Understanding differences, and an ability to shift perspective is central to professional learning and development, and this is a transformative process in that it requires professionals to modify taken for granted assumptions preconceptions. Transformative learning, defines this kind of learning it as a process by which individuals change their 'meaning schemes'. Mezirow (1990) in the development of his theories – defines 'meaning schemes' as sets of habitual expectations and beliefs that drive individual behavior. In a professional context the differing meaning schemes of individuals provides fertile ground for conflict.

In developing an understanding of relational issues professionals need to be able to recognize conflict, respond appropriately and develop resiliency. We had learned through DRACON work with young people that this requires the ability to reflect constructively on interpersonal relationships, and that drama was a powerful way of fostering engagement and reflection (Chaps. 3 and 4). The research confirmed that drama provides a safe place for individuals to take risks and explore ideas and issues through engagement in role, and it can help create new insights for participants as they unify their own lived experience with experiential fictional experience.

Conceptual understanding is needed to drive transformative learning yet it cannot be taught in traditional ways, and innovative strategies are required that can engage the whole person- feelings, thoughts and actions. Applied drama is one approach that can foster this kind of engagement. Applied drama, although closely related to educational drama, is broader in terms of its contextual application. Several definitions and descriptions of applied drama or applied theatre could be used (Ackroyd 2007; Neelands 2007; Nicholson 2005; Taylor 2003). In this Chapter we use the terms 'applied drama' and 'drama' to describe a set of discursive drama practices employed in a training context to advance personal awareness through action and reflection.

8.3   A Workshop for Professional Development: Enhanced Forum Theatre

A model for using drama as a learning medium for the development of professional relational skills, including conflict management was developed in collaboration between researchers from Australia, Sweden and UK – Bruce Burton, Margret Lepp and Morag Morrison, all of whom were involved in the DRACON project and are academics in the fields of Teacher Education and Nursing Education. The model illustrated below evolved as a result of workshops with teachers and nurses aimed to incorporate a theoretical understanding of Conflict, with practical, interactive strategies which would develop personal understanding, and foster understanding and perhaps a change in individual meaning schemes.

The model serves to illustrate the basic structure of a number of workshops used in learning situations in nursing and teacher education in a number of professional training contexts. What can be seen is that it brings together interactive drama strategies, theory and performance and offers participants the opportunity to collaboratively reflect on the explorations they have made through drama. Reflection is a central component in learning through drama because it is not only the experience itself, but the reflection on that experience which fosters understanding (Morrison 2004). While the workshop model has been utilized in training programs with nurses and teachers; some individual strategies were also explored in adult education and particularly teacher professional development, and this chapter highlights how some elements have been incorporated in a professional development programs for teachers in Kazakhstan. All the explorations discussed in this chapter have drawn of the key strategies utilized in this workshop model (Fig. 8.1).

Fig. 8.1 Structure of workshop with four phases (ref. Morrison et al. 2013, p 68)

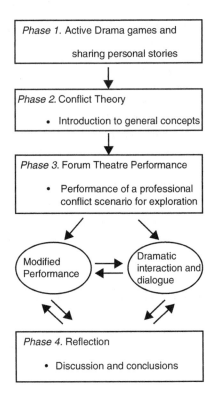

8.4 Context 1

8.4.1 Exploring Professional Conflict with Pre-service Teachers in the U.K.

In this exploration a research study involving pre-service teachers was the focus and the workshop model illustrated above was used to develop an understanding of conflict and conflict competency during a Professional Skills conference day. Although the 'Enhanced Forum Theatre' performance that formed the base for the last part of the workshop was performed by trainee Drama teachers, it was decided they should not be part of the study, so data was not collected from them. Our interest was to see how drama would work in a professional education context, and it was felt Drama students may already have some bias in terms of their appreciation of the form. Participants were all trainees undertaking their postgraduate year in the Faculty of Education, University of Cambridge, U.K. The trainee teachers were offered a range of workshops throughout the day and were able to select on the basis of which they might find most valuable. A large number – 64 in all selected this workshop, and participants were drawn from across a range of subject areas in the secondary school curriculum and they were not familiar in working through drama.

The trainees came from the United Kingdom and Ireland, as well as a small number from other parts of the world. The 64 trainees included 43 females and 21 males), ranging in age from 21 to 44 years, and they participated in the workshops and completed a questionnaire directly after finishing the drama workshop. The questions concerned their experiences of participating in the workshop. Content analysis was used as a methodological approach as described by Graneheim and Lundman (2004). In this analysis we looked for common issues mentioned by participants either within their response to the questionnaire, or in interview following the workshop and these issues clustered into a broad theme that could be broken down into categories reflecting the outcomes of participation in the workshop.

One main theme – *the nature of learning through the medium of drama* – and three related categories emerged from the analysis of the open ended questions. The three categories are:

- Bridging theory and practice in teacher education
- Fostering courage and self-esteem
- Cognitive engagement, shifts in perspectives and empathy.

8.4.2 Key Theme: The Nature of Learning Through Drama

The trainees participating in the workshop expressed the view that the interactive nature of the engagement it fostered bridged the gap between theory and practice. Their response illustrated that they both enjoyed he workshop and found it valuable:

I am not usually a fan of Drama, but I really did enjoy this session! (Modern Languages trainee)

   Some of the changes we made 9in the Forum theatre Performance) and solutions will be useful, especially what we can do as a trainee to change things. (Music trainee)

Drama activities and working in role had provided the necessary distance to think more deeply and reflect on the actions and opinions of others in relation to their own perspective on a situation. This illustrated that empathy was valuable in fostering understanding.

8.4.3 Bridging the Gap Between Theory and Practice

Because the scenario illustrated in the workshop had been developed by teacher trainees, it was based on real experiences. A number of trainees expressed the view that they found one of the biggest challenges in their training was navigating power relationships within the hierarchical structures of some schools. Sometimes mentor expectations in terms of workload could overburden them, and senior management in the school were often unaware of this or too busy with their own professional pressures to assist. Trainees sometimes felt powerless to challenge or even ask questions of school colleagues, and so small problems could grow into more serious issues.

   In the scenario developed as the base for the enhanced forum component of the workshop, a trainee faced a problem with one of the teachers she needed to work with in the school. The teacher expected her to take on the workload of a fulltime teacher, and offered little practical support for her to develop resources. The trainee felt uncomfortable about approaching the teacher for help, for fear she would look incapable, and was reticent to raise the issue with her mentor, a close friend of the teacher. As she struggled under the weight of expectation with little practical support, the teacher approached senior management communicating that the trainee was not performing well, raising doubts about her ability to cope in the classroom and suitability for the profession. The situation undermined the trainee's confidence and ultimately led her to doubt her own career decision to train as a teacher.

   Participants could see this and recognized how the in exploring the performance they could learn themselves.

   It is a situation you might find yourself in as a trainee, so you can both identify with the conflict being portrayed and learn how perhaps to handle the situation should you find yourself in it. (Classics trainee)

   Very useful in that it reflected an experience encountered by many of us. (Modern Languages trainee)

What was clear was that trainees were also learning theory through the experiences provided in the workshop; as well as it being deemed fun and 'refreshing', it was considered an effective way of learning:

I found it more effective than theoretical sessions I have attended (Music trainee) another said it *…easier to relate to than theoretical teaching.* (Music trainee)

Further to this, participants welcomed the innovative approach to the way conflict was management was taught,

We spend enough time as trainees being lectured on educational theory. (Classics trainee)

In considering the impact of using Applied Drama, and drawing on feedback, it became clear to all participants, as well as the leaders of the workshop, that the ability participants had to actively explore their own ideas and experiment with different approaches to the problem offered a less didactic form of training compared to training approaches focusing on theory in the abstract. It is here that the unique nature of engagement in Drama offers the key to why it might be an effective learning medium in contexts requiring personal reflection and empathy, i.e. qualities necessary in interpersonal understanding. In understanding that conflict empathy is key, and in bringing together the experiential opportunities of the workshop with cognitive engagement requiring critical thinking and reflection, trainees developed their understanding of the perspectives of others.

Participants in this workshop were required to work in role, but these roles were not so far removed from their own experience. They were in fact bringing their own perspectives and understanding, shaped most recently by their introduction to conflict theory in the earlier part of the workshop, to practical activities such as the Forum Theatre. Drama education theorists have written extensively on the affective and intellectual power of subject-learning through working in role, and working in role is a form of 'experiential' learning which fosters empathetic connections to the human experiences of others (e.g. Bolton 2012; Morgan and Saxton 1987; Edmiston 2013). It could be argued that all the trainees in this study had to move out of their comfort zones as passive learners; they were asked to turn their intellectual reflections on a problem into action. The experience of being 'in the moment' is powerful and easy solutions were not always found.

8.4.4   Fostering Courage and Self-Esteem

One of the opportunities provided in the workshop was for the trainees to test out responses in a safe environment. Given that power relationships in school are often complex, trainees welcomed the chance to try out responses that they were not confident to make in the real world. Through the Enhanced Forum presentation they could dare to speak up and challenge those deemed to have greater power or control. It allowed them to practice courage and this seemed an important factor in developing their understanding of power relationships in conflict. One participant states

It was useful to realise that trainees sometimes have to speak up to resolve latent conflict and avoid confrontations (Modern languages trainee)

Another added that it was helpful because she was usually quiet and the workshop taught her she needed to

..communicate more confidently with other members of staff (Classics trainee)

Others spoke of

...being more assertive, and the need to *make sure you are confident.*

The workshop had offered opportunities for participants to build courage and self-esteem. Through experimenting with different possibilities they could see how they could take back power for themselves in given situations. In the workshop the trainees had had the opportunity to explore conflict through exercising their imagination in the pursuit of finding alternative outcomes to interpersonal professional issues.

8.4.5 Cognitive Engagement, Shifts in Perspective and Empathy

In the workshop participants had had to engage very actively. This kind of engagement required them to really listen to others in order to respond. But they were not just asked to respond to others, they also were offered opportunities to question themselves. In one of the earlier activities in the workshop the participants told each other a story from their own experience; the twist was that the story had to be retold by their partner as a first person narrative. This required to them to reflect with some distance on their own problem. One reflection was

Hearing your own story back to you really helped you to think a lot and gain perspective on the conflict in question. (History trainee)

The same participant was impressed by how this form of cognitive engagement could provide clarity through distance,

Allows you to see it from another angle, it takes the emotion out and allows you to think more clearly. (Music trainee)

Participants also reflected on the role empathy had played in how the presentation evolved. As different approaches were tried out to try and find a resolution, the trainees could see different perspectives and attitudes in play. Role play strategies were seen as providing emotional insight,

Putting yourself in someone else's place, acting back the story is good for empathy. (Classics trainee)

Participants in the workshop were watching action from the inside and outside, and experimenting with different views and perspectives. There was time for discussion and reflection and this brought together cognitive engagement with the experiential learning that had taken place in the drama activities: Being able to identify with another person's position, and understand the emotions and feeling that can impact on behavior, was a very valuable learning experience for the trainees. Lessons learned brought the personal to the professional in a very meaningful and valuable way.

8.4.6   Conclusions for Context 1

Importantly, trainees agreed that drama had not only provided a very useful way into conflict theory, but it had made the theory visible,

> *..seeing how the choices affected results in a way you usually wouldn't get to do'* (Maths trainee)

It is important for teachers inside and outside the classroom to develop empathy and understanding. These are qualities that provide insight in professional contexts where interpersonal skill is vital. The study yielded a number of important implications for teacher training.

Implications for Teacher Training

- Applied Drama pedagogy can provide unique opportunities for learning and developing vital relational skills.
- The use of Drama promotes courage and self-esteem.
- Complex learning can be achieved by unifying theory with practice, and this is effectively possible through the medium of Drama.
- There is a strong link between empathy, understanding and personal empowerment. Drama fosters emotional engagement and empathy, and as a result participants can experience shifts in perspective.

8.5   Context 2

8.5.1   International Collaboration in Nursing Education in Sweden

The focus of this study was on how nurses, nurse educators, and doctoral and masters students from three universities and three countries, Germany, Jordan and Sweden experienced learning through drama in the field of nursing education. A long-term collaboration was already established between the three participating universities. In 2008, an international, collaborative, interactive educational conference, called 'Drama and Learning Across Borders' (D-LAB) was born (Lepp et al. 2011). In total 14 participants met in Sweden and participated in the 2-day program. Even though English was not their native language, all participants could speak, read and write in English. The first day of the program consisted of a drama workshop which included an exploration of key ideas through EFT conflict management and the second day comprised of research presentations and academic work involving further collaboration.

The program was undertaken at the University of Borås, in western Sweden. The two other participating universities were the University of Jordan in Amman, Jordan and the University of Witten/Herdecke in Germany. All universities had nursing programs at undergraduate, masters and doctoral levels. The study was qualitative, building on the participants' involvement in a drama workshop, and the participants utilised reflective journals. Drama was used as the main language to communicate and share experiences such as dilemmas and conflicts that are common in the field of international nursing and nursing education.

8.5.2 The Drama Workshop

The drama workshop was conducted at the university, in a classroom cleared of tables with plenty of room for movement and performance. The workshop lasted for 1 day. It started with participants sitting in a circle, sharing presentations and expectations, followed by warm-up games, stories of participants' names and life histories (in pairs), and image theatre performances in groups related to themes such as caring, suffering, curiosity, anger and hope.

The ABC-model (See Chap. 2) was introduced based on conflict theory: escalation, de-escalation and conflict resolution. Elements of conflict management theory, were explained, including the three stages of conflict discussed in Chap. 3, latent, emergent and manifest. Then the term Enhanced Forum Theatre was introduced and utilised in the same form as in the DRACON project. Situations drawn from the participants' own lives, related to conflicts and ethical dilemmas in health care the scenes were improvised and illustrated. The forum-plays utilised open-ended dramatised stories to invite participants' reactions to possible change – for example, in the process of the conflict – or to explore and possibly reduce the conflict being represented through various actions. The participants in this study responded positively to this model. Three forum-plays were performed, and the three situations from the forum-plays were used for further exploration and discussion as follows. All three situations were recognized by all the participants as common situations that did happen in their countries as well.

Situation 1
Conflict between a physician and a nurse about a patient in pain. The question for the nurses was how to convince the physician to give more pain relief to a patient in deep pain. The conflict related to inter-professional communication and difference in power related to hierarchical health care organisations where physicians traditionally have more status and power than nurses.

Situation 2
A teacher and a nursing student had a negative encounter. The student was disrespectful to the teacher during the class in front of other students. The questions raised were: How do you create a learning environment as a professional teacher and at the same time satisfy every student's need for attention? How should or could the teacher

have responded instead of getting angry? And why did the teacher become upset in the first place? The conflict related to teacher–student relationships and negative interaction in the classroom.

Situation 3
A teacher and a student were complaining about the negative workplace environment at the director's office. The questions related to how to get your voice heard and your needs taken into consideration at work.

8.5.3   Journaling as Data

Journaling was used as a method for data collection and as a pedagogical tool for reflection. The participants were asked to reflect and write about their drama experiences directly after the workshop. The journals from the 14 participants were exposed to a quality content analysis.

8.5.4   Results

Two categories and five sub-categories emerged in the analysis of the participants' journals. The category *Creating a Learning Environment* consisted of two sub-categories: the role of the drama teacher, and a universal nursing language, which covered statements related to how a learning environment is created and how to communicate in the field of nursing education. The category *Opening Doors* is described in three sub-categories and levels: a pedagogical level, a group level and a personal level.

The participants stated that no specific cultural differences that arose surprised the group. It was all about meeting people and being human. Participants also acknowledged that there were situations in their professional lives that were not easy to solve:

> The forum-plays were constructed situations that participants had experienced in their professional life on a daily basis. Sometimes, finding solutions to the problems we face is not always easy.

In this specific context, drama was identified by the participants as a form of interaction that international nurses could use to communicate, and to understand each other, independently of cultural or language differences.

Drama was also described by the participants as a democratic process of learning, as it created feelings of equality independent of profession within the group, making the environment feel more collegial and less hierarchical: According to the journal statements, the dilemmas in the forum-play revealed that there were many similarities among the participants from the three countries, and only a few cultural differences. The journals also revealed that drama increases the ability to be prepared to act in the future. It also helps individuals to see new possibilities:

I was astonished at the amount of problems and scope of solutions that were discussed.

According to the participants, an international group is effective for pedagogical activities. Drama helps to reveal the diversity of the group members as individual people, but also allows them to share their experiences within the group: "I felt integrated in the group and felt the democratic process of learning".

After this day, many questions are answered. All started with a real feeling of being welcome. The international group has a very high effect on me – explaining the meaning of a Christian name to a number of participants from an Islamic religion was not easy ... However, it was a basic action to confidence.

Participants spoke of the humanistic side of being a learner in the drama program. They felt that often they not only belonged to a certain team, country, ethnic group or culture, but also shared the feeling of belonging to what can be called a 'culture of nursing'.

8.5.5   Conclusions for Context 2

The use of drama in this study assisted the participants overcome different obstacles among professions, cultures, language, experiences, social status and academic status. Participants in this study described drama as going beyond verbal language, using non-verbal communication, role-play, gestures and dynamic actions that made language a universal context beyond nationality and culture. The participants identified 'caring elements' as 'universal connections', regardless of their mother language, culture or experiences. This study has implications for nursing education and curriculum activities and development.

8.6   Context 3

8.6.1   Employing Drama Teacher Professional Development in Kazakhstan

The final exploration into adult professional learning through Drama has been based in Kazakhstan; the research is in its early stages, although already there are some interesting observations and conclusions to be drawn. Whilst teaching conflict management through Drama has not been the explicit focus of the research, there have been opportunities to draw on some of the strategies developed through DRACON to support broader professional learning, and it is teachers' responses to learning concepts through these strategies that will be explored here.

8.6.2 Background

In 2011 Cambridge University, Faculty of Education was approached to devise a program of teacher professional development to enhance the pedagogic skills of the nation's current teaching workforce. This was to be delivered through a cascading model of training i.e. a team of Cambridge university personnel would train and mentor an initial group of Kazakh teachers who would in turn each train a group of colleagues in their regions to also become trainers, and so on. An initial group of 320 teachers undertook the first stage of the program and by the end of 2014 more than 23,000 teachers will have received training. The necessity for such a program of development is an interesting one, and worth explaining in a little depth in order to frame the later discussion in terms of how Drama has been a very valuable vehicle of support in this context.

Following independence in 1991, Kazakhstan found itself needing to establish its own education system. In common with much of the country's tired infrastructure, it had inherited a soviet model of education; and while there were many strengths to this system, such as equality of access and high literacy and numeracy rates, there were also some elements missing for a nation that wished to develop a workforce to compete in its own right on a world stage. When the country's top school graduates were sent to study abroad it was recognized that they faced many challenges. In western universities where critical and creative thinking was valued, and where students were expected to think and work both collaboratively and independently, Kazakh students struggled. It was clear that the kinds of skills needed for twenty-first century learning were not being offered in the schools, and teachers would need to modify their approach to pedagogy to address this issue. Traditional didactic forms of tuition were not serving students well, and while teachers may have felt comfortable in recreating the classrooms of their own youth, and offering models of classroom practice similarly traditional and teacher-centred, this approach could not deliver what was needed.

In collaboration with representatives from Kazakhstan, specialist teachers from the Faculty of Education, Cambridge, developed began to a three stage training model, based on developing a paradigm of pedagogy which acknowledge that a teacher needs more than subject knowledge to be effective. Shulman (1998) states that teaching involves three key aspects; professional understanding, the head; practical skill, the hand; and professional integrity, the heart. All these aspects are focused in relation to the learner. It was recognised that one of the fundamental shifts currently serving teachers in Kazakhstan would need to make was in terms of their understanding of how learners learn, and the importance of acknowledging the interplay of all three domains, social and affective, as well as cognitive in the effective education of young people.

In this framework it was decided by Kazakhstani government there were a number of core areas that needed to be developed to enhance the professionalism of Kazakh teachers and an important place to start would be developing teachers understanding. This would include an understanding of how critical thinking skills can be developed, and new approaches to teaching and learning that would enhance more pupil-centred collaborative and dialogic approaches to teaching. Morag Morrison was pleased to be invited by the one of the project leaders, Elaine Wilson, to join the project. Along with Fay Turner, Elaine was one of the driving forces behind developing the training program that would be delivered in the country by a team of experienced teacher educators from Cambridge, and project leaders had to work with extraordinary logistic challenges and formidable time-frame expectations to roll out the program. All materials had to be translated into two languages, Kazakh and Russian; project leaders in Kazakhstan were under considerable pressure to move the program out quickly, and thus time frames were short for the development and production of plans and materials. Furthermore, face to face delivery of training was conducted via translators in either Kazakh or Russian, the two main languages of the country, a teaching experience very few of the team were familiar with. However, balanced against this backdrop of enormous challenge, was enormous opportunity, and it became clear from the outset that drama pedagogic skill could be very valuable in developing pedagogy integrating skill, knowledge and understanding, 'head, hand and heart.'

8.6.3   A Multiple Role for Drama in Developing Pedagogic Change

Once on the ground in Kazakhstan it very soon became apparent to the Cambridge researchers that many of the ideas the teachers were being introduced to were challenging in terms of the teaching culture currently embedded in the country. Teachers did not find it easy to accept that they may need to rethink how they saw themselves as teachers, and yet it was essential to shift their mindset away from the belief that primary purpose of a teacher was to deliver information, to a more holistic approach focused on the needs of the learner. Teachers themselves were steeped in a very competitive and hierarchical professional environment and against this backdrop it was a challenge for some teachers to relinquish long established expectations and behaviours, their individual 'meaning schemes' (Mezirow 1990), referred to earlier in this chapter, in order to transform their practice . Education theorists from Dewey onward have acknowledged the complexity and challenge of the teacher's role, and central to this is how teachers see themselves (Freire 2007; Greene 1995; Giroux 1997, 2011; McIntyre et al. 2008). So before any change in practice could be established, Cambridge trainers recognized that the Kazakh teachers would need to see themselves as collaborative learners and commit to the ethos of the program. They would need to be convinced that new ways of working in the classroom could be more effective for learning and a more democratic classroom could be both enjoyable and productive.

   Clearly the best way of communicating this to the teachers was to have them experience it for themselves, therefore central to the training was the modeling of approaches and behaviors in the classroom that would break down barriers to learning and develop a more 'dialogic' (Alexander 2006) and collaborative approach to teaching. Here is where drama came to the fore because experiential learning is the heart of any drama experience, and dialogue and reflection also are key elements of the drama process. During the training Drama strategies served two very important purposes. Firstly, through interactive games, workshops and activities, Drama offered a vehicle to break down personal barriers and create a more democratic and enjoyable learning environment and secondly, some of the strategies provided invaluable opportunities to develop the reflective skills of teachers. Among the strategies used by some of the trainers for fostering reflection were role-play and hot-seating, and in sessions conducted by Morag Morrison, her background in DRACON work (Chap. 3) enabled her to utilise Enhanced Forum Theatre as a key strategy in a number of learning contexts, most notably when teachers were exploring relationships in mentoring and coaching.

In the first instance, drama games and active collaborative activities helped forge bonds between the groups of teachers being trained. Most sessions started with what were called 'ice-breakers' and it cannot be overestimated how important these simple active and fun games were in breaking down hierarchical barriers in each group. Whether it was a simple game of musical chairs, a name game or creating a human knot, the teachers seemed to revel in the 'silliness' of letting go and enjoying the moment, and personal and professional boundaries began to break down. As one teacher said, 'the ice is thawing'. The climate in each classroom began to improve and these activities also served a vital purpose in establishing energy and enthusiasm. Cambridge trainers had only expected these kinds of activities would be needed on the first day or so, but it soon became clear how vital they were in establishing group cohesion, and they became an on-going feature throughout the training program. In time the teachers began to enjoy finding their own warm-up games and took turns in leading their group. The teachers learning was in fact facilitated by an increase in their positive disposition toward working with each other and this seemed to flow into developing more positive and 'open' attitudes to ideas being introduced in the training program.

The second way in which drama was utilized in the training was to develop reflective practice. One of the key challenges the Kazakh teachers faced was in acknowledging some of the more subtle links between their pedagogic choices and the learning of their pupils. In a system where little differentiation was made between learners, many teachers simply blamed the pupil for any shortcomings in their learning experience. Pupil behavior, good or otherwise, was for many teachers seen simply as the result of a child's personal choices; so one of the key issues to address was how teachers could develop a deeper understanding of their role in pupil engagement. As highlighted earlier in this chapter, the drama approach of Enhanced Forum theatre has provided an excellent springboard in a number of professional contexts for reflection and this was utilized on numerous occasions, both to explore classroom practice and wider professional issues. One example of the former, is where the Kazakh teachers developed short role-plays on teaching and learning scenarios involving a set of fictitious pupils, each with a particular kind of barrier to their learning. Examples of scenarios exploring professional issues included situations where teachers had to face a challenging mentoring situation with a colleague, or had to deal with a less supportive member of the school management team in order to foster confidence in the training program.

8.6.4   First Research Steps as Teachers Reflect on Learning

Although formal research into how the use of drama strategies in the Kazakhstan teacher development context is only in its early stages, data collected to this point has supported the anecdotal evidence from trainers in their classrooms. In 2012 a survey of 125 teachers who had just undertaken training simply asked teachers to rank in order strategies and techniques utilized in their own training in terms of what they found best supported their own learning, and also which of these strategies they might use themselves in their training of others. In addition eight teachers, representing a range of participants, male and female, Russian and Kazakh speakers, were interviewed following their final days of training. Teachers on the course were also required to keep a 'training journal' where they were asked if they would be prepared to share some of their reflections on the drama strategies used in training.

In one journal entry a teacher echoed some of the sentiments expressed by the trainee teachers in the project described earlier in this chapter i.e. the link drama could make between theory and practice,

> *Under such circumstances a role play enables teachers to reflect on what is seen, and theoretical material is remembered and comprehended much better in this case.* (Nazulan, Journal entry)

One teacher, following her school-based period after the first stage of training, where she herself at the opportunity to train others, tried some of the activities she had been introduced to and reflected on what they had brought to her classroom.

> *My conclusions were proved by further events as my experience showed that exactly those (drama) activities were effective and helpful for deeper understanding of the program (ideas of topics/modules). All trainers noted an extreme cohesion of the group, good psychological climate/atmosphere, mutual readiness to help as well as empathy between group-mates. (Botogoz Journal entry)*

Reinforced in this entry is the perception that drama strategies were valuable in breaking down barriers and improving classroom climate, but also clear is the link the teacher has been able to make between this and the development of 'deeper understanding' through more interactive strategies.

Enhanced Forum Theatre had a very powerful impact on the Kazakh teachers and it was borne out in several interviews when teachers were asked to consider some of the strategies they had found most effective for their learning. One commented that,

> *...it was an interesting method the result of which we could not predict (Sergio, Journal entry).*

What the teacher is revealing in this comment is not only how interesting she found the approach, but that she was comfortable with the unexpected and unplanned. Many teachers in the initial stages of training had expressed some unease with activities that were not tightly controlled or where the outcome was unknown, so this of itself marks a shift. Another teacher interviewed also observed that after an Enhanced Forum Theatre activity where they were asked to observe a teacher, deep reflection on the problem was stimulated,

> ...there was another shift towards the teacher and her actions, requirements and feelings. It was great to consider (as mentors) teacher's behaviour (sic) and come up with an idea about a complex problem to be solved for sure. It made us think what changes were necessary. (Katrine Interview)

Also clear in this response is the role of empathy in understanding a problem. Teachers acknowledged that through the drama activities,

> ...we identified a whole tangle of complex and complicated problems, such as professionalism, responsibility, personal involvement and interest for a lesson. (Gulnara Interview)

It appeared that the participatory form of Enhanced Forum Theatre had supported their learning. What was interesting to learn in the interviews was that some teachers had experienced role play before; and several had been on training courses where they had been asked to participate or watch a scenario played out.

> The strategies were not new- I had seen these strategies before, but the difference in the Cambridge training was all this reflection. Whatever we do there was reflection. (Katrine Interview)

This respondent was asked to explain further how this form of reflection was different from her previous experiences,

> It is more philosophical. Of course I had used some of these active ways before, but it was not in such a philosophical way and such a way that my attitudes changed somehow. It was not interactive work for the sake of interactive work. It was important; the outcome of this- understanding and better communication. (Katrine Interview)

Another teacher also noted how engagement in the activity had fostered empathy and understanding,

> In the role play, where I was the teacher playing the student and a teacher was scolding the student for their behaviour, I would not do this in my practice again – I felt how it would be to be scolded, de-motivated. (Olga Interview)

In both of these comments it is clear that the teachers were acknowledging some from of transformative learning; could it be that their engagement in drama was fostering a shift in what Mezirow (1990) had identified as individual 'meaning schemes'? There was no doubt that the specific characteristics of some of the drama approaches, particularly Enhanced Forum Theatre, were memorable and fostered deep professional reflection.

8.6.5   Conclusion for Context 3

Many of the drama activities were based on ideas used in DRACON (Chaps. 2 and 3) workshops. Enhanced Forum Theatre as a strategy was borrowed directly and it was invaluable as a teacher development training method. But the value of Enhanced

Forum Theatre and other drama strategies in professional learning, should come as no surprise – indeed drama as a way into experiential learning reinforces Dewey's (1933, 1973) well-established views on effective teaching and learning practices i.e. the power of learning that engages the whole person.

During the training in Kazakhstan, despite the challenges of working through a translator, drama games and activities were embraced by teachers. Enhanced Forum Theatre, a complex strategy to explain even to an English speaking group, was inherently understood as ideas unfolded, and teachers' engagement deepened. It is very satisfying to know some of them will endeavor to use the strategy in their own practice; but even if this does not happen, very important personal and professional learning resulted from their own experience of the form as it deepened their ability to reflect on teaching and learning. To paraphrase Dewey, individuals do not learn from experiences but from reflecting upon them (1933). Given that the Cambridge Teacher Development project is seeking, in collaboration with education authorities in that country, to transform professional practice, this goal appears well supported by such strategies as Enhanced Forum Theatre.

8.7 Context 4

8.7.1 Involving Patients and Their Caregivers in a Drama Program in Sweden

In Sweden, persons with dementia live at home as long as possible with the help of home assistance services. Dementia has many causes, the two most common being Alzheimer's disease and vascular dementia. As a result of higher ages and increase in survival rates, after different diseases, the prevalence of older people with dementia is expected to increase. However, as the disease progresses, they are often admitted to hospitals or nursing homes. There is currently no pharmacological treatment to cure or prevent dementia, although there are indications that some medications may retard the progression of the disease. The greatest losses older adults face in long-term care communities is the loss of community, family, and home, and the increase sense of isolation (Rollins 2013). Alternative treatments and participating in creative activities may contribute to an increase in the quality of life of persons with dementia and thereby permit them to maintain their dignity in old age (Anderberg et al. 2007). Engaging in the arts can help establishing a sense of identity and community, increase socialization skills, and enhance quality of life (Boyer 2007).

8.7.2 The Study

The study was part of a research project DRAMA-GER and supported by Stockholm County Council's Research Program "Arts in Hospital and Care as Culture". The focus of this study was on developing a drama program designed for patients with dementia. The content of the program was on dance, rhythm, song, storytelling and conversations. The aim was to describe how a drama program for patients with dementia and their caregivers was experienced by the caregivers. The project team consisted of two researchers (Lepp M and Ringsberg KC) and two drama teachers (Holm A-K and Sellersjö G).

Twelve strategically selected patients, 10 women and 2 men aged 73–95 years, with diagnosed middle and severe dementia participated in a drama program, as did their 7 female nursing assistants/caregivers. The selection of the patients was based on their capacity to take part and be able to talk and understand Swedish. They were all registered at a home care centre for older people. A nurse who specialized in dementia assisted with the selection of the patients. Verbal and written information about the project was given to the caregivers, the patients and their relatives. The Research Ethics Committee, Göteborg University, approved the study.

8.7.3   The Drama Program

The patients and their caregivers were randomly allocated to two programs A or B, led by different drama teachers. In program A the focus was on dance, rhythm and songs well known to this age group. The content was taken from themes from everyday life, such as love, the seasons, nature and the four elements (fire, water, air and earth). The participants danced, sang, played and talked about memories they associated with these different themes, using props such as clothes, hats, fruit, vegetables and 'old things'. In program B the focus was on storytelling, stories with themes influenced by Erikson's (1982) theory of the eight life cycles, themes such as childhood, adulthood and marriage. Each group met on six occasions over 2 months. The two groups had the same external structure; the meetings lasted for 1½h, including a 30-min coffee break during which the conversation continued. All participants received small gifts, such as flowers and shells related to the contents of the meeting, as confirmation of having attended. The meetings took place at the same day, place and time, once a week.

8.7.4   Interview with the Caregivers

A focus group interview was held by the two researchers with the caregivers 1 month after the program had ended. The interview was semi-structured, informal and conversational in style and lasted for 90 min. The interview focused on the caregivers' various experiences and concepts of the drama program. The interview was tape-recorded and transcribed verbatim. The data were then analysed according to the principles of phenomenography, that is to capture people's concepts of various aspects of the world. The analysis resulted in two comprehensive categories and five descriptive subcategories. The categories represent qualitatively different ways of experiencing the drama program.

8.7.5 *Interaction and Professional Growth*

Two categories, *Interaction* and *Professional growth*, with their attendant subcategories, representing different concepts of having participated in the drama program emerged in the analysis of the interviews with the caregivers.

The category *Interaction* covers concepts that emphasize that both the patients and the caregivers interacted in different ways during the drama meetings. They shared joy and sadness as an example of fellowship. The caregivers felt that communication between the patients became stronger between the first and the last drama meetings. The caregivers emphasized that the drama program had an effect on the patients' behaviour, such as greater communication and a reactivation of their memory. The patients expressed their feelings, positive and negative, and showed greater interest in other people and a better self-confidence. It may be that when they felt confirmed the patients dared to show their feelings. The caregivers stated that the patients also showed knowledge and abilities that were unknown to them before the drama program was held. This finding is important, as the caregivers might be able to use this knowledge in their caring interaction with the patients.

As the patients and their caregivers developed fellowship and greater communication, one consequence was that the caregivers got access to what they termed their patients' reactivated memory, which they used in other caring settings. There was a great deal of laughter and this created a feeling of fellowship between the participants:

> We kept following this story and many people talked. We started to sing children's songs and recite children's poems. It was a lot of fun and we laughed a lot.

Having interacted with the patients, on a level other than their everyday dealings, gave them satisfaction on both the personal and the professional levels:

> When my patient has so much fun, I also have fun.

A special kind of fellowship developed between the caregivers and the patients because the caregivers participated in the drama program. The patients slowly started to seek contact with one another and later on communicated spontaneously so communication between the patients developed during the course of the drama program. Relatives of the patients had also noticed that the patients took more interest in their surroundings and had mentioned this to the caregivers. As the patients engaged in greater communication with their surroundings, some behavioural changes took place. For example, the caregivers reported that the patients demanded less attention from them in the home environment:

> I have to say that I think she's opened up. Become a little happier, a little more open.

By participating in the drama program the patients appeared to increase their ability to communicate. This may have strengthened their self-confidence and ability to show greater interest in their surroundings than before. The caregivers increased their communication with their patients during the program and even in other settings. The interaction in the drama activities brought the patients' memory to life. From the story's symbols, the patients continued to offer to the other group members stories and events from their own lives. They made further associations with what the drama teacher had brought up during the meeting:

> *They built upon the story and one thing led to the next and it came to include fantastic things, but the whole thing had to do more with times past, because the story she (the drama teacher) told was well thought out. It had very much to do with real life and they could connect it to their lives from the time they were children and right through with one thing leading to another.*

The caregivers were surprised when the patients showed skills and knowledge that they had not displayed before. With the help of thoughts and ideas brought up during the drama meetings, the patients were led to make associations with other situations in life and in that way they reactivated their memories. By participating in the program, the caregivers learnt new things about their patients, which they could use in other settings in their interaction with them.

In the second category, *Professional growth*, the caregivers stated that they felt confirmed as caregivers through their participation in the study. The caregivers realized that they were important to the patients in terms of functioning and serving as a link to everyday life. The patients needed the caregivers to feel safe in new situations, such as during the drama meetings described here. The caregivers learnt new things about their patients during the drama meetings and, as a result, started to reflect upon their own role as a caregiver. The participation in the drama program spurred them to reflect upon themselves, the patients and how to use drama within the field of caring. They began to see that the use of drama and cultural activities has potential as an alternative treatment method. The caregivers reflected upon the way in which they could continue to use drama activities in everyday caring situations, as they had experienced this way of working with patients with dementia as meaningful.

The presence of the caregivers not only created a safe space for the patients but also offered the caregivers and the patients mutual experiences which could later be talked about in the everyday setting. In the current program, efforts were made to stimulate as many of the patients' senses as possible, through song, rhythm, dance, storytelling and conversation. In the research on the program, the caregivers were involved in the program, as participants. In all the drama activities, the focus was on the interaction between the individuals in the group. The findings of this study indicates that the interaction between the patients, and the patients and their caregivers improved through participating in a drama program. The whole process strengthened their professional self-confidence; they felt confirmed and viewed drama as a possible treatment method. Their participation in the program gave them a new attitude towards their profession including seeing the patient from a holistic perspective and giving the patients a sense of security by being present during the six meetings.

Before the program started, the caregivers expressed doubt as to whether it was possible at all to carry out a drama program for this patient group. After a few meetings they felt that this was possible after all and felt inspired to continue holding similar activities:

It has to do with everyday culture, how we meet people and that we can create small groups of this kind very easily and make them meaningful for the people living here and stimulate them to maintain the skills they have.

The caregivers noted and reflected upon the relationship between the drama teachers and the patients. In this way they became a model for other caregivers in the terms of their professional relationships with the patients:

What was so wonderful with this group was that it was on their – the patients'- conditions and that the leader was sensitive to that and observed which of them wanted to tell a story. It's something to think about in the group situation.

Although the caregivers were doubtful at first about the use of drama, their feelings had changed by the end of the program. They discussed how they could use drama activities in practical terms. They gave suggestions about what could be included in the activities; such as pictures, music, stories and the participants' own musical instruments. The caregivers emphasized the importance of meeting the needs and using the capabilities of each patient as a starting point for the drama activities:

So you have to have some different types of activities depending on their needs and interests, what they are able to do.

One caregiver suggested that the patients could be divided into different groups on the basis of their needs and interests. Another caregiver stressed the importance of helping the patients to maintain their interests in spite of living in a care setting. Involving the caregivers in the program raised their interest in starting an alternative treatment method such as a drama program.

8.7.6   Conclusion for Context 4

Involving the humanities such as drama, culture, song, dance and storytelling, seems to increase the quality of life in patients with dementia. Using a specific approach towards the patients, which included affirmation and being authentic, the caregivers began to see the importance of meeting each patient as an individual with his or her own personal history. Thus this approach helped the caregivers to grow professionally.

8.8   Final Reflections on the Four Journeys

The four projects explored in this chapter were based in very different contexts, yet all have ultimately drawn very similar conclusions about how transformative learning is possible through applied drama practices. Drama offers the opportunity to transcend cultural and language differences to uncover and question, to foster collaboration, communication and seek insight and understanding. Pre-service teachers, nurses, caregivers and experienced teachers all undertook a journey in transformative learning. German, Jordanian and Swedish nurses found universal connections as they explored the challenges of their caring profession, likewise pre-service teachers in the U.K. and experienced teachers in Kazakhstan found applied drama strategies, such as Enhanced Forum Theatre, generated empathy and understanding and offered fresh insight for their development as professionals. Caregivers in Sweden found that providing a drama program as an alternative treatment seems to increase the quality of life in patients with dementia.

Exploring through engagement in drama would appear to create a level 'playing' field, where language, communication, cultural and status differences are transcended. Kolb (1983) in his analysis of experiential learning highlighted that behavioral learning theories emphasis cognition over affect and devalue the role subjective experience can play in the learning process. Central to all four explorations was affective engagement, the core of learning through drama and the key to transformative learning and practice.

For Interested Readers

A more detailed account of the project described in Context 4 may be found in:

Holm, A.-K., Lepp, M., & Ringsberg, C. K. (2005). Dementia – Involving patients in storytelling: A caring intervention. A pilot study. *Journal of Clinical Nursing, 14*, 256–263.

Lepp, M., Holm, A.-K., Ringsberg, K. C., & Sellersjö, G. (2003). Dementia – Involving patients with dementia and their caregivers in a drama program: The caregivers' experiences. *Journal of Clinical Nursing, 12*, 873–881.

References

Ackroyd, J. (2007). Applied theatre: An exclusionary discourse. *Applied Theatre Researcher, 9*, n.p.

Alexander, R. (2006). *Towards dialogic teaching: Rethinking classroom talk.* Thirsk: Dialogos.

Anderberg, P., Lepp, M., Berglund, A.-L., & Segesten, K. (2007). Preserving dignity in caring for older adults: A concept analysis. *Journal of Advanced Nursing, 59*(6), 635–643.

Bolton, G. (2012). *Selected writings on drama and education.* David Davis (Ed.) London: Trentham.

Boyer, J. (2007). *Creativity matters: The arts and aging toolkit.* New York: National Guild of Community Schools of the Arts.

Dewey, J. (1933). *How we think.* Lexington: D.C. Heath.

Dewey, J. (1973). *Experience and education* (16th ed.). London/New York: Collier Mc Millan.

Edmiston, B. (2013). *Transforming teaching and learning with active and dramatic approaches.* London: Routledge.

Erikson, E. H. (1982). *Identity and the life cycle* (Psychological issues Vol. 1, No. 1). New York: International Universities Press.

Freire, P. (Ed.). (2007). *Education for critical consciousness.* New York: Continuum.

Giroux, H. (1997). *Pedagogy and the politics of hope.* Boulder: Westview Press.

Giroux, H. (2011). *On critical pedagogy.* New York: Continuum.

Greene, M. (1995). *Releasing the imagination: Essays on education, the arts, and social change.* San Francisco: Jossey-Boss.

Graneheim, U. H., & Lundman, B. (2004). Qualitative content analysis in nursing research: Concepts, procedures and measures to achieve trustworthiness. *Nurse Education Today, 24*, 105–112.

Grossman, P., Compton, C., Shahan, E., Ronfeldt, M., Digra, I., & Shiang, J. (2007). Preparing practitioners to respond to resistance: A cross-professional view. *Teachers and Teaching: Theory and Practice, 13*(2), 109–123.

Kolb, D. (1983). *Experiential learning: Experience as the source of learning and development.* Englewood Cliffs, NJ: Prentice Hall.

Lepp, M., Abdalrahim, M. S., Halabi, J. O., Olausson, S., & Suserud, B.-O. (2011). Learning through drama in the field of global nursing. *Applied Theatre Research*; nr 12, article 5.

McIntyre, D. J., Fieman-Nemser, S., & Cochran-Smith, M. (2008). *Handbook of teacher education: Enduring questions of challenge.* Abingdon: Routledge.

Mezirow, J. (1990). *Fostering critical reflection in adulthood.* San Francisco: Jossey-Bass.

Morgan, N., & Saxton, J. (1987). *Teaching drama: A mind of many wonders.* London: Hutchinson.

Morrison, M. (2004). Risk and responsibility: The potential of peer teaching to address negative leadership. *Improving Schools, 7*(3), 217–226. Sage.

Morrison, M., Nilsson, E., & Lepp, M. (2013). Bringing the personal to the professional: Pre-service teaching students explore conflict through an applied drama approach. *Applied Theatre Research, 1*(1), 63–76.

Neelands, J. (2007). Taming the political: The struggle over recognition in the politics of applied theatre. *Research in Drama Education, 12*(3), 305–317.

Nicholson, H. (2005). *Applied drama: The gift of theatre.* New York: Palgrave Macmillan.

Rollins, J. (2013). *Bringing the arts to life. A guide to the arts and long-term care.* Washington, DC: Global Alliance for Arts & Health, IDEAS Institute, and Hulda B. & Maurice L. Rothschild Foundation.

Shulman, L. S. (1998). Theory, practice, and the education of professionals. *The Elementary School Journal, 98*(5), 511–526.

Taylor, P. (2003). *The drama classroom: Action, reflection, transformation.* London: Routledge.

Chapter 9
Conflict Competency in Nursing Education: An International Collaborative Project

9.1 Introduction

A health care professional such as a registered nurse, nurse manager, nurse educator and preceptor in the globalized world faces challenges in communication. The hospital and academic settings of health care deal with relational misunderstandings and conflicts on a daily basis. For example it is vital that preceptors in both settings understand not only how students learn, but also how power relationships operate. For example the relationships between health care provider and patient, and also between preceptor and student are asymmetric. To be able to manage conflict is a core skill required for functioning effectively as a professional. This chapter is about a study using drama as one of several pedagogical methods in the development of Core Conflict Competency in a preceptor training program on Clinical Nursing Education in Jordan, in collaboration with Sweden. However, the collaboration started earlier, within another project: *A Model for International Nursing Collaboration*. Therefore, this chapter will start with a brief introduction of that project followed by the preceptor training program study.

9.2 A Model for International Nursing Collaboration

The development of a model for international nursing collaboration was one outcome of a project between Jordan and Sweden, involving an international exchange program and a collaborative model for exchanging experiences among Jordanian and Swedish nurses, nurse managers, and nurse educators in the hospital and academic settings (Halabi et al. 2011). It was funded by the Swedish International Cooperation Development Agency (SIDA), the Swedish Hospital Fund, and the University of Jordan. SIDA is a government agency organized and financed by the Swedish Ministry of Health that offers many scholarships for international exchange

© Springer International Publishing Switzerland 2015   143
B. Burton et al., *Acting to Manage Conflict and Bullying Through Evidence-Based Strategies*, DOI 10.1007/978-3-319-17882-0_9

programs. International education projects in nursing offer excellent possibilities for multicultural healthcare workforces to achieve intercultural competence (Koskinen et al. 2004).

The idea for the project started in 1993 when a Jordanian faculty of nursing held its first international nursing conference in Amman, Jordan. A dialogue about nursing care started among faculty members from Jordan and Sweden. These discussions led to exchange visits to both countries in 1995. The aim of the visits was to discuss forthcoming collaboration, become oriented to nursing practice, leadership and management, and nursing education in both countries. The visits resulted in a joint agreement to collaborate in three main areas: (1) clinical nursing care, (2) nursing management and leadership, and (3) nursing education. A pilot project was started to create mutual confidence, build trust, and develop a structure for international collaboration.

The collaboration project was ongoing from 1998 to 2007 and was realized in four phases between 1998 and 2007. When the collaboration started nursing care provided in Jordanian hospitals was mainly medically oriented, meaning that the nursing and medical care followed the physicians' orders. Hence, there was a need to develop and implement a more patient-oriented system of high-quality care. The Swedish participants wanted to gain knowledge about caring for patients from Islamic cultures and traditions, in addition to further developing nursing care by reflecting on the care provided.

The four phases consisted of different activities such as: 'careful selection of participants in the exchange program; participants' observations and studies of caring in nursing practice in the other culture; keeping a diary about one's own reflections, thoughts, and questions; and participation in reflective dialogue and meetings with colleagues' (Halabi et al. 2011, p. 154). In addition lectures, seminars and workshops were held in both countries.

The concepts for the model are based on theories about learning through sharing and exchange of experiences, and transforming nursing through supervision and reflective practice (Rolfe 1997, 1998). In addition, Freire's (1972) theory of dialogue and Dewey's (1964) theory of learning by doing provided a foundation. To turn experience into personal knowledge and provide new perspectives, the experiences must be processed and reflected on. This reflection implies exposing, confronting, and understanding the contradiction between actual and desired practice, and how to integrate theory and practice. Freshwater (1999) points out that reflection on experience makes practitioners more self-aware. In addition, Johns (1998) states that reflection on experience should be guided to fulfil its learning potential, since attempting to reflect by oneself may be difficult. Through reflection with others, nurses are confronted with their own beliefs, values, and routines in practice. They gain critical self-awareness and may begin to see the world differently. Nurse educators assisting students to develop as reflective practitioners need to clearly indicate the purpose of reflection and the aims of reflective strategies. Reflection can be a technique and a purposeful inter-subjective process. The concepts developed for the Core Conflict Competency research explored in Chap. 7 were applied as reflective tools to explore how contradictions or conflicts empower practitioners to take actions to change practice.

One of the outcomes of the project was the recognition of differences in nursing legislation and regulation in the two countries. Another outcome of the last phase during 2005–2007 was the highlighting of two areas: (1) nursing leadership and management, and (2) nurse education in practice-preceptorship. The Jordanian clinical instructors and preceptors from the faculty and hospital agreed to come to Sweden for further training to increase their pedagogical competency and nurse education in practice-preceptorship. This was followed by several workshops in Amman in 2006 and 2007. The focus during these years was on preceptorship and in-depth training in pedagogical methods. A course for nurse preceptors was developed to improve the clinical training of nursing students in Jordan. This is described in the following section: a preceptor training program.

9.3 A Collaborative Preceptor Training Program

As mentioned, the study regarding a preceptor training program is part of a larger international collaboration project between higher nursing education in Jordan and in Sweden. The necessity to develop a preceptor training program for clinical supervision in Jordan was identified within the international project. Literature supports the importance of having mandatory and formal program to preparing preceptors. It is therefore important to understand how the preceptors feel about training programs and what kind of support they need. The aim of the study was to develop, implement, and evaluate a preceptor training program to enhance pedagogical strategies for student-centred nursing education in Jordan (Halabi et al. 2012). A three-phase program was developed and implemented in 2006–2007. To better understand the study it needs to be put in its context. Therefore a brief introduction of nursing education in Jordan and a definition of preceptorship is given. Thereafter the design of the study, data collection and analysis, and the results are presented and finally discussed.

9.3.1 Nursing Education in Jordan

Jordan is a low- to middle-income developing country with limited resources. Human resources are seen as the most valuable asset in Jordan. It is estimated that 90 % of the population living in Jordan is Sunni Muslim and Islamic law guides their lives. There are clear and definite obligations for Muslim conduct. Islam means a submission to the will of God (*Allah*) (Barakat 1993). Family laws are prescribed which govern gender roles, marriage, childbirth, divorce, custody, and obligations to extended family (Bowen and Early 1993).

Nursing education started with the beginning of BSc education in 1972 (Jordanian Nursing Council (JNC) 2004, 2006). The profession of nursing used to be seen as a female dominated profession. In 1982, male students started to be accepted into the program where they initially formed 20 % of students. As a comparison, men comprised only 5.7 % of all registered nurses in the USA in 2006 (US. Department of Health and Human Services 2006). However, during the last two decades, nursing in Jordan has moved from a female-dominated profession to one in which male nursing students outnumber females (Ahmad and Alasad 2007).

With the formation of graduate nursing programs, nursing education in Jordan has advanced and improved strongly over the last two decades. Despite its stable development, nursing education faces numerous challenges such as the increasing number of students in the BSc program, the high ratio of students-to-faculty members, the inadequate education opportunities, and limited clinical sites available for clinical training (Al Maaitah and Shokeh 2009). The Jordanian Nursing Council (JNC 2003) published a job description for Registered Nurses (RNs) and emphasized the need to make the education of nursing students' part of nurses' daily work. However, educating nursing students is not yet fully incorporated in the description of nurses' responsibilities in Jordan. Therefore, faculty members from the university and preceptors from different healthcare institutions take the responsibility for educating nursing students in clinical settings (Halabi et al. 2012).

Nurses in Jordan face many challenges which require a high level of competency in managing conflict situations of all kinds. These include poor working conditions and high rates of turnover and attrition (Mrayyan 2006). Clinical practice education faces several problems such as the large number of students, teacher-centred learning over student-centred learning, and often lack of a learning environment in health care practice. These conditions require suitable pedagogical methods in nursing education. These include a student-centred approach involving a philosophical belief and vision to create learning environments that allow learners to develop their professional competence through experiential learning. Crucial to this approach is the need to become skilled at conflict management at all levels.

9.3.2   Preceptorship

In the literature the terms clinical instructor, clinical teacher, clinical supervisor, mentor, and preceptor are often used synonymously for preceptorship. Preceptorship is defined as a one-to-one relationship between a student and a staff nurse related to a specific clinical experience and evaluation of outcome objectives (Udlis 2008). This concept has been thoroughly described by Luhanga et al. (2010) in a review of the literature in different countries. They have concluded that the value and outcome of preceptorship experiences were positive and effective in nursing education.

In Jordan, the term preceptor refers to a Registered Nurse (RN), who has completed a teaching, assessment, and preceptor training program and is involved in the education of nursing students in the clinical practice part of the Bachelor of Science

(BSc) program. The traditional one-to-one preceptorship is not possible due to some challenges such as the number of students. Therefore, preceptorship in Jordan takes the form of a group of students who are assigned to a preceptor during a specific course time limit. Preceptorship is considered to be an organized process, in which nurses at the clinical sites are responsible for the education of nursing students. The goal is to achieve an ideal learning environment with the cooperation of faculty members by bridging the gap between theory and practice.

9.4   The Design of the Study

9.4.1   The Location

The location for the study on the preceptor training program was the faculty of nursing at a large public university in the capital, Amman, in Jordan that offers undergraduate, graduate and PhD programs in nursing. As part of its role in serving the community, the faculty involves nurses from different hospitals in training activities and programs to assure the quality of students' education.

9.4.2   Participants

Twelve RNs, all in the role of a preceptor, (six working at the university, and six from different clinical areas in private and governmental hospitals in Jordan), were invited to participate in the program. All twelve were involved in the education of nursing students in the clinical practice part of the BSc program. The RNs were either working at the faculty or at the hospitals involved in training the university students. The RNs were willing to take part in the training through the three phases of teaching periods of the preceptor training program. Their selection was based on their working experience with students and familiarity with the collaboration project with Sweden. They were all females, aged 20–50 years, with seven BSc and five master degree holders with a minimum of 5 years' experience as an RN (Halabi et al. 2012).

9.4.3   The Preceptor Training Program

In the International Nursing Collaboration project, a core group was formulated at the faculty to run the preceptor training program at the intended university. The core group, **an international teaching team including both Jordanian and Swedish members,** were the leaders of this program and therefore, coordinated several programs for training clinical teachers and nurses.

The development of the preceptor training program was linked to the feedback from pilot studies at various points of the collaboration during 2005 and 2006 with 150 nurse participants from different health sectors in Jordan. The program consisted of three teaching phases, lasting one week each. The focus of the program was on integrating theory and practice in nursing education through pedagogical methods, tools and activities such as experiential learning and reflection, and educational drama, case method, photolanguage and diaries for reflection.

9.4.4   Educational Drama

In this study, several drama workshops were performed in a classroom free from tables. The drama consisted of warm-up games, image theatre performances in groups related to caring themes, improvisation, role-play, and enhanced forum theatre.

In addition participants were introduced to some of the main structures and exercises used within the Swedish DRACON classroom program, for example; the ABC-model of conflict theory, and the third party sculpture activity (See Chap. 2, pp. xx) They also enacted roleplay in pairs, applying the ABC Model, for example exploring the situation of a nurse in an argument with the physician (focus on attitude); a nurse acting as a lawyer for the patient in a meeting with the health care team (focus on behaviour); a nursing student telling her preceptor about something unethical (focus on content); a repentant student listening to the preceptor (focus on de-escalation of the conflict). This prepared the ground for enhanced forum theatre with third party intervention (for detailed description of this more complex technique see Chaps. 2 and 3).

For the forum theatre work the situations were drawn from the participants' own stories and from their real lives, such as conflicts or ethical dilemmas related to health care education. The situations and the scenes were improvised and illustrated. Open-ended dramatized stories were performed, to invite participants' reactions to change: for example, the process of the conflict, or to explore and possibly reduce the conflict through various actions. The participants in this study responded positively to this model. Several forum-plays were performed, and the conflict situations from the forum-plays were used for further exploration and discussion. The following five conflict situations are some examples of many among those presented.

Situation 1
A nursing student is handing out correct prescribed medication; however, he gives it to the wrong patient. The patient does nod when asked for his name. To be explored through EFT: *What are the roles of the preceptor and the student? What measures of safety should be included? How to effectively teach and facilitate learning? How is the student thinking and feeling?*

Situation 2

A patient (female) refuses to take the medication from a nursing student (female). The patient is sitting on a chair; the student, clinical teacher, and preceptor are standing around the patient. To be explored through EFT: *Is it the best way to communicate with the patient? What are the legal rights for patients receiving medications and the international safety goals related to administering medication? Does the patient have enough information about why the medication has been prescribed, and if so, who did inform her? How? What does she think and feel?*

Situation 3

A nursing student full of energy arrives at the clinical department for his training; nobody is there to receive him. To be explored through EFT: *What are the proper educational measures used when receiving a new student in the practice area? How important are the collaboration and communication between the Hospital and the University in students' training? How does the student feel?*

Situation 4

In situations where there are many students with only one preceptor, it is common to see some students get bored as they cannot hear or see what the preceptor is showing. One of the students is shown leaving the ward for a cigarette. To be explored through EFT: *What is the role of the preceptor? How does the structure and organization of the learning environment affect students' learning? Should the preceptor try to approach the student? In what way? How can we motivate the student?*

Situation 5

A patient within a psychiatric ward is sitting in her room very sad. A nurse student (female) approaches and provides support. She puts her arm around the patient's shoulder. To be explored through EFT: *In which situations would this action be considered appropriate? Discuss it from cultural and gender points of view? As a professional caregiver, how could you become aware (judge) its appropriateness?*

9.4.5 Case Method

Case-method is inductive and experiential and prepares learners for a world that demands critical thinking skills and the ability to create convincing arguments (Lynn 1999). Case-method teaching is an active, discussion-oriented learning mode, organized by a case problem drawn from the complexity of real life (Christensen 1994). Case problems are subtle, complex, and persistent. They have no easy, definite, or correct solutions. Discussions are facilitated in which the students analyze a situation, a case problem, often through collaborative work, role-play, and intensive discussions, debate and dialogue.

9.4.6 Photolanguage

Photolanguage is a training tool comprising a method for group work based on 50 black and white photos of nature and people (Belisle et al. 1991). It requires time for reflection, is influenced by one's life history as well as personality and emotional intelligence. The participants in the study were guided to thoughtfully select photos that showed their response to everyday nursing situations as a preceptor. Each participant discussed the personal meaning of the selected photo with the other participants. The use of both verbal and visual expressions can result in richer introspection and sharing.

9.4.7 Diaries for Reflection

In the project diaries were used as a pedagogical tool for reflection. Journaling is a form of diary, often handwritten, in the individual's authentic voice (Kerka 2002). Diaries used as learning journals (Hancock 1998), and for written reflection (Jasper 1999) are considered as essential for both professional and personal growth. In the last phase of the project, the Jordanian participants were involved in drama workshops while visiting Sweden. This is an example of reflection from one of the participants:

> I learned about the use of drama. Drama and its performance called attention to some situations in which appropriate patient care is not given. Using role-play is helpful because it facilitates deeper understanding and leads to a discussion of viewpoints for the employer and the employee. Using reflection is helpful in addition to role-play and drama. I hope I will be able to apply role-play and reflection when I go home (Jordan).

9.5 Interviews and Findings

An external researcher conducted three 30-min tape-recorded focus group interviews (with four participants in each). All participants were involved in the interview that took place in a classroom at the university. The main interview question was, 'What did you gain from this program?' followed by probing questions to encourage discussion. All the three focus group interviews were transcribed verbatim and imported to the data program NVivo as described by Bazeley (2007). The analysis of the interviews showed that participating in the program had an effect on their personal and professional growth, the students' learning and the quality of health care.

9.5.1 Effect on Personal Growth

Participants expressed the view that the new methods of teaching had positive effects on their personalities, for example related to daring to explain opinions, which could have an effect on their conflicts and conflict handling. One participant commented:

I gained many things from this program. First, my personality has changed. I am usually a shy person, but this program gave me more self-confidence. I now know how to state my feelings, explain my opinions, and express myself with other people.

According to another participant role-play helps in understanding other people. Being in someone's shoes is often used as a term in drama and related to empathy:

Using role-play as a method, we have to play some part of other people's life for a short time so we can understand them. Being in someone's shoes makes it easier to understand how other people might view the world and make decisions.

9.5.2 Effect on Professional Growth

The participants described the perceived effect of the program on their professional work, such as learning to adjust teaching strategies in order to individualize their teaching:

I believe that applying the strategies learned in this program would help us to better understand our students and their feelings.

The generation gap between the older teacher and the younger student was reported as a conflict based on difficulties of understanding the other's perspectives and values in life. The participants reported that using these teaching strategies helped them to bridge the generation gap between the older teacher and the younger student, and contributed to their professional growth. According to their statements, the participants were able to redefine their traditional educational strategies during the program. Planning lessons using new teaching methods such as case-method and drama helped to use class time more efficiently. In addition, most of the participants noted that they became better prepared for managing challenging learning situations, such as ethical conflicts and dilemmas of patient care.

Sometimes, we want to raise some issues, such as ethical considerations in dealing with patient, and discuss them with students, but we do not know how. In the program, we wrote scenarios for some ethical dilemmas that occur in clinical practice. We think that this would help students to put themselves in the patients' positions and how it would feel to face the problem.

9.5.3 Effect on Students' Learning Process

Methods used in the program and subsequently in the teaching increased students' participation in the learning process. Conflicts between colleagues using different teaching approaches such as teacher or student centred learning became apparent. The participants stated that learning became easier and more fun when their students could share their ideas in a group discussion:

The new methods were fun and beneficial to students who enjoyed learning. They were not just sitting and looking, as it is the case in the traditional way of education. They were more actively participating in the learning process.

9.5.4   Effect on Quality of Health Care

According to the participants' statements, the new drama-based pedagogical strategies presented in this program assisted them to narrow the gap between theory and practice – a gap that causes many conflicts between the hospital and the academic setting. Participants reported wider networking as well as improved communication skills with colleagues, students, and hospital staff. For example, the clinical instructors from the university built new networks, and developed effective channels of communication with preceptors from the hospital:

All of the benefits we gained from the program would help the patients and improve health care delivery. The final output from this program would be more effective clinical training, with more competent students. This would improve the quality of care offered.

9.6   Discussion

The findings from the interviews supported the contribution of the program towards development of preceptors' competency including core conflict competency. The participants of the program perceived that they were able to encourage the imminent potential in their students, as well as in themselves. Participating in drama helped participants actively reflect on dilemmas and conflicts from health care and nursing education. A safe environment for exploration and learning was created.

The findings from the study showed three areas of perceived impact of a preceptor training program on various dimensions of nursing education and practice: the preceptor, the student, and the nursing care provided. From the preceptors' statements, participating in the program influenced the communication, the networking, and the ability for decreasing the gap between theory and practice and thereby the quality of healthcare. Furthermore, they believed they would increase students' empathy and deepen the understanding of their needs. As their comments above indicated, the preceptors had recognised that stepping into others' shoes and exploring power relationships through drama gave the nurses the training in empathy which would assist them to deal coolly and sensitively with the inevitable conflicts that would arise in the intensely interpersonal relationships and hierarchies of the profession they were embarking on. Consequently, better-prepared nursing students could offer quality nursing care to their patients. However, some of the participants expressed the need for continuous support for the preceptors in order to improve their clinical teaching and be able to use the pedagogical strategies learned in the program.

During the project Jordanian and Swedish nurses shared their experiences and knowledge of nursing practice and developed friendship built on mutual respect, confidence, trust, willingness to work democratically, and active involvement in the program. This sharing of dilemmas, conflicts, values and beliefs has also increased the nurses' respect for and confidence in their leaders at the universities and hospitals at both countries. The project helped to recognize the value of international collaboration and education between Islamic and Western cultures. This kind of collaboration requires the careful establishment of relationships built on trust and ongoing teamwork. This project study involved different countries, cultures, and languages. However, the similarities were greater than the differences, and the project helped to build bridges collaboratively, by sharing teaching and learning across borders.

It is important for future nurses to become oriented to their active role in learning and reflection. In conclusion, this international education study enabled multicultural health care workers to gain intercultural competence, and offered an opportunity to influence the clinical education and pedagogical competency of their preceptors.

References

Ahmad, M. M., & Alasad, J. A. (2007). Patients' preferences for nurses' gender in Jordan. *International Journal of Nursing Practice, 13*(4), 237–242.

Al Maaitah, R., & Shokeh, D. (2009). *The nursing workforce in Jordan: A policy oriented approach.* Amman: JNC.

Barakat, H. (1993). *The Arab world: Society, culture, and estate.* Berkeley: University of California Press.

Bazeley, P. (Ed.). (2007). *Qualitative data analysis with NVivo.* London: Sage.

Belisle, C., Baptiste, A., Pechenart, J., & Vacheret, C. (1991). *Photolanguage, une methode pour communiquer en groupe par la photo.* [Photolanguage, a method to communicate in group by photograph]. Paris: Editions d'Organization.

Bowen, D. L., & Early, E. A. (1993). *Everyday life in the Muslim middle east.* Bloomington: Indiana University Press.

Christensen, C. R. (1994). Teaching with cases at the Harvard Business School. In L. Barnes, C. R. Christensen, & A. Hansen (Eds.), *Teaching case method.* Boston: Harvard Business School.

Dewey, J. (1964). The need for a philosophy of education. In R. D. Archambault (Ed.), *John Dewey on education: Selected writings.* Chicago: University of Chicago Press.

Freire, P. (1972). *Cultural actions for freedom.* London: Penguin.

Freshwater, D. (1999). Communicating with self-trough caring. The student nurse's experience of reflective practice. *International Journal for Human Caring, 3*(3), 28–33.

Halabi, J., Majali, S., Carlsson, L., & Bergbom, I. (2011). A model for international nursing collaboration. *Journal of Continuing Education in Nursing, 42*(4), 154–163.

Halabi, J. O., Abdalrahim, M. S., Length Persson, G., Hedemalm, A., & Lepp, M. (2012). The development of a preceptor training program on clinical nursing education in Jordan in collaboration with Sweden. *The Journal of Continuing Education in Nursing, 43*, 3.

Hancock, P. (1998). Reflective practice: Using a learning journal. *Nursing Standard, 13*(17), 37–40.

Jasper, M. A. (1999). Nurses' perception of the value of written reflection. *Nurse Education Today, 19,* 452–463.

Johns, C. (1998). Opening the doors of perception. In C. Johns & D. Freshwater (Eds.), *Transforming nursing trough reflective practice* (pp. 1–20). Oxford: Black well Science.

Jordanian Nursing Council (JNC). (2003). *Job description for registered nurses.* Retrieved from http://www.jnc.gov.jo/english/publications/jobdescriptionRegisterdnurse.pdf

Jordanian Nursing Council (JNC). (2004). *Situational analysis report on nursing in Jordan in 2004.* Jordan: JNC.

Jordanian Nursing Council (JNC). (2006). *Action plan for nursing development.* Jordan: JNC.

Kerka, S. (2002). *Journal writing as an adult learning tool* (Report No. ED-99-CO-0013). Washington, DC: Office of Educational Research and Improvement.

Koskinen, L., Jokinen, P., Blackburn, D., Gilmer, M., & McGill, J. (2004). Learning intercultural competence in a transatlantic nurse education project. *Diversity in Health and Social Care, 1,* 99–106.

Luhanga, F. L., Billay, D., Grundy, Q., Myrick, F., & Yonge, O. (2010). The one-to-one relationship: Is it really key to an effective preceptorship experience? A review of the literature. *International Journal of Nursing Education Scholarship, 7*(1), 115.

Lynn, L. E., Jr. (Ed.). (1999). *Teaching and learning with cases: Guidebook.* New York: Chatham House. Seven Bridges Press.

Mrayyan, M. (2006). Jordanian nurses' job satisfaction, patients' satisfaction and quality of nursing care. *International Nursing Review, 53*(3), 224–230.

Rolfe, G. (1997). Beyond expertise: Theory, practice and the reflective practitioner. *Journal of Clinical Nursing, 6,* 93–97.

Rolfe, G. (1998). The theory-practice gap in nursing: From research-based practice to practitioner-based research. *Journal of Advanced Nursing, 28*(3), 672–679.

Udlis, K. A. (2008). Preceptorship in undergraduate nursing education: An integrated review. *Journal of Nursing Education, 47,* 20–29.

US. Department of Health and Human Services. (2006). *The registered nurse population: National sample survey of registered nurses.* Preliminary findings. Available from: http://bhpr.hrsa.gov/healthworkforce/reports/rnpopulation/preliminaryfindings.htm

Chapter 10
Acting Against Relational Aggression and Cyberbullying

10.1 Introduction

The Acting Against Bullying research explored in previous chapters in this book focused on all bullying as a single phenomenon, and did not differentiate between the genders in developing an effective, evidence based approach to bullying management. However, as a result of the success of the program as a whole, the Griffith University researchers were approached to investigate specific forms of relational aggression and cyber bullying amongst female students at a large, private, girl's school. This chapter details how these covert forms of bullying were revealed as endemic amongst the older adolescent girls in the school, and evaluates the success of action research in producing transformational changes in behaviour in this specific group.

10.2 The Research Project: Uncovering and Managing Covert Bullying

The research site was a large, elite private, girls' school with students ranging in age from 5 to 18 years old. There had been isolated instances in the past of serious bullying in the school amongst the older girls, and the Dean of Students had detected a serious degree of disharmony and conflict amongst the current senior cohort of girls in Year 11 aged between 15 and 16. However, there was no actual evidence of systematic bullying, and there had been no specific complaints from the senior students about conflict or bullying issues. Nevertheless, the administration of the school was aware of the extensive evidence world-wide that indicates bullying in schools is both widespread and escalating (Statistics on Bullying NSPCC 2013; Bullying Statistics 2010; McDougall et al. 2009).

Like most other educational institutions, the school had no comprehensive anti-bullying program in place. Because the Acting Against Bullying program

© Springer International Publishing Switzerland 2015
B. Burton et al., *Acting to Manage Conflict and Bullying*
Through Evidence-Based Strategies, DOI 10.1007/978-3-319-17882-0_10

developed at Griffith University had received extensive exposure in the media and at conferences on bullying and child safety, Professor Bruce Burton was approached to investigate the real extent of bullying in the school and implement the Acting against Bullying program at all year levels.

This project therefore provided the opportunity to evaluate the effectiveness of the Acting Against Bullying program in a different environment from the co-educational state schools that had constituted the previous research sites. It also offered the chance to investigate the specific nature and extent of covert bullying amongst adolescent girls as part of addressing the bullying occurring in the school. Within the overall implementation of the program, 3 action research cycles were therefore conducted to reveal and address the extensive relational aggression and cyber bullying amongst a particular cohort of older adolescent girls.

The implementation of the overall program was led by Professor Burton and conducted by a team of two graduates and four final year students from the Applied Theatre degree at Griffith University who were particularly interested in the field, plus two experienced Drama teachers. The Acting Against Bullying program was implemented throughout the school over a 2 year period using the combination of formal teaching, improvised drama, Enhanced Forum Theatre and peer teaching that had proved successful in the range of conflict and bullying management research projects reported in this book. However, the initial focus of the research became centred on the extent of social and cyber bullying amongst the older adolescent girls, and evolved to experiment with ways of empowering these students to manage the covert bullying that was revealed.

Action research was therefore the methodology chosen, and improvised drama activities were used extensively, especially in the first 2 cycles, to uncover the covert bullying, and then to enable the students to find ways of managing it. There is extensive evidence that improvised classroom drama has the power to generate behavioural change in adolescents in schools, allowing them to experience reality from different perspectives – creating the distance that is needed for them to see themselves as others and appreciate different points of view (Bolton 1998; Burton 1991; Neelands 2009; Fleming 1998). Furthermore, Crothers, Kolbert and Barker (2006) claim that secondary school students themselves prefer the use of drama strategies when learning about real world problems such as bullying in comparison with other forms of instruction.

10.3   Covert Bullying: Relational Aggression and Cyber Bullying

The issue of aggression amongst teenage girls has only become the focus of extensive research over the past 25 years, partly due to its covert nature in comparison with the physical and verbal bullying most common amongst boys (Besag 2006). It had traditionally been assumed that boys were the primary perpetrators of bullying and violence. However, there is now an increasing body of literature on the subject of how girls bully, and the nature of relational aggression between girls (Crothers et al. 2005; Besag 2006; Leenaars et al. 2008; Underwood 2003). Studies on girls' aggressive behaviour in a number of countries (Björkqvist et al. 2001) have produced consistent findings that girls are aggressive toward each other in covert, indirect ways which are motivated by relational goals concerned with friendships (Archer and Coyne 2005; James and Owens 2005; Randall and Bowen 2007).

Relational aggression occurs between girls of all ages but is most intense during adolescence. Messerschmidt (2011: 204) reports that: 'interviews with 421 young women in the USA found that especially during adolescence, girls frequently find themselves "dancing through the minefield" of primarily verbal and social forms of bullying'. The fact that girls' friendships are so intimate means that relational aggression is very effective when a bully uses it to hurt another girl (Bright 2005; James and Owens 2005; Remillard and Lamb 2005). Within the school context, acts of relational aggression include gossiping, spreading rumours, ignoring, exclusion from friendship groups, isolation, alienation, writing hurtful letters and text messages, and stealing friends or boyfriends (Crothers et al. 2005). Relational aggression is associated with the formation of social cliques and subtle verbal and psychological tactics used to injure other girls' feelings of social acceptance. Wood (2007: 165) argues that because girls are discouraged from direct, overt aggression, "they develop other, less direct ways of expressing aggression". These indirect forms of aggression are covert and subtle forms of attack, difficult for teachers and other adults to recognise and manage (Bauman and Del Rio 2006). In a research study, pre-service teachers were given written descriptions of physical, verbal and relational bullying. Their responses indicated less empathy for the victims of relational bullying and demonstrated that they were least likely to intervene in incidents involving relational bullying (Bauman and del Rio 2006). In issues related to sexuality, teachers may even be hostile to students being bullied. Smith (2013: 84) notes: 'In secondary schools, children maybe teased about their sexual orientation, and even physically assaulted or ridiculed about this by other pupils or teachers.'

Adolescent girls are increasingly using forms of verbal violence through electronic media such as the Internet, email and mobile phones (Kowalski et al. 2007). Cyber bullying is rooted in relational aggression and is a growing issue, especially amongst adolescent girls, because of their extensive access to a range of ways to communicate and broadcast information among their peers. Li's (2006: 160) research found. : "about one in four adolescents are cyber victims and they experience various negative consequences, particularly anger and sadness." Recent international surveys confirm this figure Hinduja and Patchin 2013) with 24 % of all adolescents in 8 different studies over 7 years identified as victims of cyber bullying, whilst 17 % of subjects identified as cyber bullies.

Ponsford (2007) found that teenage girls use electronic media to engage in social exclusion or the demotion of other girls from the social hierarchy. and their on-line communications are more extreme and direct than in the real world, focusing on gossip, criticisms of appearance, attacks on sexuality, declarations of disloyalty, and statements about desiring physical violence. Smith et al. (2008) in their extensive studies of cyber bullying amongst girls in the UK found that it was less prevalent than traditional bullying, but still appreciable, and that most of it occurred outside school. They also found that most of the cyber bullying was done by one or a few students usually from the same year group as the victims. Recent statistical evidence (Cyber Bullying Statistics 2010), confirm these findings. Each of these findings was clearly confirmed by the action research reported in this chapter.

Recent research indicates that Australia has very high rates of cyber bullying (Owens et al. 2000). "The most targeted victims are those who are also commonly victimised off-line, including those of different sexuality or with a disability. It is more common among the middle-school age range" (Nicol 2012: 4). They who cyber bully often have communication problems off-line and many bullies are also victims and they will often alternate roles (Nicol 2012). In his survey of current research on cyber bullying, Smith (2013: 87) notes: "In cyber bullying gender differences vary consider-ably between studies, but relatively girls may be more involved in cyberbullying and victimisation."

The negative consequences of female bullying behaviour are strikingly similar for both bullies and victims (Roberts 2006). As discussed in Chap. 5, the impacts on victims include peer rejection, anxiety and depression, low self-esteem, and even suicide (Crick and Grotpeter 1995). Equally, those who bully tend to have lower academic ability, more health problems and as adults are more likely to have been convicted of a serious crime and of drug taking. Girls who bully are also specifically linked with adult depression and a prediction of early pregnancy (Besag 2006; Miller-Johnson et al. 2005). There is also evidence of a pattern amongst adolescent girls of moving from having been bullied at school to engaging in reactive sexual offending outside of school Messerschmidt (2011: 208).

10.4   The Structure of the Acting Against Bullying Program in the School

The Acting Against Bullying program was implemented in each of the 2 years of the project with the aim of developing an effective, whole-school anti-bullying program that was disseminated within the standard school curriculum. As with previous implementations of the program (Chap. 5), the first stage of the program in each year began with a Year 11 senior secondary class learning through drama a set of concepts and definitions about the nature and consequences of bullying (Burton 2008). This cognitive understanding and a range of bullying management techniques were further explored through improvised drama (Nicholson 2005) and Enhanced Forum Theatre (Boal 1996). During this stage the first two cycles of the Action Research investigating covert bullying were conducted.

The second stage followed with groups of the Year 11 senior students teaching a number of younger Year 9 classes in the school, using the same conceptual frame-work and enactment strategies. The peer teaching took place across the school within the formal Pastoral Program that was part of the curriculum. Assisted by their classroom teachers and the older students, the younger secondary school classes developed an understanding of bullying and the use of drama to explore strategies for its effective management, then in groups prepared their own peer teaching for use with younger students.

In stage three of the program, the Year 9 students taught classes of Year 7 students what they had learned, and these Year 7 students in turn repeated the process with Year 5 classes who in then taught the Year 3 Classes in the school. The second year of the research project followed exactly the same process with the classes that had not experienced the program in the previous year.

10.5   Participatory Action Research

Because the aim of the specific research conducted within the Acting Against Bullying program in the school was to empower the students involved to manage the covert bullying that had emerged as a major issue amongst the senior students, participatory action research was the chosen methodology. An important goal of all action research is to provide workable solutions to immediate concerns and to develop human capacities (Kemmis and McTaggart 2008). Furthermore, in participatory action research the researchers and subjects actively collaborate throughout the cyclical process. The subjects offer practical knowledge forged through their struggle with real-world problems, and researchers contribute theoretical knowledge. This leads to the researchers and the subjects developing a common understanding of the problem and its solution, and they are then able implement change (Choudry 2010).

Finally, action researchers are also committed to extending the specific social theories and strategies developed in a research context to inform wider improvements in society. In this case, the researchers sought to discover effective responses to a major, global behavioral problem – the difficult and largely hidden issue of covert bullying amongst adolescent girls.

Three participatory action research cycles were planned, with the Year 11 girls who were the subjects being fully informed of the nature and purpose of the research and invited to be co-researchers in the process. Preliminary and summative questionnaires supplied the base line data that was made available to the students. This data provided valuable information on the extent of the covert bullying that was occurring, and also gave indications of the learning and behavioral changes that had occurred as a result of the action research. Detailed observation notes were kept by the researchers and teachers involved, and the students kept journals. Most importantly, extensive group and individual interviews were conducted throughout the research as an essential element in obtaining insights into the impact of the participatory action research (Zuber-Skerritt, Ortrun and Associates 2009).

10.5.1   Cycle One: Identifying the Bullying

The action research to examine the nature and extent of covert bullying amongst the senior student cohort commenced right at the beginning of the first stage in the first year of implementation of the Acting Against Bullying program. The preliminary questionnaire that had been used consistently in the previous bullying research detailed in this book was again administered to the 32 students in the Year 11 classes who were the subjects of the research. The questionnaire revealed an extraordinary level of on-going, regular, relational bullying. In the two classes surveyed, 60 % of the girls responded that they had been bullied at school during their last year, and 64 % admitted that they had bullied other students during the past year. These figures are extraordinarily high for older students, as international research indicates that bullying is most prevalent amongst it is younger adolescents: "Teens in grade sixth through 10th grade are most likely to be involved in activities related to bullying. About 30 % of students in the United States are involved in bullying on a regular basis" (Bullying Statistics 2010). The figure for the United Kingdom is 46 %, with students aged 11–15 being the ones most concerned in bullying (Statistics on Bullying NSPCC 2013).

Not only was the incidence of bullying revealed in the questionnaire very high compared with international statistics, but the percentages were higher than any other survey results from the hundreds of schools where the questionnaire was used as part of the Cooling Conflicts and Acting Against Bullying programs. As well as revealing a significant current level of bullying amongst this cohort, the questionnaire also demonstrated that students had extensive past experience of the different forms of bullying, and were aware of the reasons for bullying. When asked to define bullying on the questionnaire, most respondents described aspects of relational aggression as typifying bullying and identified the consequences. One girl wrote:

> The deliberate reducing of a person or persons' self-esteem by a person or group to make them feel excluded and unhappy.

In their responses, the majority of students admitted to using some form of bullying at some time in their secondary schooling. Of these, 70 % stated that they had used social bullying, whilst 17 % admitted to cyber bullying, and only 1 respondent said she had physically bullied someone else during her time at the school. Most of the respondents had also been subjected to a number of different forms of bullying, with Verbal, Social and to a lesser extent Cyber bullying being the most common. When asked why some students bully others, 40 % responded that the bullies enjoyed having power over others, whilst 23 % believed the bullies were showing off, and 21 % stated that the bullies did not like the students they were bullying. Only 4 % believed that the person being bullied deserved it, and only 8 % responded that they did not know why some students bullied others. Not only had the majority of respondents been active involved in bullying situations at the school, but almost 70 % of them indicated that they had been bystanders when bullying was taking place.

The evidence from the questionnaire that covert bullying was a real issue amongst these older girls was confirmed by their reactions to the initial teaching about bullying. In the 15 years of research that has investigated the implementation of the Cooling Conflicts and Acting against Bullying program in hundreds of schools, the senior secondary male and female students that have been the first classes to experience the program in their schools have been enthusiastic, focused and fully – engaged. However, the Year 11 girls in the research school reacted entirely differently. The detailed observation notes taken by the researchers revealed that they were reluctant to respond to questions or discuss bullying, they resisted improvising bullying situations suggested to them, and they were initially unwilling to engage in the dramatisation of fictional bullying scenarios that might be relevant to their age group.

When asked to work in groups to devise fictional improvisations that generically illustrated the three parties to bullying (bully, bullied and bystander), and the stages bullying escalates through (latent, emerging and manifest), the majority of the students constantly watched the reactions of three girls in the class to these improvisational activities, even when these girls were not in their groups. Some of the students chose not to participate in the drama activities, but were active in the discussions about bullying. Although the facilitators had indicated that the bullying scenarios being constructed should be fictional and used as illustrations of the explicit teaching about bullying that had taken place, some of the participants chose to improvise situations they insisted were real. The observation notes recorded:

> The students appear subdued, inhibited and reluctant to become involved in the discussion and the process. This could be partly due to both classes being combined and taught by a stranger in an unfamiliar space and observed by a number of other teachers.
>
> It's becoming evident that there are serious bullying issues within this group. This is revealed by the way the students surreptitiously look at certain girls when bullying is being discussed, and their reluctance to provide any information about bullying issues.
>
> The drama activities are revealing more. Despite being asked to improvise fictional bullying situations, some of the students chose to identify and improvise specific bullying treatment they had experienced.

Discussions were held with the Dean of Students and senior school teachers after this session to determine what issues needed to be addressed and what changes to the program might need to be made in the light of the extraordinary response of the students to the workshop. The discussion revealed that there was in fact awareness amongst some of the teachers that systematic long-term bullying could be occurring amongst the Year 11 students, and some the girls suspected of being the ring leaders were in the Drama classes that were involved in the Acting against Bullying program in the school. The extraordinary responses of the participants in the first workshop may have been related to the power these bullies could exercise because as Bright (2005), James and Owens (2005) and Remillard and Lamb 2005) all observe, the intensity and intimacy of adolescent girls' friendships makes relational aggression very effective when a bully uses it to hurt another girl. The teachers had no concrete evidence that these girls were guilty of organising the bullying, nor of its extent. Furthermore, the classroom teachers did not feel they were competent to recognise or manage covert bullying. Besag (2006) notes that it can be extremely difficult to identify the instigators of gossip and rumours, and teachers are unsure how to challenge a group who have deliberately excluded a girl from their friendship circle. The literature indicates that adolescent girls often bully others covertly through the use of personal opinions such as criticism of physical attributes and personal characteristics, which makes it difficult for the victim to challenge or for adults to intervene (Bauman and Del Rio 2006). Whilst girls are more likely to report bullying than boys, they are still very reluctant to do so to parents, teachers or other adults (Li 2006).

It appeared to be significant that these older students, who had been so reluctant to discuss or enact any bullying situations in the classroom, were willing to identity and quantify the extent and seriousness of the bullying occurring in their classes on the anonymous questionnaire, which was confidential and administered by the applied theatre team in the absence of the teachers. This suggested that the students were genuinely concerned about bullying but reluctant to expose themselves to further covert bullying by revealing their experiences publicly in the classroom. It also seemed especially significant that a number were prepared to identify themselves as bullies on the questionnaire, or at least to admit to covert bullying behaviour.

Interestingly, on the pre-questionnaire, 63 % of the students stated they would intervene in a bullying situation if they saw one happening, and tell the bully to stop, whilst 32 % believed that the bystander had the most chance of stopping bullying. Given the extreme levels of bullying reported by the students and their reluctance to engage with the subject of bullying in the first workshop, these positive responses seemed to be an anomaly. However, as the questionnaire revealed, most of the bullying that was occurring was social and cyber bullying, and this meant that it was covert and therefore difficult to confront. Furthermore, the workshop and the action research cycle which followed revealed that a number of the students were in fact unwilling to confront the bullies in their cohort, even though they believed they should.

10.5.2   Cycle Two: Revealing the Bullying

In the light of the initial observations and particularly the data from the questionnaire, it was decided to make more extensive use of classroom drama techniques in the project, before introducing enhanced forum theatre. The strategies utilised included the construction and performance of dramatic narratives about bullying by the students. Bolton and Heathcote (1998) believe that individuals behave in certain ways based on their personal belief systems and their cultural belief systems, and the dramatisation of real and fictional situations allows students to express these beliefs. This cycle of the research also engaged the students in a number of process dramas, led by the teachers and researchers in role, and beginning with a bullying pretext (O'Neill 1995). In both these forms of classroom drama, emotional distance may be increased, so that the student learners can de-centre themselves from their own point of view (Byram 1997).

The action research therefore sought to explore the impact of covert bullying on individual girls and groups of students by providing opportunities for them to de-centre from their own personal and cultural codes by using improvisation and role to explore covert bullying. By later reflecting on these positions and critically analysing personal responses to them, the students appeared to achieve a deeper understanding and appreciation of both self and other (Young 2000). Indeed, Neelands (2009) argues that through drama young people can be led to imagine and look for new ways of living together rather than against each other; to find a shared understanding and to create new models of pluralist community.

In a series of 1 h workshops, the students discussed and dramatised a range of bullying scenarios, both spontaneous and prepared, that explored the nature of the bullying they believed was occurring at their school. The intention was to offer the students the opportunity to investigate the causes and consequences of covert bullying by creating narratives based on personal experiences, but performed in the safe, fictional environment of drama. The fictionalisation and dramatisation of personal narratives offered the students a genuine choice about their level of involvement in the construction and performance of the narratives, and the extent to which these narratives were fiction. This appeared to be the best way to create the conditions for the students to explore and reflect on the covert bullying that was occurring, whilst providing them with protection any negative consequences.

In the third 1 h session of the action research cycle, a technique from the conflict resolution strategies used in the Cooling Conflicts research reported in this book generated a significant change in the commitment and engagement of the students. The students were asked to analyse the motives, attitudes and behaviours of bullies, people being bullied, and bystanders in any bullying situation. The observation notes reveal that an intense discussion took place where the students decided that the motives and attitudes of the all three parties to bullying were very similar, with only some of the behaviour being different. The students were fascinated by these conclusions, and in the construction of the dramatic narratives that followed, there was an intense concentration on the motives and emotions of the three parties to the bullying. The intensity, involvement and energy observed in the creation of these narratives were of a qualitatively higher order than any previous drama work by the group. Increasing empathy was evidenced, and overtly stated, for students being bullied, but there was also dramatic and reflective understanding expressed about the motives of the bullies, and their need for positive support to change their behaviour, as well as sanctions.

They feel really low and embarrassed and rejected, because they are pretty much powerless to the bully. (Amy 16)

The bully won't be able to stop without intervention from another. The bystander needs to make them realise the severity of the situation and the consequences, and offer help. (Sarah 16)

Although they do hurt people, I believe some bullies are just misunderstood and are acting out because of family/personal problems. (Trish 16)

In the four 1 h workshops that were conducted in the following weeks, a series of spontaneous dramas were created dealing with a range of relational aggression behaviours that the girls identified as of concern to them. During these sessions the Applied Theatre team increasingly became actively involved as participants in the improvisations and process dramas at the invitation of the girls. The school students initiated and directed the improvisations and performances, instructing the young, female applied theatre researchers in the roles and the behaviours they wished to explore. In turn, the researchers used questioning and modelling both within and outside their fictional roles to enhance the structure, performance and meaning of the dramas.

A number of the improvisations that were created in this process involving the researchers as participants contained incidents of cyberbullying, including sending abusive texts and placing text, photos and other material on Facebook and uploading films recorded on mobile phones on YouTube. Some of this cyberbullying was identified by the students in class and in interview as having actually occurred during the current school year. However, none of the cyberbullying activity revealed in the drama had occurred in isolation, but was portrayed and described as an outcome of relational aggression occurring at school or in social situations. This is consistent with the research into cyberbullying which indicates that up to 80 % of all electronic bullying has its origin in face-to-face bullying. Li (2005) found that traditional bullies are also more likely to engage in cyberbully activities and that there is a close relationship between bullying, cyberbullying and victimization.

Many of the spontaneous bullying improvisations that the students created were related to intense relationships between girls and friendships with boys, often with a strong sexual element involved. The research suggests there is often a sexualised dimension to bullying amongst older adolescent girls, including accusations of being a lesbian or of heterosexual promiscuity (Duncan 2004). The girls themselves were surprised and even confronted at times when these themes emerged from their own spontaneous improvisations, but were able to acknowledge that much of the relational aggression occurring amongst their peers did arise from intense relationships with boys and other girls, creating the 'minefield' of verbal and social bullying identified by Messerschmidt (2011) as confronting adolescent girls. Increasingly, the improvised dramas developed by the Year 11 girls explored ways of acknowledging and dealing with jealousy, sexuality and competition in relationships, and some of the spontaneous solutions that emerged were both creative and effective.

One particular bullying scenario resulted in significant changes in the attitudes and behaviour in the participants to bullying. Jessica, one of the most articulate and active girls in the class, organised a group to enact a drama about some bullying she had experienced related to her relationship with a boy. As Crothers et al. (2005) note boyfriends and sex major focuses of teenage relational aggression. Jessica asked Tony, one of the adult male researchers, to take the role of her boyfriend. This appeared to be for support and assistance with the drama, as she was very nervous about structuring the improvisation and then performing it for the whole class, but she was determined to attempt it. Tony suggested that someone else in her group should play her role as the victim of bullying in order to distance the experience of the drama from her, but Jessica refused. She explained that she wanted to reveal to her class mates the bullying that had occurred and then change what actually happened to demonstrate how to deal with this kind of bullying. She also requested that Martha, who had been identified as one of the three highly active bullies in Year 11, should take the role of the bully in the improvisation, because she had in fact been one of the girls involved in the attacks on Jessica about having a boyfriend. Martha was reluctant to take the role but agreed when Tony talked to her about committing to the drama process as part of her learning.

The improvisation that followed was believable and intense, with Martha acting out spying on Jessica and her boyfriend at a school dance, and then texting friends with fictional sexual details of Jessica's behaviour, and over time spreading rumours at school, placing photos on Facebook and sending insulting texts to Jessica. A scene was then improvised involving a scenario that had never occurred, where after weeks of systematic bullying Jessica confronted Martha at school about the bullying. During this enacted confrontation, a number of other girls spontaneously intervened in role, supporting Jessica and criticising Martha. An extended discussion followed this drama involving the whole class, where a number of the girls acknowledged that they had known about the bullying and in some cases had taken part in spreading rumours and sending texts. They indicated that they now wished they had intervened instead to support Jessica, as they did in the drama. Martha remained silent during the discussion, but afterwards apologised to Jessica, who accepted the apology and declared that actually portraying the bullying she had experienced to the rest of the class and then changing the outcome had really empowered her to deal with its impact on her self-confidence and self-image.

Jessica's use of improvised drama and then performance recalls in microcosm the way the participants in the Moving On project addressed their trauma. Jessica had been negatively affected by the bullying she had suffered, and she wanted both the bully and her peers to recognise this. By telling her story and then changing it in performance to empower herself, she found a way to move on from the hidden hurt she had experienced. In a later interview, Jessica observed that the rest of her class had been made to acknowledge the bullying that was rife in their year level, not just because of the drama about her, but because of the Acting Against Bullying program as a whole.

I think the Year 11s have become aware of it. I think that the connections that have been made are the most positive experience from it

It also emerged at this stage that in a school notable for its emphasis on academic achievement, part of the covert bullying the workshops revealed actually involved contempt and exclusion for girls who were perceived as unintelligent and low achievers (Volk et al. 2012), which in some ways reflected the ethos of the school and would not necessarily have been recognised by the teachers as bullying.

This finding is supported by Duncan (2004), who argues that the competitive element in schools where students are encouraged to compete for grades and in sport is a contributing factor to the increase in bullying amongst teenage girls: "this competitive, combative culture might be heard as the echo of the national culture of competition in education"(p. 149). The participants in the workshops acknowledged that social bullying based on perceived intelligence was common, and in improvisation and discussion they condemned it, some of them admitting they had been responsible for this kind of bullying in the past.

Another important aspect of the engagement of the students in the dramatisation of bullying narratives was the desire to explore the full range of roles implicit in bullying situations – the bully, the victim and the bystander. Individual girls chose to experiment with role reversal, choosing to portray bullies carrying out the kind of bullying they had actually experienced. In interviews conducted during this research cycle, one student observed:

> *Because I have been able to play the three roles: bully, bullied and bystander, I've been able to get into their heads to understand what they are really thinking. (Sarah 16)*

The students in the Year 11 Drama classes were experienced in educational drama practices, and were able to exploit the possibilities for personal learning that were available (Morrison et al. 2006). Warner (1997) notes that "participants in drama are very aware of their own elaborate engagement patterns. They are also very conscious of how they personally learn best and what kind of methods work to enhance their learning."

The observation notes reveal that in the final stage of this cycle, the students began to use the drama activities to actually address the relational aggression that had been occurring. Particular students were nominated by different groups to take on the roles of girls being bullied, often with the clear indication that the students enrolled as victims of bullying in the drama were in fact bullies in reality. Initially, these girls were reluctant to accept the roles of victims or engage in bullying scenarios that were based on actual relational aggression and cyber bullying experiences. However, as the improvisations increasingly focused on exploring and managing a range of bullying situations, the observation notes and interviews indicated that the girls identified as bullies willingly accepted the roles and acted them out with both conviction and commitment. There was also increasing observational evidence that all the students were manipulating the context of the drama to developing a more sophisticated understanding of the nature of covert bullying itself.

10.5.3   Cycle Three: Peer Teaching About Covert Bullying

Given the increasing commitment of the Year 11 students to the Acting Against Bullying program, and their demonstration of effective learning and some behaviour modification in relation to covert bullying, the final cycle of the action research was implemented to track the students as they planned and conducted the peer teaching of the Year 9 classes in the school. The girls who had been identified as the ones mainly responsible for the relational aggression that had been revealed in the earlier cycles of the research were encouraged to take leadership roles in teaching the younger students about the nature of bullying and in performing a prepared piece of enhanced forum theatre about bullying. As they planned the peer teaching and the creation of the forum theatre performances, the Year 11 students revealed that they had been able grasp the concept of covert bullying and to make sophisticated judgements about its nature and consequences, as well as a sense of competence in dealing with their own experiences of bullying. In particular, the data indicated that the level of identification generated by the drama now allowed them to empathise with and understand the behaviour of bullies, the bullied and bystanders.

The peer teaching of the Year 9 students offered the strongest confirmatory evidence that their exploration of covert bullying through drama had transformed the behaviour and attitudes of the Year 11 students. The observation notes revealed that despite limitations of time for preparation, and numerous timetable clashes, the peer teaching was remarkably successful. Without exception, the Year 11 peer teachers were able to explain and demonstrate to the younger students the nature of bullying and the behaviour and feelings of the participants. The Year 11 peer teachers also offered the younger girls a number of valuable strategies for dealing with relational aggression.

The level of commitment by all the Year 11 students was also notable. In the first two cycles of the action research there had been numerous absences amongst the students, particularly involving the girls who had been identified as bullies. During the entire time of the peer teaching, only one Year 11 student was absent from one session, and she contacted her teacher in advance to explain her absence and to ask if she could still do the peer teaching if she was able to arrive during the session. Some of the most effective and enthusiastic peer teachers were girls who had been identified, or who had self-identified, as bullies, or were perceived by their teachers as disengaged from their schooling. This finding is consistent with previous implementations of Cooling Conflicts and Acting against Bullying and the research into negative leaders reported in Chap. 4. One Year 11 student who self-revealed in an individual interview that she had been involved in serious bullying, stated that doing the peer teaching had been extremely valuable for her, and not just in learning about bullying.

And it's really helped also with leadership because I mean we are going in to grade twelve now and we've got grade tens that will be able to talk to us and come to us.

The engagement of the Year 11 students in the final action research cycle was also clearly indicated by the impact of the peer teaching on the Year 9. Interestingly, the observation notes and the questionnaire applied to the Year 9 students revealed a much lower level of relational aggression amongst the younger girls than had been occurring in Year 11. The observation note reveal that the Year 9 students were exceptionally enthusiastic and engaged, and the level of their responses, both spoken and improvised, demonstrated a real commitment to learning, and an increasing understanding of bullying management which was remarkable in comparison to the implementation of the program in this phase in other contexts. The excitement and enthusiasm evidenced by the Year 9 students, and their liking and admiration for their Year 11 peer teachers, appeared to enhance the quality of the peer teaching and the engagement of the Year 11 students The Year 11 peer teachers also demonstrated real concern for the Year 9 girls when the questionnaires and the drama activities revealed that some covert bullying was occurring at this level. When asked their responses to the younger students who had revealed they were being bullied, two of the Year 11 students responded:

> *Sympathetic that they often can't stand up for themselves (Jo)*
> *More sympathetic, but at the same time they do have the ability to change things. (Annie 16)*

10.6   Outcomes

In the 6 months following their involvement in the project, there were no reported incidents or observable indications of relational aggression amongst the Year 11 drama students. Their classroom teachers also reported an improvement in attendance and in commitment to their studies by the students in the second half of the year. In contrast, there was continuing conflict and bullying observed and reported amongst the Year 11 girls not involved in the project.

Further longitudinal evidence of the impact of the research was provided a year later in an interview with Delia, the school counsellor who had initiated the project in the school. She stated that there had been very little reported or observed bullying of any kind amongst the current Year 11 classes, and no evidence of serious bullying had emerged from the latest iteration of the Acting Against Bullying program during the previous year. Delia noted that the girls now in year 11 had been the Year 9 students who had been peer taught and had in turn taught younger girls in the school in the research. In her role as counsellor, she had observed that the Current Year 11 students appeared to have better social relationships with their fellow students and stronger mentoring bonds with the younger girls than any comparable year level she had experienced.

A number of the Year 11 girls confirmed in their summative interviews that they believed there had been a change in the culture of the school, because girls being bullied now felt empowered to act, and in particular, to seek out help from teachers and other students who had been involved in the Acing Against Bullying program.

> *I think the fact that the victim in a situation now has the ability to go to someone and to say "look this is happening, and I feel that it is negatively affecting my life". I think the fact that they have the ability to do that is a positive influence on our general school environment*

Strong mentoring relationships developed and continued between the Year 11 and Year 9 students, especially in regard to bullying, and again, some of the year 11 girls identified as bullies have been proactive in the development of these mentoring relationships

> *I've spoken to some of the girls in grade nine that we taught in class and I got in contact with some of the girls that I haven't spoken to in ages and have learnt from them. Basically, I got in contact with them and they were saying it really helps them out in dealing with some of the issues. (Alice 16)*

Perhaps most significantly of all, more than 50 % of the students answered positively the question on the summative questionnaire about what they would do in future if they encountered bullying. The students were able to identify and generalise about the nature and consequences of covert bullying for those being bullied, and to offer strategies for dealing with it. The answers indicated an increased sense of informed competence in dealing with relational aggression:

> I am often a bystander so I now am informed if various ways in which I can stop bullying or support the bullied. (Amelia 16)
> I would report to an adult or get directly involved by trying to reason with the bully and bullied and sort out the problem (Isabelle 16)
> There are various ways, but the bystander can usually talk to the bully or the other bystanders. However, they can also inform someone out of the situation such as a parent, teacher or counsellor. (Danni 16)

In their summative responses to the project, a number of the students also indicated that they had come to understand the behaviour of bullies, and to identify more clearly the reasons for their actions. A number of students recognised that as bystanders they had the power to both report the bullying but also to intervene to discourage the bullying or negotiate between the parties involved.

> Report the bully to someone in authority. Also intervene by discouraging the power of the bully.
> Report to an adult or get directly involved by trying to reason with the bully and bullied and sort out their problems.

An awareness of the bully's motives and concern for their wellbeing which had emerged in the final cycle of the action research was widespread in the summative questionnaire and interview data.

> Yes, because I now understand that they could be bullying because of family troubles and they need help. (Amelia 15)

10.7   Wider Implications

The three cycles of action research clearly indicate that relational aggression amongst older female adolescents may well be much more widespread and intense than the general data for bullying in schools is revealing. The extent of the covert bullying occurring amongst the 15 and 16 year old girls in the all-female environment of the school also indicates that further research is needed in this area.

Despite intense media concentration on cyberbullying as a new and separate phenomenon, the scope and nature of the cyberbullying that was identified by the action research was demonstrated to be a direct result of the relational aggression that was occurring amongst the girls at school. This confirms other research in the area of cyberbullying, which suggests that most cyberbullying is an extension of face-to face-bullying in schools. This is obviously significant in addressing the causes and manifestations of bullying.

Finally, the action research clearly demonstrates that the conceptual framework and techniques of the Cooling Conflicts and Acting Against Bullying programs investigated in previous chapters were equally effective in uncovering and managing covert bullying amongst adolescent females. However, just as in previous implementations, it was necessary to adapt the structures and techniques to the specific context, and to conduct on-going research that provided evidence of outcomes and identified effective adaptations to enhance the success of the program.

References

Archer, J., & Coyne, S. M. (2005). An integrated review of indirect, relational & social aggression. *Personality and Social Psychology Review, 9*, 212–223.

Bauman, S., & Del Rio, A. (2006). Preservice teachers' responses to bullying scenarios: Comparing physical, verbal and relational bullying. *Journal of Educational Pyschology, 98*(1), 219–231.

Besag, V. E. (2006). Bullying among girls friends or foes? *School Psychology International, 27,* 535–551.

Björkqvist, K., Oesterman, K., Lagerspetz, K. M. J., Landau, S. F., Caprara, G. V., & Fraczek, A. (2001). Aggression, victimization, and sociometric status: Findings from Finland, Israel, Italy, and Poland. In J. M. Ramirez & D. S. Richardson (Eds.), *Cross-cultural approaches to research on aggression and reconciliation.* New York: Nova.

Boal, A. (1996). Politics, education and change. In O.'. T. John & D. Kate (Eds.), *Drama culture and empowerment: The IDEA dialogues.* Brisbane: IDEA Publications.

Bolton, G. (1998). *Acting in classroom drama: A critical analysis.* Trentham: Stoke-on-Trent.

Bolton, G., & Heathcote, D. (1998). Teaching culture through drama. In B. Michael & F. Michael (Eds.), *Language learning in intercultural perspective.* Cambridge: Cambridge University Press.

Bright, R. M. (2005). It's just a grade 8 thing: Aggression in teenage girls. *Gender and Education, 17,* 93–101.

Bullying Statistics. (2010). http://www.bullyingstatistics.org/content/bullying-statistics-2010.html. Accessed 9 Sept 2013.

Burton, B. (1991). *The act of learning: The drama-theatre continuum in the classroom.* Melbourne: Longman Cheshire.

Burton, B. (2008). Acting against bullying in schools. In A. O'Brien & K. Donelan (Eds.), *The arts and youth at risk: Global and local challenges* (pp. 139–155). Newcastle upon Tyne: Cambridge Scholars Publishing.

Byram, M. (1997). *Teaching and assessing intercultural communicative competence.* Clevedon: Multilingual Matters.

Choudry, A. (2010). Education, participatory action research, and social change: International perspectives. *International Education, 39(2),* 72–76 (Spring 2010).

Crick, N. R., & Grotpeter, J. K. (1995). Relational aggression, gender and social psychological adjustment. *Child Development, 66,* 710–722.

Crothers, L. M., Field, J. E., & Kolbert, J. B. (2005). Navigating power, control and being nice: Aggression in adolescent girls' friendships. *Journal of Counselling and Development, 83,* 349–354.

Cyber Bullying Statistics. (2010). http://www.statisticbrain.com/cyber-bullying-statistics. Accessed 9 Sept 2013.

Duncan, N. (2002). Girls, bullying and school transfer. In V. Sunnari, J. Kangasuuo, & M. Heikkenin (Eds.), *Gendered and sexualised violence in educational environments* (pp. 106–122). Oulu: Femina Borealis.

Fleming, M. (1998). Cultural awareness and dramatic art forms. In B. Michael & F. Michael (Eds.), *Language learning in intercultural perspective.* Cambridge: Cambridge University Press.

Hinduja, S., & Patchin, J. (2013). Cyberbullying Research Center, www.cyberbullying.us. Accessed 7 Oct 2013.

James, V. H., & Owens, L. D. (2005). They turned around like I just wasn't there: An analysis of teenage girls' letters about their peer conflicts. *School Psychology International, 26,* 71–88.

Kemmis, S., & McTaggart, R. (2008). Robin participatory action research: Communicative action and the public sphere. In N. K. Denzin & Y. S. Lincoln (Eds.), *Strategies of qualitative inquiry*. Los Angeles: Sage Publications.

Kowalski, R., Limber, S., & Agatston, P. (2007). *Cyberbullying: Bullying in the digital age*. Malden: Blackwell Publishers.

Leenaars, L. S., Dane, A. V., & Marini, Z. (2008). Evolutionary perspective on indirect victimization in adolescence: The role of attractiveness, dating and sexual behavior. *Aggressive Behavior, 34*(4), 404–415.

Li, Q. (2005). New bottle but old wine: A research of cyberbullying in schools. *Computers and Human behaviour, 23*, 1777–1791.

Li, Q. (2006). Cyberbullying in schools : A research of gender differences. *School Psychology International, 27*, 157–170.

McDougall, B., & Chilcott, T. (2009, June 1). Bullying is out of control in schools. *The Courier Mail*. Brisbane: Associated Newspapers.

Messerschmidt, J. W. (2011). The struggle for hetero feminine recognition: Bullying, embodiment, and reactive sexual offending by adolescent girls. *Feminist Criminology, 6*, 203–233.

Miller-Johnson, S., Moore, B., Underwood, M. K., Cole, J. D. (2005). African-American girls and physical aggression: Does stability of childhood aggression predict later negative outcomes. In J. Pepler, K. Madsen, C. Wester, K. Levene (Eds.), *The development and treatment of girlhood aggression* (pp. 75–89). New York: Psychology Press.

Morrison, M., Burton, B., & O'Toole, J. (2006). Re-engagement through peer teaching drama – Insights into reflective practice. In P. Burnard & S. Hennessy (Eds.), *Reflective practices in arts education*. Netherlands: Springer.

Neelands, J. (2009). Acting together: Ensemble as a democratic process in art and life. *Research in Drama Education: The Journal of Applied Theatre and Performance, 14*(2), 173–189.

Nicholson, H. (2005). *Applied drama: The gift of theatre*. Basingstoke: Palgrave Macmillan.

Nicol, S. (2012). Cyber bullying and trolling. *Youth Studies Australia, 31*(4), 3–4.

O'Neill, C. (1995). *Drama world: A framework for process drama*. Portsmouth: Heinemann.

Owens, L., Shute, R., & Slee, P. (2000). Guess what I just heard!: Indirect aggression among teenage girls in Australia. *Aggressive Behaviour, 26*, 67–83.

Ponsford, J. (2007). *The future of adolescent female cyber-bullying: Electronic media's effect on aggressive communication*. Honors thesis, Texas State University.

Randall, K., & Bowen, A. (2007). *Mean girls 101 ½ creative strategies and activities for working with relational aggression*. Chaplin: Youth Light Inc.

Remillard, A. M., & Lamb, S. (2005). Adolescent girls coping with relational aggression. *Sex Roles, 53*, 221–231.

Roberts, W. B., Jr. (2006). *Bullying from both sides: Strategic interventions for working with bullies and victims*. California: Corwin Press.

Smith, P. K. (2013). School bullying. *Sociologica, 71*, 81–98.

Smith, P. K., Mahdavi, J., Caryalho, M., Fisher, S., Russell, S., & Tippett, N. (2008). Cyberbullying: Its nature and impact on secondary school pupils. *Journal of Child Psychology and Psychiatry, 49*(4), 376–385.

Statistics on Bullying NSPCC. (2013). www.nspcc.org.uk/inform/.../bullying/bullyingstatistics. Accessed 9 Sept 2013.

Underwood, M. K. (2003). *Social aggression among girls*. New York: The Guilford Press.

Volk, A. A., Camilleri, J. A., Dane, A. V., & Marini, Z. A. (2012). Is adolescent bullying and evolutionary adaptation? *Aggressive Behavior, 38*(3), 222–238.

Warner, C. (1997). The edging in of engagement: Exploring the nature of engagement in drama. *Research in Drama Education, 2*(1), 21.

Wood, J. (2007). *Understanding and addressing attendance problems in schools*. Charlotte: Information Age Publishing.

Young, D. (2000). Reality drama: The drama classroom as a place for disclosure. *NADIE Journal Drama Australia, 24*(1), 111–122.

Zuber-Skerritt, Ortrun and Associates. (2009). *Action learning and action research: Songlines through interviews Rotterdam*. Boston: Sense Publishers.

Chapter 11
Conflict and Bullying Management for Adolescent Refugees

11.1 Introduction

This chapter investigates another recent application of the research, this time working with newly- arrived adolescent refugees as the subjects. A number of positive outcomes are identified, as are the particular problems and constraints of working with this group. The project involved the combination of explicit teaching about conflict and bullying combined with the use of drama to provide experiential understanding and expertise, that was used in previous projects. The data clearly indicated that this model again proved effective in enhancing conflict and bullying management in the refugee participants.

However, the use of peer teaching, whilst still effective in increasing knowledge and confidence, emerged as less successful than in the previous studies explored in this book due to language and cultural factors and lack of time. A number of other positive outcomes were observed, including increased self – identity and the development of language and socialisation skills.

11.2 The Research Project: Arrivals

The research analysed in this chapter was part of The Arrivals project (2010–2013), funded by the Australian Research Council, which aimed to design, implement and evaluate a drama- based program to support refugees and develop resilience in their first 12 months of settlement. The outcomes were intended to identify the efficacy of such programs and their applicability to other situations and settings, and to synthesise a model of effective practice using drama-based interventions with refugees. The industry partner in the research was Multi-Link, a government-funded organisation responsible for assisting refugees to re-settle in Australia, and three case

© Springer International Publishing Switzerland 2015
B. Burton et al., *Acting to Manage Conflict and Bullying Through Evidence-Based Strategies*, DOI 10.1007/978-3-319-17882-0_11

studies were planned, one with primary school children, one with refuge female adults, and one with refugee teenagers, the case study reported in this chapter.

The participants in this case study were newly arrived adolescent refugees between 14 and 17 years of age who had been assigned to an additional languages unit at Riverside State High School, a large Brisbane secondary school in a very low socio-economic area with a significant refugee population. The majority of the 32 students in the case study were from African nations, but a number of other cultures were also represented including 7 students from Burma, plus individuals from Thailand, Cambodia and China. Some of the students had been in refugee camps overseas for a number of years before arriving in Australia, a number of them spoke almost no English, and many had experienced very difficult childhoods, such as being child soldiers in The Sudan.

The director of the school language unit, the classroom Drama teacher and the supervisors and counsellors responsible for the refugee students requested that the research project should include the application of the Acting Against Bullying program (Chap. 5). Their call for this approach was based on the fact that many of the young people in the language unit had experienced significant conflict situations since their arrival in Australia, or been the targets of bullies from both within the school community and beyond it. They believed that the refugee students needed greater competence in handling conflict and bullying and in forming positive social relationships if they were to develop the self-esteem and sense of identity that would enable them to operate effectively in the mainstream of the school when they were moved out of the language unit at the end of the year.

The primary aim of the case study was therefore to determine whether the conceptual framework and strategies developed in the Cooling Conflicts and Acting Against Bullying programs (Burton and O'Toole 2009) could enhance the present and future development of the refugee adolescents in the language unit. Given this aim, a deliberate decision was made before the research began not to make their experiences before they came to Australia the subject matter of the workshops. This was not only because of the ethical problems related to re-traumatisation. Matthews (2008, p. 40) argues that: "Refugees have already shown reliance, resourcefulness and strength ..practical and emotional support measures are required that do not overstate vulnerabilities and helplessness, but build on strength and resilience." Recent literature on the adjustment of adolescents to re-settlement strongly supports this approach (Kovacev and Shute 2004; Ferjoa and Vickers 2010).

There is also increasing evidence that the experiences of young people after resettlement are actually more important in their psychological development and adjustment than their previous experiences in refugee camps and war zones (Phan 2003; Fazell et al. 2005). In their study, Guerrero and Tinkler (2010) found in their research that: "Despite the young people in this study's undeniable experiences of injustice and trauma, they did not identify themselves as victims. The youth instead saw themselves as capable actors in their world." Other studies have concluded that integrating refugee adolescents into the society they have joined, whilst valuing the cultures they bring with them, is the most beneficial approach to settlement (Berry et al. 2006).

11.3   The Refugee Experience

The extensive literature dealing with refugees emphasises the considerable challenges faced by them when resettling in a new country, and there has been a particular focus on the difficulties encountered by adolescent refugees. "Displaced youth represents a particularly vulnerable population forced to adapt to a new way of life whilst also undergoing important developmental changes" (Guerrero and Tinkler 2010, p. 55).

Recent reviews of literature about the re-settlement of young refugees has identified the importance of the school in the process, with Taylor (2008, p. 58) stating that: "Studies have highlighted the crucial role that schools could play on facilitating the transition from refugees to participating citizens." A number of studies of refugee re-settlement in different countries confirms this research, and Rossiter and Rossiter (2009, p. 412) discovered that for refugee youth at risk: "One of the most critical factors in a successful transition to Canadian society is education". This is confirmed by Matthews (2008, p. 39) who argues that "A broad range of interventions including the development of safe and nurturing educational environments ….. are key to best practice".

Onsando and Billett (2009, p. 87) argue that: "Students from refugee backgrounds that may be facing socio-cultural and possible psychological issues require the experience of transformational learning curriculum that will enable them to have a greater sense of purpose and meaning". Yohani declares that: "A strengths-based approach does not imply ignorance of vulnerabilities, but instead broadens our perceptions to include the positive attributes of children" (2008 p. 321).

However, the extensive literature on the teenage refugee experience makes it clear that the preparation young people are given for settlement in Australia and elsewhere is most often inadequate. "Resettlement policies and programs for refugee youth, for the most part, fail to recognise and build on the considerable resources these youth bring to their new country and miss opportunities to develop their leadership potential "(Correa-Velez et al. 2010, p. 1399). In particular, Ferjoa and Vickers (2010, p. 150) note that:

> Existing research has found that 4 terms of attendance at Intensive English Centres in standard high schools is insufficient to prepare many refugee students for a successful transition to mainstream classrooms. This transition is difficult for students in terms of their learning and acculturation needs, as well as for many of their teachers.

Significantly, the recent research and literature in the field identifies conflict and bullying as major factors in determining the success of resettlement for adolescent refugees. Correa-Velez et al. (2010, p. 1404) found in their research on the well-being of youth from refugee backgrounds that: "Being bullied was negatively associated with happiness. Perceived discrimination was also a significant predictor, with young people who had experienced discrimination scoring lower in their physical and environment domains." Matthews (2008, p. 38) insists: "Anti-bullying, harassment, anti-racism and cultural inclusivity policies and training are important steps towards countering marginalisation and exclusion."

Correa-Velez et al. (2010) argue: "Sense of control plays a key role in the rebuilding of a meaningful life amongst those who have survived forced displacement" and they emphasise the significance of a supportive school environment and note that: "Bullying at school has a negative impact on well-being among youth" (p. 1401).

11.4 Drama and Refugees

The use of arts-based interventions to assist young refugees has been trialled in a number of countries. However, these interventions have tended to focus on the use of visual media to explore narratives of re-settlement. The Hope Project in Canada (Yohani 2008) used visual art, photography and crafts with groups of young children and adolescents, whilst Rodriguez-Jimenez and Gifford (2010) encourage adolescent Afghan refugees to make films, as did Harris (2009) with Sudanese girls. Photography was also the medium for the project conducted in the USA and Columbia by Guerrero and Tinkler (2010).

The personal and cultural learning that Drama in the classroom can provide (Bolton and Heathcote 1998) has received attention from researchers in the field of cultural conflict and exclusion in schools (Kana and Aitkin 2007). Lee and De Finney (2005) in Victoria, Canada, worked with adolescent girls from racial and cultural minorities, some of them refugees, using theatre performance composed of three short play to demonstrate the girls' experiences with racism and gender discrimination, including racial bullying. One of the plays, Popularity, contained a forum theatre component. "The expressive and transformational nature of popular theatre was particularly well-suited for involving young people in developing critical consciousness about their marginalization and working collaboratively to develop concrete strategies for social change" Lee and Finney (p. 96).

Forum theatre (Boal 1979, 1996) has been performed by professional TIE actors with refugee students in schools in the UK "Students claimed repeatedly that the Forum Theatre workshops had altered their perception of refugees ..". Day concluded: "Valuable interventions enabled progress within the play by displaying positive moral conduct. From these interventions, students could potentially learn ways of dealing with similar situations in their own lives" (2009, p. 29).

Rousseau et al. (2005) from a therapeutic standpoint found that: "Drama therapy workshops facilitate the adaptation of young immigrants and refugees to their new environment through creative work on identity issues related to migration ad status as a cultural minority (p. 25). However, they queried: "how much do the workshops influence the well-being and adjustment of the teens to their new environment?" (p. 25). The fact that the Acting Against Bullying program actually teaches conceptual understanding and competence in managing conflict and bullying was significant in the adolescent refugees in the Arrivals research believing that their well-being had improved and they were able to manage these issue in their ne environment.

11.5   The Arrivals Research

The case study involved a sequence of one and a half hour drama workshops delivered by a research team each week over a period of one semester. The goal of the research was to determine the effectiveness with adolescent refugees of the model for managing conflict and bullying that is the subject of this book. In particular, the research investigated the efficacy of drama and peer teaching in empowering the refugee students by giving them a voice within conflict and bullying situations they may be encountering or might encounter in future.

The research team was comprised of five research assistants who were final year Griffith University students (participating as part of required work integrated learning practice) and three more experienced Applied Theatre researchers The workshops were conducted for our months across the second half of the school year. Each workshop ran for an hour and a half on a Monday and Tuesday, and a third class each week on a Friday was run by the Drama teacher and followed up on the learning covered in the two earlier sessions. During this time three action research cycles were implemented and evaluated using a range of approaches and techniques in response to the needs and the requests of the participants, and the advice of their mentors and teachers.

11.6   The Case Study Process

This research began with overt teaching by the research team and the classroom teacher about the nature of conflict and bullying, and English language competence immediately emerged as an issue. The basic conceptual structure that has informed all the research reported in this book was taught, including the three stages of Latent, Emerging and Manifest conflict, and the three parties involved – bully, bullied and bystander. However, most of the refugee students had arrived in Australia in the past 12 months and had been at the school for just 6 months. Furthermore, almost half the 32 students had only begun to learn English in these 6 months before the project began. The 7 Burmese students and the Thai and Cambodian boys in particular struggled to understand even simple instructions and were very reluctant to answer questions, or indeed, speak at all in the first few workshops conducted for the research. Whilst the African students were much more fluent in English, for some of them it was still their third spoken language after Swahili and French.

The overt teaching about conflict and bullying was therefore done in groups, with each group led by one of the young researchers, who explored the nature of the issues with their groups, and told stories about their own experiences and knowledge of conflict. They helped the refugee students to identify some key features such as the deliberate misuse of power, the on-going and escalating nature of both bullying and conflict, and the harm caused. They encouraged their groups to talk about, and enact, their experiences of conflict and bullying since coming to Australia.

The workshops in this initial phase focused on a range of Drama activities and exercises, including freeze frames, mime, spontaneous improvisation and dramatic storytelling. None of the students had studied Drama as a subject before they came to Australia, and they had acquired only limited experience in improvisation and performance of dialogue in their first drama classes. Initially the students chose to work in their ethnic groups, facilitated by the researchers and research assistants. When asked to share some of their improvisations in the early workshops, a number of the students were reluctant to do so, and the performances were very brief, sometimes only a matter of seconds in length. To engage the students initially and encourage them to take on roles and become involved in fictional situations, a number of classroom drama games and activities were used, and students were encouraged to share games and enact stories from their own cultural backgrounds with the whole class.

Specific drama concepts and techniques proved particularly successful for the students who had no background in Drama, not only in developing drama skills but in enhancing conceptual understanding of the effectiveness in exploring human issues. The use of transformation as developed by Grotowski and Brook (Burton 2011, pp. 194–200) was explicitly taught in one session, with the students transforming chairs, rostra blocks, lengths of material and their own bodies to create the settings, costumes, characters and creatures for a range of dramas. A genuine level of engagement and enjoyment quickly developed, and as the students became more confident, cross-cultural groups were structured placing the articulate African students in groups with the less fluent Asian students. In informal interviews conducted at the end of the first 4 weeks, all the students except one indicated their approval of the workshops and their desire for them to continue. The one exception was a Chinese boy who joined the project in the third week and who spoke no English. When the whole group was offered the opportunity to do visual art instead of Drama, this boy was the only one who took up the offer.

The use of enacted stories, told both by the students and by the researchers, formed the heart of the improvisations dramatising conflict and bullying. Storytelling was the technique Liebmann (2004) found most useful in her arts approaches to conflict, and it was particularly effective with the Burmese refugee students when the storytelling was followed by enactment. Working in small groups, the Burmese girls told stories of their lives, both before and during their time in Australia. From these stories fictional scenarios were created of conflict and bullying situations the girls were interested in exploring. These scenarios were turned into group performances that were shared with the rest of the class.

When I was in primary school, like year 6, and like I got my photo taken, and then I was like holding my photo on my hand and an old girl came and she took my photo, and then she ripped the plastic bag and my photo flew away. I never told my teachers. (Ka Mai)

This was one of the very few cases where a participant went back to their childhood experiences to illustrate their understanding of bullying. It was acted out by a group of the Burmese girls, much of it in their own language, with great enthusiasm and embellishment, and directed by Ka Mai, but not performed by her. This approach, where a refugee who really wanted their story enacted became the director of the performance, was used consistently throughout the project, providing distance and safety (Hunter 2008). After the improvisation that dramatised this story, Ka Mai went on to say that she thought the whole school should do the Acting Against Bullying program, and she articulated her own learning from the experience:

Interviewer: What would you do now?
Ka Mai: I would say to her. I would say: "Stop doing that to people. How will you feel if people do that to you?" So ..like, they will not bully other people, and they will not hurt other peoples' feelings.

The last part of this phase was devoted to Enhanced Forum Theatre. The research team prepared and performed a play in three scenes about a serious bullying situation involving cultural issues. The first scene presented the latent stage of the conflict, scene two developed the emerging stage, and the final scene showed the manifest stage when the bullying was at its most serious. The play was performed three times as part of the Enhanced Forum Theatre structure. The refugee students watched the first performance through, then hot –seated and thought- tracked the characters during the second performance. Many of the questions asked in these process drama interventions demonstrated clear understanding of the nature and impact of bullying and conflict.

During the third performance of the play, members of the audience were able to intervene to take on the role of any of the characters and to try and de-escalate the situation. This was accepted by a number of the students with great enthusiasm, and some of the interventions were successful in reducing the severity of the bullying, at least temporarily. All the interventions clearly demonstrated at least some authentic learning and a genuine desire to find strategies to manage the problem.

In the final phase of the research, in the last month of the project, the refugee students took responsibility for sharing their knowledge and expertise about bullying and conflict through peer teaching another class. This involved not only the teaching of the bullying concepts and the use of improvised drama, but the preparation and staging of forum theatre performances (Burton 2012). Before the refugee students took on the role of peer teachers, the research team worked with them in groups to help them develop their peer teaching about bullying and conflict, and to create their own enhanced forum theatre pieces to perform. In this phase the students were much more willing to work across cultural divides and across gender boundaries than they had been in earlier phases of the research.

As Kana and Aitkin (2007) found, using the safety and distance of Drama allows students to take on leadership roles and to articulate issues of social justice. The refugee students in *The Arrivals* project were able to perform their forum plays effectively for the Year 8 class and to lead reflective discussions on the issues and consequences of bullying.

11.7   Data Collection and Analysis

As with previous implementations of the Acting against Bullying program, pre and post questionnaires were administered to all the participants in order to identify changes in understanding, attitude and behaviour as a result of the research process. Observation notes were written by each of the researchers for each session, and the classroom teacher also kept a research diary. All the workshops were filmed. Semi-structured group interviews were conducted at the end of the first two phases of the research and summative group and individual interviews were conducted with all participants after the final session.

The preliminary questionnaire was administered in the third week of the research, after the specific teaching about the nature and key features of bullying, so that the students had some understanding on which to base their responses. Because of the range of cultural backgrounds and English language abilities, the questionnaire was administered to groups which were facilitated by researchers who assisted with the understanding of the questions. The questionnaire was similar to previous surveys used in the Acting Against Bullying program and asked the students to identify their experiences with bullying, to describe how they had coped with these experiences, and indicate what they considered the most effective ways of managing bullying.

The survey revealed both commonalities and differences in comparison to the data from previous conflict and bullying research. Almost 50 % of the students stated that they were currently experiencing bullying at school, and the same percentage had been bystanders in bullying situations during the past year. This is consistent with international research findings on bullying in secondary schools (McDougall and Chilcott 2009; Burton 2008; Roberts 2006; O'Toole et al. 2005). However, only 10 % of the refugee students admitted to bullying any one or being involved in bullying during their time at the school, which is far lower than the incidence generally found amongst secondary school students. This finding is however consistent with studies of the refugee experience, where newly – arrived refuges are found to be the targets of racial harassment bad aggression, and are far less likely to be the aggressors in conflict situations.

The preliminary questionnaire also revealed that the students believed that the bully or a teacher were the most likely to be able to stop bullying from occurring and in this initial survey only 10 % of the students believed the person being bullied could stop it from happening, and only 7 % of the respondents believed that a bystander could effectively stop bullying. A third of the respondents identified the enjoyment of power as the reason people bully others, which appears to be a response to the overt teaching about bullying which emphasised the miss-use of power as a key element.

The observation notes revealed that at the midpoint of the project, after 7 weeks of workshops, the students were freely and enthusiastically engaging in a range of drama exercises, activities and improvisations. In performances of their rehearsed improvisations, the students increasingly became more verbal and more expressive, including those with very limited English. In terms of learning about bullying and conflict, a number of the students in the on-going group interviews spoke at unusual length and with some passion, attempting to overcome the language barrier and clearly revealing their developing understanding of bullying and conflict management.

One Burmese girl observed:

> *Bullying is when you hurt someone's feelings or harm them in any way, cyber, emotionally, physically, and socially.*

Also at this mid-point in the research a significant incident occurred that offered real-world evidence of the efficacy of the process for one of the participants. A Sudanese refugee (identified by the pseudonym Ali) arrived late for one of the workshops and with blood staining his trousers. He initially explained that he had fallen over and injured himself. However, during an exploration of group bullying activities, it was observed that Ali had initiated an improvisation about a gang of youths physically bullying a teenager, with himself in the role of the victim. Alerted by the intensity of Ali's emotional involvement in this improvisation, the researchers conducted a discussion with the performance group. Ali then revealed he had been experiencing on-going serious bullying by a group of older Sudanese adolescents who were trying to force him to leave school and join their gang. He acknowledged that he was actually using drama within the workshop to explore how to cope. He agreed to go with the classroom teacher to talk to the school counsellor immediately. With the support of the school and the involvement of the police and the Sudanese community, the bullying ceased altogether.

When asked in a summative interview at the end of the research about his learning in the project, Ali responded:

> *I have more ideas about bullying, and then how to solve bullying. Then what are the different kinds of bullying. You can learn that someone can hurt someone's feeling and then what type of bully there is, and how bully take...um. . Bully topic. Make me know what is a solution, and then it gets bigger, just as the three stages of bully which is latent, emerging and also manifest*
>
> *So I don't bully people, because I've been bullied... when they bully me I have an idea how to solve it, to stop the bully so that they can't bully me any one. Ya.*

It became increasingly apparent that the crucial factor in the developing engagement and competence of the students was the use of drama as the central learning technique. A group of 4 African girls were eager to list the reasons for their enthusiastic involvement in the project:

> *I like the acting. It's so cool.*
> *I like the acting and when we first started learning about bullying*
> *And I like the...acting about our language stuff.*
> *And I like acting about bullying*

This enthusiasm for the project in the early stages had a substantive outcome. At the half-way point of the research project, after 2 months of workshops, this group of girls requested that they be permitted to talk about bullying at a full school assembly and perform some of the bullying scenarios they had developed in the workshops. This was approved, and the performance was received with enthusiasm by both the teachers and the students of the school. The actual performance used the structure of Enhanced Forum Theatre in depicting a conflict scenario in three scenes, showing how the conflict escalated form latent to emerging to manifest. There were no interventions from the audience however.

The classroom teacher and the refugee support staff were both surprised and impressed by this initiative. The girls explained in interview why they had taken this initiative.

Della: *Cause we got to know everything about the bully. How we can stop it.*
Kamu: *Ya, we felt like… we should tell, like people, like the bullies…Like how the victim will feel.*
Della: *Because lots of people do the bullying at the school, so you can stop it if you do it in front of the whole school.*
Sema: *Ya, and then, like give time for the bully, to think about it. How people will feel when they bully people*

In contrast to this interim positive outcome, the peer teaching in the final phase of the research was extremely difficult for the refugee students. With 4 weeks to go in the final cycle of research, as part of the participatory nature of the action research, the participants were consulted to decide whether to teach a mainstream Year 8 class in the school what they had learned about bullying and conflict. As in previous projects (Chaps. 4, 5 and 10) this peer teaching involved not only the teaching of the concepts and the use of improvised drama, but the preparation and staging of enhanced forum theatre plays depicting conflict and bullying situations, where members of the Year 8 audience would be invited to intervene in role. The refugee students were intimidated by the demands of the task, but were determined to attempt it with the help of the research team and their class teacher.

The peer teaching proved even more challenging than anticipated. The difficulty many of the refugee students had with spoken language meant they struggled to communicate effectively with their peer learners, and they completed the formal teaching they had planned within 20–30 min of the hour long class. This problem had arisen in the early stages of other Acting Against Bullying programs (Chap. 5) and had been overcome by allowing more class time for groups of students to prepare their peer teaching and to practice it on each other. Due to lack of available time, the peer teaching preparation by the refugee students was brief and hurried. The lack of material to teach and the skill to teach it effectively to the Year 8 class was therefore an acute problem.

A second constraint was the fact that the class chosen as peer learners was not, as planned, an ESL class composed of students similar to the participants, but a mainstream Year 8 class that contained a number of students with learning and behavioural difficulties. The refugee peer teachers were therefore confronted with class control issues and with differentiating their teaching to meet the needs of individual learners. These are major challenges for even experienced teachers, and in the first peer teaching session the refugee students became increasingly frustrated and disappointed with the behaviour of their peer learners.

Despite their sense of failure following their first attempt at peer teaching, the refugee students insisted that they wished to continue. In a planning meeting, the groups decided to make much more use of improvised drama with their peer learners, teaching the conflict and bullying concepts through action rather than formal teaching. This approach had worked well with one of the groups in the first session, and the others all adopted it. As a result, the second peer teaching session was characterised by numerous drama activities and improvisations that demonstrated high levels of enthusiasm and involvement amongst the peer learners.

In workshop three with the Year 8 class, groups of the refugee students performed their forum theatre plays for their peer learners and invited them to intervene by replacing one of the characters in the action of the plays and deal with the bullying being portrayed. The enhanced forum plays proved to be effective in demonstrating different bullying scenarios, and in engaging the Year 8 audience. A number of peer learners in each group chose to intervene in the action of the plays, and in each case the interventions attempted to de-escalate the conflict and bullying being represented. Despite the constraints of language learning difficulties there was worthwhile discussion between the peer teachers and the peer learners about how to manage conflict and bullying.

The refugee students were much more positive about the outcomes of this session of peer teaching, and there was a clear sense of accomplishment and self-confidence expressed in the planning session that followed. They were excited that they had been able to perform their forum plays effectively for the Year 8 class and that they were able to conduct reflective discussions on the issues and consequences of bullying.

However, the final session raised again the issue of adequate preparation of the peer teaching for this particular group of subjects to work effectively. In this workshop, the refugee students assisted the Year 8 peer learners to prepare their own peer teaching for another class. The refugee students did not have the pedagogical skills or the language to teach this component effectively. Again, much more time was needed to provide the refugee students with effective teaching strategies and class management techniques. Because of time constraints and organisational issues, the Year 8 class did not get the opportunity to teach another class.

The peer teaching component was implemented in the research because it had proved so successful in all the previous projects where it had been applied (Chaps. 4, 5 and 10). However, the context in which the peer teaching took place in this project severely limited its success in terms of increasing the expertise and confidence of the peer teachers in dealing with conflict and in empowering the peer learners. The lack of time, the communication difficulties faced by refugee students and the nature of the class chosen for the peer teaching were all serious constraints Nevertheless, the refugee students were positive about their learning through the peer teaching whilst acknowledging the difficulties they encountered.

Interviewer: So you all enjoyed teaching the class. What was your favourite part
              about teaching the class next door?
Ali: Well I enjoyed everywhere. I enjoyed being the host, and to direct,
              how to help my friends, to make the play up, to learn a thing, outside
              making the play, to explain to the students we teaching, what's hap-
              pening and asking questions. I enjoyed doing that, I was so happy
              and shouldn't be bully., when I was doing the bullying and then with
              this assistance how bully started and how it gets escalated and then
              keeps going keeps going and then we shouldn't and then just us
              when its started- 1,2, 3 just like that. how bullies get to us.
Interviewer: So what did you like about teaching the other class Tan?
Tan: Everything. It make me to know how to teach others.

A group composed of two African and three Burmese girls was placed with a
large group of Year 8 boys, and although they encountered some problems with peer
teaching them, they felt a strong sense of accomplishment after the session. When
two more girls joined the peer group, the refugee students were able to identify the
fact that one of them was a bully, and they actually used one of the key techniques
they had learned, Hot Seating, to attempt to both engage and teach this girl. Hot
Seating involves asking questions of a character in a drama about their behaviour
and motivations . Although they did not achieve a breakthrough with this particular
girl, they felt that they had succeeded in peer teaching effectively, and their
conscious use of Hot Seating demonstrates a sophisticated understanding of the
technique and also their ability to identify bullying behaviour.

Interviewer: Okay..., we just kind of talked about this but did you have any
              problems when you were teaching the other class?
Mary: Yes. Yes. All group did the first time.
Samu: No.
Deela: No not us.
Zema: The first time-
Deela: It's the last time. You Know the big girl join in and she-
Zema: But she was not there when we were doing like-
Deela: Ya.
R: She's a real bully.
Zema: She say bad words. She, she say...she keep say "shut up, shut up".
Regina: She's a real bully.
Zema: Ya she's really, really bully.
Interviewer: So How did you, how did you try and teach her-
Zema: You know like when-
Regina: It's hard.
Zema: When, when the other people ask us like to, who's going to be like in
              the hot seat, and then we chose her and then she say, and then she
              didn't answer and she just be bully.
Deela: She just say "I know that, I know that".
Interviewer: So you think she's a bully in real life?
Regina: Ya she a real bully.

11.8 Findings

The post-project questionnaire and individual interviews subsequently confirmed that the impact of the Acting Against Bullying process was comparable with this cohort of newly – arrived refugees to the outcomes from previous implementations with large numbers of mainstream school students reported in this book.

Almost all the participants were able to identify the significant conceptual information they had learned about the nature of bullying, and the majority were able to apply this understanding in identifying key strategies to manage bullying effectively. On the summative questionnaire, 92 % the respondents were able to identify and explain the characteristics of at least one form of bullying, and were confident that they could describe to others exactly what bullying involved. Furthermore, 85 % of respondents were able to of identify the three stages of bullying and the order in which they escalate, and 77 % were able to write down the three categories of participants in bullying situations – bully, bullied and bystander. 11 % of students misunderstood the questions (possibly due to language difficulties) and wrote down answers that actually described another aspect of bullying, or did not respond.

Bullying is when someone gets power over other people. Sometimes more than one person bullying one person. They think they are the strongest people in the school.

Bullying is using your strength over someone or hurting them in some kind of way, like using technology, and saying mean things to them.

To physically, verbally, emotionally socially or cyberly (sic) harming someone.

When asked on the questionnaire if they now noticed bullying situations more as a result of the project, 40.5 % responded yes, another 40.5 % responded no, and 19 % did not respond. Again, it is difficult to know to what extent lack of language influenced their answers. However, 50 % of the total respondents did state that they could identify bullying when it was happening and provided examples of bullying situations they had observed since beginning the program.

More significantly, most of the participants felt empowered to manage bullying situations more effectively. On the summative questionnaire, 77.7 % responded that they now believed that bullying could be prevented or de-escalated, and when asked if they themselves were more likely now to intervene in a bullying situation in order to de-escalate it or end it, 56 % of the respondents said they would.

A major positive finding was the fact that 81 % of respondents identified the bystander as the one most likely to be able to change a bullying situation. This is a significant change from the 10 % who identified the bystander as the most effective agent of bullying management on the initial questionnaire.

The bystander is very important. Bystander can change the bully situation.

Bystanders can stop the bullying because they are allowed and they can tell someone and they can help.

A significant number of the refugee students indicated a willingness to take an active role in de-escalating the bullying, and their responses indicated that they understood that that there were a number of strategies available to them.

These responses were a clear indicator of their confidence that they had learned how to manage bullying more effectively.

> *I can stop the bully when you really want to stop the bully, we have to talk to the person and make the person smile*
> *Because I will tell someone what is going on especially my parents and teachers.*
> *Because the good bystander can stop them bullying the person and if they don't listen, maybe the person who was the bystander can tell the police and the police can stop the bullying.*

Those who wrote that they would attempt to persuade the bully to stop their activities emphasised the importance of convincing bullies to empathize with their victims. This was an interesting finding given that their first responses in the early workshops to any kind of bullying portrayed in a drama. Both as individuals and as groups, boys and girls had responded physically, acting out separating the bully and the victim, often using force to restrain the bully. On the final questionnaire and in summative interviews they revealed much more thoughtful responses to dealing with bullies.

> *Because I can't stand there and watch someone being bullied because it is not fair.*
> *A bystander would do this by telling the bully to stop, and ask … "how would you feel if someone did that to you. Think about what you are doing before you do it. It's not right to bully other people. You hurt their feelings".*
> *Maybe the bystander can be the best friend and the bystander can say to them. 'If you don't stop bullying them I'm not going to be your friend anymore'.*

This element of empathizing with those involved in bullying emerged as an important thread in the learning of the refugee students. All of the participants indicated concern and sympathy for those being bullied, and none believed that victims were in any way responsible for the bullying they experienced. However, a number of the refugee students also believed that bullies needed advice and support because their behaviour was a result of inadequacy or unhappiness, and could lead to serious consequences, and 67 % of respondents on the summative questionnaire stated that they now understood why some people become bullies.

> *I feel bad for the bully and victim because the bully is trying to make they look good, and the victim is getting embarrassed.*
> *Because the bullies think that they are more powerful and smarter, That is why they want to bully, they get jealous of other people.*
> *I would explain like bullying don't(sic) have to happen anywhere and you would end up in jail for bullying someone*
> *Some people want help to change life and they don't want to bully anymore because they want help to be a good person..*

As well as feeling empowered to function as positive bystanders, a majority of the students felt competent to deal with bullying they might be directly involved in, and 59 % believed they had learn how to manage personal bullying experiences more effectively, including some who identified as being bullies in the past.

I have been bullied in primary school and never told anyone but now if it would happen again I would tell someone

I have learnt how to avoid and de-escalate the situation.

I want to stop bullying people because on Uganda I used to bully my friend, saying bad words.

One day some of my friends they were fighting in school and I try to stop them, but the bully refused to stop so I took the victim to the ESL office. Then the bully got angry at me and he say he go to fight me after school and I told one of the teachers and she took me to the school officer and solve the situation.

In the summative group interview with 4 Burmese refugees, 2 boys and 2 girls, they explained what they had learned from the project. The transcript of the interview reflects their struggle to explain in limited English what they had learned, both in terms of identifying and managing bullying, but also the difficulties they sometimes encounter in their relationships with other students.

Kim: *Like, if people bully. I don't know. Like when people bully you, like you feel sad. Like you don't have to like, bully them back. You just say 'Stop it!'*

Li: *You can help someone. When you saw someone, you don't have to stand and watch it. You have to go and stop the bully, When... When he or she started to bully you. But it's the same, you have to help someone*

Tan: *You don't have to be scared of bully. You have to go, and just say that I'm going to help someone. You don't have to say: I'm scared of the bully– she punches you whatever.*

Li: *But you know that bully, they never respect you. And then you know when we go to say stop, stop, they never listen to you. They say "you just go away or something like that to us.*

Sim: *It's like the cyber bullying. They make you feel like you're the...I mean the social. They make you, really hurts your feelings.*

Kim: *When it walks away, they start talking about you. Laughing. So, ya. You have to talk to someone, and then they will help you*

11.9 Outcomes

First of all, the refugee adolescents were able to explore a range of real and fictional bullying situations in the safe environment of drama. The range of Drama activities allowed all the students to create and enact completely fictional scenarios, as well as revisiting past experiences, providing a range of reflective opportunities both in the action of the drama and outside it. They were also able to experiment with changing the bullying being enacted, thereby learning both how, and how not, to deal with a range of bullying experiences The program gave students the opportunity to change actual bullying situations and to act differently in the drama, exploring ways they could have acted differently in the real life experiences. The summative interviews confirmed that these forms of reflection had occurred, and all the students were

emphatic that they had acquired valuable information and skills which they believe
had empowered them to deal with conflict and bullying issues.

R:	*I like the teaching.*
Z:	*I like being bully.*
M:	*Ya the teaching part that's good.*
Interviewer:	*Would you like to do more Acting Against Bullying? Or no?*
M:	*I would love to.*
S:	*It's fun.*
Z:	*It's fun.*
R:	*Because it's fun.*
M:	*Because it help you learn more-*
Z:	*Ya learn more about bully, like how...*
R:	*Because it helps us to learn, and...Ya. And how to stand, stand for others if they're, like, in trouble or something.*
M:	*How you can solve the problem.*
E:	*Um. So it like, I get to learn more. Like, like how the big people, the old people know more things about bully.*
M:	*Confident.*
Z:	*Confident and everything in drama.*
R:	*In drama.*
E:	*Not just in drama, everywhere.*
E	*So that when someone bully me I can stand for myself.*
K:	*Ya.*
E:	*And tell them "stop!"*

From her on-going observations during the research, not only in the workshops
but in normal classes with the refugee students, the classroom teacher identified a
major general outcome of the project as helping the students realise they can change
their behaviour not just in drama, but in the school and in their lives. She observed
that the students were demonstrating an increased interest in, and commitment to
their school.

The students themselves stated that doing *Acting Against Bullying* had actually
changed their behaviour at school and this was confirmed by a group of the refugee
students in the summative interviews, despite their very limited English.

Interviewer:	*In what ways have you changed?*
Nema:	*Behaviour.*
Interviewer:	*In a good or a bad way?*
Nema:	*Good. I wasn't listening to the teachers, when they were like, when the teacher was talking to me.*
Interviewer:	*And now you listen?*
Nema:	*Ya*
Dees:	*now I don't talk back to teachers.*

Interviewer:	*Did you before?*
Dees:	*Ya*
Interviewer:	*Now you're better behaved?*
Dees:	*I just say yes. I just do whatever they want.*
Kasha:	*My behaviour is a bit better*

Finally, the *Arrivals* research provided further evidence of the need to adapt the *Acting Against Bullying* program to the needs of each participant group. In this case, the differing English language levels of the students and their lack of experience with classroom drama meant that a number of new strategies had to be implemented. These included some overt teaching of improvisation and enactment skills such as the use of transformation, and also encouraging groups of students to perform in their own languages. These modifications to the program allowed the students to feel more confident in their use of drama and enhanced their confidence and self-esteem in regard to performance.

References

Berry, J. W., Phinney, J. S., Sam, D. I., & Vedder, P. (2006). Immigrant youth: Acculturation, identity, and adaptation. *Applied Psychology: An International Review, 55*(3), 303–332.

Boal, A. (1979). *The theatre of the oppressed*. London: Pluto.

Boal, A. (1996). Politics, education and change. In J. O'Toole & K. Donelan (Eds.), *Drama culture and empowerment: The IDEA dialogues*. Brisbane: IDEA Publications.

Bolton, G., & Heathcote, D. (1998). Teaching culture through drama. In M. Byram & M. Fleming (Eds.), *Language learning in intercultural perspective*. Cambridge: Cambridge University Press.

Burton, B. (2008). Acting against bullying in schools. In A. O'Brien & K. Donelan (Eds.), *The arts and youth at risk: Global and local challenges* (pp. 139–155). Newcastle: Cambridge Scholars Publishing.

Burton, B. (2011). *Living drama* (4th ed.). Melbourne: Pearson Education.

Burton, B. (2012). Peer teaching as a strategy for conflict management and student re-engagement in schools. *Australian Educational Researcher, 39*(1), 45–58.

Burton, B., & O'Toole, J. (2009). Power in their hands: The outcomes of the acting against bullying research project. *Applied Theatre Researcher 10*(1), 1–15.

Correa-Velez, I., Gifford, S. M., & Barnett, A. G. (2010). Longing to belong: Social inclusion and well-being among youth with refugee backgrounds in the first three years in Melbourne. *Australia Social Science & Medicine, 71*, 1399–1408.

Fazel, M., Wheeler, J., & Danesh, J. (2005). Prevalence of serious mental disorder in 7000 refugees resettled in western countries: A systematic review. *The Lancet, 365*(9467), 1309–1314.

Ferjoa, T., & Vickers, M. (2010). Supporting refugee students in school education in Greater Western Sydney. *Critical Studies in Education, 51*(2), 149–162.

Guerrero, A. L., & Tinkler, T. (2010). Refugee and displaced youth negotiating imagined and lived identities in a photography-based educational project in the United States and Colombia. *Anthropology & Education Quarterly, 41*, 55–74.

Harris, D. A. (2009). The paradox of expressing speechless terror: Ritual liminality in the creative arts therapies' treatment of posttraumatic distress. *The Arts in Psychotherapy, 36*(2), 94–104.

Hunter, M. (2008). Cultivation the art of safe space. *RIDE, 13*(1), 5–21.

Kana, P., & Aitkin, V. (2007). She didn't ask about my grandmother: Using process drama to explore issues of cultural exclusion and educational leadership. *Journal of Educational Administration 45*(6), 697–710.

Kovacev, L., & Shute, R. (2004). Acculturation and social support in relation to psychosocial adjustment of adolescent refugees resettled in Australia. *International Journal of Behavioral Development, 28*(3), 259–267.

Lee, J.-A., & De Finney, S. (2005). Using popular theatre for engaging racialized minority girls in exploring questions of identity and belonging. *Child and Youth Services, 26*(2), 95–118.

Liebmann, M. (2004). *Arts approaches to conflict*. London: Jessica Kingsley.

Matthews, J. (2008). Schooling and settlement: Refugee education in Australia. *International Studies of Sociology in Education, 18*(1), 31–45.

McDougall, B., & Chilcott, T. (2009, June 1). Bullying is out of control in schools. *The Courier Mail*. Brisbane: Associated Newspapers.

Onsando, G., & Billett, S. (2009). African students from refugee backgrounds in Australian TAFE institutes: A case for transformative learning goals and processes. *International Journal of Training Research, 7*(2), 80–94.

O'Toole, J., Burton, B., & Plunkett, A. (2005). *Cooling conflicts: A new approach to conflict and bullying in schools*. Sydney: Pearson Education.

Phan, T. (2003). Life in school: narratives of resiliency among Vietnamese-Canadian youths. *Adolescence, 38*(151), 555–566.

Roberts, W. B., Jr. (2006). *Bullying from both sides: Strategic interventions for working with bullies and victims*. California: Corwin Press.

Rodriguez-Jimenez, A., & Gifford, S. M. (2010). Finding voice learning and insights from a participatory media project with recently arrived Afghan young men with refugee backgrounds. *Youth Studies Australia, 29*(3), 33–41.

Rossiter, M., & Rossiter, K. (2009). Diamonds in the rough: Bridging gaps in supports for at-risk immigrant and refugee youth. *International Migration and Integration, 10*, 409–429. doi:10.1007/s12134-009-0110-3.

Rousseau, C., Drapeau, A., Lacroix, L., Déogratias, B., & Heusch, N. (2005). Evaluation of a classroom program of creative expression workshops for refugee and immigrant children. *Journal of Child Psychology and Psychiatry, 46*(2), 180–185.

Taylor, S. (2008). Schooling and the settlement of refugee young people in Queensland :The challenges are massive. *Social Alternatives, 27*(3), 58–65.

Yohani, S. (2008). Creating an ecology of hope: Arts-based interventions with refugee children. *Child and Adolescent Social Work Journal, 25*, 309–323.

Chapter 12
Conclusion

This book has investigated nine related research projects conducted over two decades in a number of countries and a range of settings which were aimed at empowering both children and adults to effectively manage the conflict and bullying they may encounter in their lives. The most significant outcome of this extensive and various research has been identified as the development of research-based effective strategies for conflict and bullying management that have proved successful in different cultures and a number of educational and professional contexts. The strategies developed during the 20 years of research are currently being applied in contexts as diverse as nursing education in Jordan, in-service training of teachers in Kazakhstan, teacher training in the UK, undergraduate Sociology and Nursing Education in Sweden, and addressing cultural and gender bullying in an Islamic school. Aspects of the projects utilising the outcomes of this research continue to operate in schools in two states in Australia, and the book concludes with a brief overview of a number of new initiatives that are emerging.

Four core strategies were developed in the initial projects and were intensively evaluated and refined in the projects that followed.

- The projects have involved *formal, structured teaching* about the nature of conflict, and several have focused on bullying, with participants learning the core concepts upon which managing and resolving them depend.
- The use of *Drama* as the central learning technique provides participants with a safe and creative structure to enact realistic events and characters involving conflict and bullying. Through diverse forms of Dramatic enactment, participants re-enforce their understanding of the nature and consequences of conflict and bullying. Furthermore, they are able to experiment with managing the relationships and events they have created.
- *Enhanced Forum Theatre*, involving the improvised performance of a realistic play in three scenes, allows participants both to demonstrate and further enhance their knowledge base, by representing specific stages in the escalation of the conflict they are exploring, and by depicting the three parties involved. The

© Springer International Publishing Switzerland 2015
B. Burton et al., *Acting to Manage Conflict and Bullying
Through Evidence-Based Strategies*, DOI 10.1007/978-3-319-17882-0_12

interventions in the performance by members of the audience generate a reflective dialogue between actors and audience that stimulates further understanding.

- *Peer teaching* empowers the students acting as teachers, enabling intellectual, social and personal growth and an increasing sense of mastery and self-esteem in conflict and bullying management. For the students being taught, there is an increase in positive attitudes to their learning, and being helped by older children acting as peer teachers motivates younger children to adopt a helping relationship towards others, which is particularly significant in conflict and bullying management.

12.1   Core Pre-conditions

As well as the implementation of these essential strategies, the research demonstrates that some core conditions must be met in order for the strategies to succeed. The first is the involvement of the whole organization in the conflict or bullying management project. Every student or employee must be actively involved and have the opportunity to develop and practice the skills and if possible have the opportunity to teach them to others. In schools, the peer teaching component is especially significant, and it is only when the students have taught the strategies to others that they become knowledgeable about conflict or bullying and adept at dealing with it.

Secondly, the conflict or bullying management program must be included as part of the compulsory or standard activities of the participants. In schools, this means that it must be part of the curriculum, taught and learned within academic subjects. In professional and industrial organisations the project should be a necessary part of professional training or in-servicing, and required as a skill base for all employees. In its therapeutic use, the strategies required the engagement and commitment of both the participants and their counsellors.

Finally, the program must have the active support of the managers, directors or employers where it is being implemented. This means school principals and hospital managers as well as senior administrators in state, non-governmental or commercial organizations. That support must be realized through the appointment of responsible program coordinators answerable for the effective running of the program.

12.2   The Nine Projects

The DRACON Project aimed to find effective means of dealing with conflict in schools in Sweden, Malaysia and two states of Australia. The researchers engaged in the project in each country experimented with a number of approaches which led to the creation of research paradigms with a number of common features., These included the collection of baseline data on young people through surveys and focus groups, action research in classrooms or similar educational contexts.... and a number of Drama techniques that informed the later research. All used some Drama techniques in common, including a diversity of forms of role-play and improvisation, and developing unscripted forum-type performances. In Sweden and Australia, initially independently, several of these techniques emerged to form the Enhanced Forum Theatre that was used as a key strategy in most of the later projects.

Cooling Conflict initially employed the effective strategies developed in the DRACON research to implement a successful conflict management program in a country school in Australia where a serious racial conflict between Aboriginal and other students had spread to the town. A characteristic of this research was the identification, through longitudinal follow-up spanning more than 2 years, of significant long-term behaviour change in a number of key students. Cooling Conflict then became a major research project in five schools in Sydney that developed into a program which was eventually implemented and sustained in over 100 schools in New South Wales, Australia.

The Negative Leaders case study was conducted as part of a major research project at Cambridge University in the UK and demonstrated how peer teaching and Drama can transform the behaviour of aggressive and disengaged female school students.

Acting Against Bullying was a major, 3-year action research project conducted in a total of 18 schools, in Queensland, Australia. The success of the four key strategies in reducing bullying is revealed in the extensive data from the action research, and reinforced in the specific outcomes of three case studies in individual schools. There was strong evidence in one of these schools of a sustained change for the better in the ethos of the whole school, in terms of conflict and bullying, with a major reduction of incidents of both. This has been reinforced by anecdotal evidence in other schools in this project and *Cooling Conflict.*

Moving On From the Trauma of Childhood Abuse was another 3 year action research project using drama processes and theatre performance, but in an entirely different context from the earlier projects in schools. This time the subjects were the adult survivors of childhood abuse, and despite serious issues with re-traumatisation, they developed a range of skills and new and effective behaviours through drama workshops and theatre performance that significantly enhanced their lives.

Drama for Learning in Professional Development Contexts: a Global Perspective demonstrated how those same effective Drama strategies for conflict management that had been developed in the earlier research could be applied to professional training in four quite different cultural and professional contexts; initial teacher education in the UK; teacher's in-service professional learning for radical change in Kazakhstan; and an international and intercultural workshop with university nursing students from Sweden, Germany and Jordan.

A more extensive project also set in Jordan investigated the improvement of communication in training of nurses, and focused on training the trainers (preceptors). *The Use of Core Conflict Competency in Nursing Education in Jordan* researched the impact of Drama as one of several pedagogical methods in conflict management for these senior health care practitioners.

Acting Against Social and Cyber Bullying was a case study of intense covert bullying amongst older adolescent females which demonstrated how the four strategies could produce positive transformational changes in behaviour in this specific group of female students.

Conflict and Bullying Management for Adolescent Refugees was another case study of the impact of the four strategies on newly-arrived adolescent refugees. Despite the constraints, the core strategies for conflict and bullying management empowered them in similar ways to previous subjects of the research.

12.3 Outcomes

This continuous sequence of connected research and practice over almost two decades has naturally produced numerous reports and other outcomes, project by project. This book is the first synthesis of all of them, and also contains extensive new material.

So far over 100 papers and conference presentations of all kinds have been produced. These have varied from fully refereed journal articles to 'how-to' practical handbooks for teachers, nurses, administrators and school students. The presentations have also taken place on all continents, and ranged from academic keynotes to workshops, demonstrations and ongoing Special Interest Groups.

Three books have been produced on earlier aspects of the work. These are: the already mentioned final report of the project (Löfgren and Malm 2005); a book in Swedish describing the Swedish DRACON program, that was translated into Danish in 2008 (Grünbaum and Lepp 2005); and a book about managing bullying and conflict in schools based on the Brisbane DRACON, Cooling Conflicts and Acting Against Bullying programs (O'Toole, Burton and Plunkett 2005). Morrison's work with negative leaders is the subject of a chapter in *Rebuilding Engagement through the Arts* (Finney et al. 2005). Training videos and DVDs have been made of the Swedish DRACON Work and Cooling Conflicts.

DRACON also inspired research about essential strategies for promoting effective collaboration and conflict resolution in international research projects. Strategies to support a fuller international engagement are: valuing diversity and developing cooperative goals, engaging in self-reflection and reflexivity, promoting collaborative dialogue and taking time and developing trust.

12.4 Successes and Challenges

This extensive list of outcomes and world-wide dissemination of what were often quite large-scale practical research projects provokes two significant questions. If the projects were mainly successful – as the research consistently indicates – what is there to show for them now? Moreover, given the constantly increasing attention being given to bullying and conflict resolution in contemporary institutions, especially educational ones, why are these four core strategies: *structures of conflict* taught through *Drama techniques*, *enhanced forum theatre* and *peer teaching*, not used more extensively around the world, particularly in schools?

12.5 Successes

The first question about the long-term outcomes of the projects can be addressed in two ways. First, there is still extensive identifiable evidence of the influence, and the on-going implementation, of the four strategies, in a number of the projects. This is evident in the changes in pedagogy of some of the nursing preceptors in Jordan and their training programs to incorporate role-play and forum theatre. Significant changes in the attitudes of student nurses in Sweden have been identified after their experience of these strategies. In the schools in, Sydney, Australia where Cooling Conflict has been integral to conflict management for more than a decade it has changed the culture of these schools. There have been sustained, positive changes in student behaviour in the Brisbane schools which have incorporated the *Acting Against Bullying* strategies into their school behaviour management plans. Major changes in behaviour occurred in the refugee students in the Arrivals project, including increasingly positive commitment to their schooling. There has been a widening use of enhanced forum theatre by professionals who have encountered it through the projects.

In terms of the project in Kazakhstan for the teacher trainers, there has been a clear positive outcome, and also firm evidence that strategies are being incorporated into pedagogy in that country by some teachers. As part of an on-going evaluation process, trainers are required to produce session plans and are observed by their international partners from the UK through a mentoring program. One of this book's authors (Morag Morrison), while visiting the country in September 2013 as a mentor, observed that those trainers she had introduced to Enhanced Forum Theatre were in fact using the form, and using it well, as one of their own pedagogical strategies. As this training is part of a cascading model of on-going teacher development, it seems probable that the strategy will continue to filter into practice in Kazakhstan through being shared with others. There are already over 15,000 teachers who have undertaken training via the program, and this numbers will expand exponentially. Even if just a small band of those initial trainers are using the ideas, the impact could be very large indeed!

In the U.K. and Sweden some strategies developed in the DRACON research, such as enhanced forum theatre, continue to be used in nursing and teacher education. As part of an on-going teaching exchange program funded through the Erasmus program in the EU, two of the books authors (Morag Morrison and Margret Lepp) continue to work on developing professional understanding of conflict through workshops delivered in the University of Gothenberg and the University of Cambridge and strategies developed through DRACON continue to form the bedrock of their teaching approach.

12.6   The Challenges

The second question, which asks why the four effective strategies for dealing with
conflict and bullying are not used more widely, especially in school worldwide, is a
complex one. The question needs widening beyond the successful projects explored
in this book to ask why both Drama pedagogy and peer teaching are taking so long
to become established as standard practice in the field of education and the training
of health care professionals. In many professions, trainers have been familiar with
and made regular use of procedural forms of role-play since at least the 1950s, and
the Viennese/American psychologist Jacob Moreno (1962) who developed psycho
Drama and socio Drama out of his own theatrical background for their use in therapy and psychiatry.

The contemporary literature of school and adult education and also teacher
education is full of theory and enthusiastic rhetoric about the need to (1) engage
students, for (2) embodied learning, for (3) dialogical teaching. As the research in
this book demonstrates, Drama pedagogy provides all three. Why is it not implemented but rather largely ignored and not taken into consideration by for example
higher Education departments and even Ministers of Education? The following
reasons were all encountered and identified during the projects and afterwards.

12.7   The Challenge of Drama Pedagogy

- Partly it is because Drama comes from a small and peripheral area of both
  curriculum and teacher education, and is easily discounted in the emphasis on
  learning the basics which drives most curriculum world-wide. For a vivid
  example, in the *Acting Against Bullying* project it was almost impossible to gain
  the interest and support of the education system concerned despite extensive
  evidence of the demonstrable power of Drama to effectively address bullying.
  Over the 3 years of the project, no curriculum officer in the local Education
  Department's Curriculum Branch could be found to take formal responsibility
  for the project for more than 6 months, none at all who brought either the Drama
  or the peer teaching into their systems and practice, and there was often nobody
  either to seek advice from or report the results to, even though the Department
  had initially enthusiastically supported the project.
- Because Drama is a form of experiential learning, it cannot be learned through
  the brain alone, but through a whole experience involving the body, the senses
  and the emotions, and must be experienced to be understood. Furthermore,
  neither the physical design, nor the schedules, of conventional classrooms
  really permit that. All the projects collected copious evidence of the changes of
  understanding, attitude and behaviour, when the participants actually experienced the holistic engagement with Drama. However, school teachers, principals, and certainly the administrators who make and carry out policy decisions,

are usually far too busy with their own priorities to give such a marginal practice the time or the space needed or to experience it for themselves. When the *Acting Against Bullying* researchers did manage to get a group of primary principals to go through a day of enhanced forum theatre, playing with their own tales of oppression and bullying, the result was an immediate request for a program specially designed for them and their schools. But such moments were rare.

• Partly too, Drama is such an ambivalent medium. As the refugee youngsters and the private school girls demonstrated, it can powerfully provide protection and the confidence to explore dangerous emotions and relationships safely. However, unprofessionally used, it can expose and embarrass participants. For the uninitiated, Drama means getting up on stage in front of a lot of people. Initially that's what many of the students and teachers we encountered throughout the projects expected, which is why so many of the projects scaffolded their early workshop sessions with safe games and discussions. Real expertise is required to use Drama as a strategy for addressing conflict and bullying. For those teachers and leaders who can make the intellectual and psychological leap to democratic learning, Drama pedagogy actually demands some knowledge of the elements and skills of Drama – skills of the playwright to structure the experience (generate the engagement, create the tension, develop the Dramatic context, identify and build the Dramatic symbols and mood), and of the performer to engage in and lead the dialogue.

12.8   The Challenge of Peer Teaching in a Teacher Centred Learning Area

Many of the same constraints and obstacles face the adoption of peer teaching. Even more than for Drama, it is hard for teachers to relinquish their belief in their real-life role that they are the keeper and provider of the knowledge – their self-esteem as teachers is vested in it, and more importantly the authority and power that resides in that role. In the school-based projects, some teachers were sceptical and reluctant to let the older students take responsibility for their students or their curriculum. Some teachers intervened prematurely and frequently, to save the peer teachers when they appeared to be struggling, or the lesson was not going as planned. Some teachers, in contrast, became passive spectators in the whole peer teaching process and were not sure when or how to assist the students when they encountered predicaments that were beyond them.

However, it appeared that the biggest factor in discouraging the use of peer teaching is the sheer logistics, including rigid timetables, of schools and to a lesser extent tertiary colleges and universities (both teaching and nursing). This problem of logistics was most clearly demonstrated by the inability of Clifton High School (Ch. 3) to cope with the organisational demands of continuing the use of the strategies once the extraordinarily effective *Cooling Conflicts* action research was over.

In spite of the immense goodwill of principal and teachers, the ongoing enthusiasm of the students, and the resounding and acknowledged success of the peer teaching, the project did not continue in the school.

The research therefore indicates that the extraordinary potential of the four strategies to address conflict and bullying is matched by the difficulties of achieving effective and sustained implementation of the strategies, especially in schools. The projects analysed in this book demonstrate that these challenges can be overcome, and the participants themselves in the numerous and varied projects provide the evidence of the effectiveness of the strategies.

12.9   The Research Continues

A number of new initiatives in diverse educational and professional settings in different countries are also using the core techniques for conflict and bullying management explored in this book. These new applications include conflict management in workplaces in Hong Kong, schools in India, Africa and the UK, a World Vision project dealing with conflict in indigenous communities in Australia, and Acting against Bullying to address cultural and gender bullying in an Islamic school in Australia. These new projects provide further evidence of the effectiveness of the strategies that have been developed, and also indicate the validity of these strategies in new and different contexts.

Hong Kong, in particular, seems to be fertile ground – indicating the potential interest in China. One of the authors (John O'Toole) of this book in 2012 demonstrated Enhanced Forum Theatre and the principles underpinning it to Hong Kong masters' students in Drama education. That demonstration led directly to two professional companies run by the student participants (one of them a former Chief of Police in Hong Hong) currently using the techniques in their ongoing community work. A decade earlier, another demonstration by the same author at a conference in the UK led a Chinese participant, then herself a masters' student at an English university, to follow up the techniques with the author on a subsequent visit to Hong Kong already in 2005, and then implement them in mainland China on behalf of a major international charity organisation.

A potentially significant international initiative, at the time of writing in its infancy and based in the UK, is the Indra Congress. According to its website,

> it is a growing, global network of young people, artists, educators and others who share a commitment to the development of the arts as a crucial resource for peace building and the non-violent transformation of conflict. We offer a range of workshop activities for teachers, pupils students and the wider school community to develop creative approaches to challenging bullying, racism, inequality and prejudice, encouraging positive perspectives on diversity, gender related issues, the school's relationship to its community and for the teaching of Global Citizenship. The Indra Congress has links with India, several countries in Africa, North and South America, as well as the UK and Northern Ireland.

The Indra Congress has adopted the term, principles and strategies of *Cooling Conflict*, with the authors' permission, as over the next year the central pillar of this work. Through the engagement with Cooling Conflict Indra will encourage schools in different parts of the world to dialogue and share their experiences of dealing with conflict, bullying and related issues in very different contexts, in the process building a global network of participating schools.

In Australia, True Quest, an organisation of teachers based in NSW and associated with World Vision, dedicated to 'empowering people and communities', has adopted *Cooling Conflict* (and in particular Enhanced Forum Theatre) as part of their work with disadvantaged Indigenous young people. Their program, named Young Mob Leaders, was first implemented with Aboriginal Youth in South Sydney, and then extended into other regions. Two separate research studies on the impact of the program concluded that the use of Drama was one of the most effective techniques in the whole program. The Young Mob Leaders program is about to be rolled out across the entire state of New South Wales in indigenous communities. All levels of this program will use Drama techniques, and the middle level of the program will use the Cooling Conflict Techniques as they were implemented in the original research project. The advanced stage of Young Mob Leaders will focus in particular on the strategy of Enhanced Forum Theatre with the participants and their communities.

A large Islamic school in Brisbane has introduced the *Acting Against Bullying* program to counter cultural and gender bullying. The initial outcomes have been strongly positive, with the older secondary students demonstrating expertise in managing cultural conflict and gender bullying, and effectively peer teaching and mentoring younger students. The administration of the school reports a significant decline in cultural conflict amongst the students involved in the project. The administration and teachers have observed that older teenage girls have taken leadership roles in countering the dominance of male students in all facets of school life. The school has decided to make the program part of its whole school behaviour management program in 2014.

The authors have demonstrated the techniques on a number of occasions in North America – originally in 2004 in Ottawa, and more recently in Kentucky at a National Conference. There is ongoing interest, although participants have indicated that the structures of formal education particularly in the USA make the kind of whole-school commitment demanded of the peer-teaching difficult to implement and sustain. However, just like conflict and bullying themselves, the four strategies that evolved in *Cooling Conflict* and *Acting Against Bullying* are still very much in evidence, and offshoots and borrowings in schools and adult education contexts continue to emerge.

CPSIA information can be obtained at www.ICGtesting.com
Printed in the USA
LVOW01*1036100815

449512LV00012B/180/P